a passion for christ

a passion for christ

An Evangelical Christology

Douglas D. Webster

Academie Books Grand Rapids, Michigan
Zondervan Publishing House

Our thanks go to the publishers who have granted their permission to quote from their copyrighted material:

"Jesus, Name Above All Names" by Naida Hearn. Copyright © 1974, 1978 by Scripture in Song—Admin. by Marantha! Music. All rights reserved. International copyright secured. Used by permission only.

Telephone Poles and Other Poems by John Updike. Used by permission of Alfred A. Knopf.

"There's Something About That Name." Words by William J. and Gloria Gaither. Music by William J. Gaither. Copyright © 1970 by William J. Gaither. All rights reserved. Used by permission.

A PASSION FOR CHRIST
Copyright © 1987 by Douglas D. Webster

ACADEMIE BOOKS is an imprint of Zondervan Publishing House, 1415 Lake Drive, S.E., Grand Rapids, Michigan 49506

Library of Congress Cataloging in Publication Data
Webster, Douglas D.
     A passion for Christ.

     Bibliography: p.
     1. Jesus Christ—Person and offices. 2. Evangelicalism. I. Title.
BT202.W423   1987   232   86–26734
ISBN 0-310-34660-6

All Scripture quotations, unless otherwise noted, are taken from the *Holy Bible: New International Version* (North American Edition), copyright © 1973, 1978, 1984 by the International Bible Society. Used by permission of Zondervan Bible Publishers.

Edited by Craig A. Noll
Designed by Louise Bauer

Printed in the United States of America

87 88 89 90 91 92 93 94 / AH / 10 9 8 7 6 5 4 3 2 1

To
Donald and Louise Webster
my parents and Christ's disciples

contents

pReface

True theological understanding stirs the heart and guides the mind. Daily obedience to the lordship of Jesus Christ is as crucial an issue in this study of the doctrine of Christ as understanding the meaning of the Incarnation. The purpose of this book is to challenge the commitment and deepen the confession of the follower of Christ.

Theological convictions need to be expressed clearly and thoughtfully as well as personally and practically. Christology may sound like an academic exercise appropriate only for intellectuals and seminarians, a study conveniently removed from the responsibility of those intent on simply following Jesus. I wish to dispel this idea. I have sought to encourage a lively exchange between a well-reasoned, heartfelt confession and a radical, costly commitment.

I begin with a critical analysis of social trends and religious pressures which scale down our sense of what it means to follow Christ. In the second and third chapters I attempt to dispel the confusion and disorientation of current attempts to recast the gospel in the mold of modernity. I argue for the normative value of God's Word. The Bible authoritatively guides our understanding and commitment in a way that is both faithful to historic Christianity and relevant in today's world.

Chapter 4 affirms the biblical pattern that unites the person of Christ with the ethic of Jesus. From there I develop an Evangelical christology, beginning with a study of the theological continuity between the Testaments and followed by chapters on Jesus' spirituality, self-understanding, and kingdom ethic. The final two chapters on the Cross and the Resurrection illustrate the strategy I have attempted to follow throughout the book. As a seminary professor, I have sought to be in dialogue with various expressions of contemporary christological thought, which I believe is important for the sake of guarding and deepening a true confession of Christ. However, as a pastor, I am concerned to discuss the practical implications of each aspect of Christ's life for daily discipleship. I trust that the reader will find this two-pronged approach helpful.

The cultivation of a passion for Christ is a personal challenge, calling for intellectual integrity, true spirituality, and ethical action. Life's intensity and fulfillment, as well as its challenge, increase as we take the truth and praxis of Jesus Christ seriously. The childhood roots of my faith in Christ sought to unite doctrine, devotion, and duty. I trust I have maintained that biblical unity in this book. My desire is that the Spirit of God will use this material to aid the reader in cultivating a passion for Christ.

Special thanks go to Ian Rennie and my colleagues at Ontario Theological Seminary for their support and a semester sabbatical to complete the writing. Paul Friesen carefully read each chapter and offered many helpful suggestions. From the beginning, Zondervan's editors Stan Gundry and Ed van der Maas, have been encouraging and enjoyable to work with. As copy editor, Craig Noll did an excellent job preparing the final version of the manuscript. By far the greatest effort was given by Ginny, who not only patiently listened, added ideas, improved my writing, and typed many portions of the manuscript twice, but served as a loving wife and mother to our three children, Jeremy, Andrew, and Kennerly.

1

to know christ

Secretly gathered together in a farmhouse in Czechoslovakia, nine Christians spend a week studying the Bible, praying, and encouraging one another in their life commitment to Jesus Christ. For the knowledge of Christ, they risk their jobs and stand against the prevailing mind-set of their culture. These Czech Christians know Christ in the power of the Resurrection. Their passion for him is marked by a single-minded desire and clarity of purpose, without fanaticism. I am impressed with their warmth, their joy, their reasonableness, and, above all, their devotion to Jesus Christ.

Hernando came to our seminary from Colombia with a zeal for Christ which he translated into action—his humor, his family, and his politics evidenced that he had been with Jesus. When his life ended in a tragic car accident in Ecuador, we mourned because, in a world where so few Christians seem really to know Christ passionately, we had lost a very special brother who challenged us with his devotion for Christ.

Nick Natola lives a few kilometers from my home. When he accepted Christ seven years ago, his life began to change. More than his soul was saved; his entire life began to change. Before, he lived to play pool and have a good time. Now, the knowledge of Christ has changed his family life, inspired a concern for others, and opened his mind and heart in worship and praise to his Creator and Lord.

Born in South Africa, Ebenson immigrated to Canada in 1980 and works in a small print shop. In the mid-1970s he was beaten and imprisoned by professing Christians in a government crackdown on dissidents in South Africa. As he told me his story I marveled how anyone as quiet and unassuming as "Ben" could pose a threat. And more important, how he could remain a Christian after being beaten senseless by regular church-going Christians. Ben responded simply by saying that the knowledge of Christ is stronger than the evil of men, even when it is done in the name of Christ.

This book is about knowing Christ in the power of the Resurrection and in the fellowship of his sufferings. Its thrust is positive and critical and aims to provoke a passion for the knowledge *of* Christ instead of merely a formal knowledge *about* Christ. The pervasiveness of nominal Christianity in many parts of the Western world keeps multitudes from knowing Christ and renders much of the church powerless.

Never have we passionately wanted so much from our culture and known so little of Christ. The "yuppie" ideal has a captivating influence on us, pervading not only the culture and the media but Christian communities as well. We are dominated by a we-expect-more-of-everything outlook. Beyond power, wealth, knowledge, prestige, and reputation, we want creativity, leisure, autonomy, pleasure, participation, community, adventure, vitality, stimulation, and tender loving care.[1] We want it all.

We have a long list of tangible and intangible requirements for a customized lifestyle that is preoccupied with self, the primary focus in today's world view. Hedonistic immaturity has been pushed to new heights by promoters who bless the quest for success. While so much of the world is in devastating political and economic turmoil, our culture is being shaped by a debilitating immaturity. Even though we have ample opportunity to know Christ, our will to know him is inhibited by forces which seem beyond our control and by our lack of spiritual vision, motivation of love, and will to discipline ourselves toward achieving high goals. We suffer from spiritual anorexia. Increasingly, our energies are spent on emotional survival, new technologies, harmless pleasures, and old idolatries such as materialism and self-sufficiency. We do not know what to say to our culture because we do not know what Christ is saying to us.

North American Christianity is facing an unprecedented crisis of meaning, far greater than the challenge of liberalism. Having absorbed the modern consciousness, we have no thirst for Christ. The failure of the Christian mind stems from our ignorance of Christ. For Christians and non-Christians alike, the combined impact of our ambitions and drives has reduced the human quest to immediate, temporal, individualistic satisfaction.

A MINIMAL JESUS

The loss of the sacred may be the single most significant phenomenon of North American culture. According to Albert Outler,

> The loss of the sacred is a code phrase for the nearly total disappearance, in the collective consciousness of "modern" man, of not only any vivid sensibility of that sacred presence in which we "live and move and have our being," but also of that sacred order by which we ought to live. It speaks of a generalized insensitivity to the Holy Spirit as God's personal presence in human life and history, and it points to a fading of the vision of the kingdom of God as the rule of his righteousness, in persons and among nations.[2]

In spite of the rise of conservative religion, it is fair to say that North American culture is rapidly dismantling anything that reflects a supernatural orientation. Morality follows social convention and sociological trends rather than precepts. Psychology rejects a biblical anthropology. Education divorces knowledge from wisdom. Commerce and industry function without a theology of stewardship. And family life has lost commitment and fidelity. Individualism reigns as the supreme norm intellectually and politically. Guilt is simply the emotional hangover of negative experiences. Death ends all. "Any serious consideration of 'the loss and recovery of the sacred' plunges us straightway into the depths of our epoch's spiritual crisis."[3]

Today's response to the spiritual crisis is particularly interesting. With remarkable ingenuity philosophers and social analysts have led the culture in scaling down expectations of the meaning and purpose of life to conform to secularized existence. The phenomenal growth of the "advice industry" is an example of our culture's search for meaning. Out of a deep sense of frustration and unsettledness, people are groping for answers. They are turning to strangers for a sense of direction and meaning.

New meanings for old words illustrate the spirit of the age. *Sacred* in this new cultural climate exchanges its theological meaning for sociological significance. The sacred no longer refers to God but to the "expressive" side of human life, in opposition to the instrumental and functional aspects of life. According to this new mode of thinking, what is sacred to one person may not be sacred to another. For many, jogging is simply good exercise, but for others it is a major component of self-fulfillment, belonging to the sacred/expressive domain of life. Theoretically, Christians maintain allegiance to the spiritual order, but in practice the new sense of the sacred beguiles them. Seekers of self-fulfillment invest the best of their creativity in inventing expressive styles of living. At the heart of the search for self-fulfillment is the moral intuition that the very meaning of life resides in its sacred/expressive aspects and that one must, therefore, fight to give these the importance they deserve.[4]

This new understanding of the sacred has diverted the attention of many believers from Christ and toward the passions of this age. In a practical way, knowing Christ no longer belongs to the sacred and expressive domain of life but fits better in the less important, instrumental and functional sphere of life. In other words, Christianity is effectively reduced to tradition and custom. It fits into the perfunctory routine of life. Consequently, many believers have a knowledge about Christ, but he is not at the heart of their search for self-fulfillment.

Commitments are being made to today's success ethic by many well-educated and highly motivated Christians who seem unaware of the difference between the world's strategy for self-fulfillment and Jesus' strategy for self-fulfillment. Decisions are often made in a person's late twenties or early thirties that take the rest of their professional lives to work out. We know what it is like to be in debt for cars and homes and education, but we must also realize that it is possible to pay the interest for these loans not only in dollars and cents but in the loss of spiritual vitality. Patterns of life are set up and goals established which may be detrimental to our own spiritual growth and to the wholeness of the church. Like the world around them, many Christians fight to infuse meaning into their lives through giving themselves to business, recreation, acquisitions, and family. Along with the culture, Christians have tended to scale down their life expectations by accommodating easily to a new quest which steals their passions and absorbs their energy.

The loss of the sacred has resulted in a new interpretation of *salvation*. In the Christian's vocabulary it is difficult to find a word richer in significance. It comprehends our deliverance from "sin and death; guilt and estrangement; ignorance of truth; bondage to habit and vice; fear of demons, of death, of life, of God, of hell; despair of self; alienation from others; pressures of the world; a meaningless life." The meaning of salvation is exceedingly positive, embracing

> peace with God, access to God's favor and presence, hope of regaining the glory intended for men, endurance in suffering, steadfast character, an optimistic mind, inner motivations of divine love and power of the Spirit, ongoing experience of the risen Christ and sustaining joy in God.[5]

Grasping the richness of the biblical view of salvation accentuates the reductionism of contemporary redefinitions of salvation. Because "life may indeed be absurd in some large cosmic sense," says Alvin Toffler, salvation means the "safe transition to a decent new civilization."[6] Successfully coping with the emergence of this new civilization is the essence of salvation. The "saved" are those who respond progressively and imaginatively to the modern evolutionary struggle by learning how to use computers to create community and how to form new structures to give life a sense of meaning and coherence.

The survival of the fittest will be predicated on constructing a coherent, meaningful picture of the world, even if in any ultimate sense such a world does not exist.[7] Scaling down the expectation of salvation to fit contemporary notions of reality usually involves a deification of technology and human autonomy. Modern men and women look to computers and to the individual self for "spiritual" deliverance. The contemporary "sacred" hope is in computers, a modern Baal, absorbing our energies and passions in much the same way that the ancient god of fertility compromised Israel's devotion to Yahweh. I am suggesting that modern technology has gone beyond functional or instrumental categories in an attempt to represent to North Americans the very means of salvation in the coming new world. No wonder it is difficult to speak of God in Christ to this generation. It is difficult to speak of Christ convincingly even to Christians.

Even though insightful social analysts borrow theological words, speculate on futuristic scenarios, and prescribe the qualities of tomorrow's new person, the real grappling comes on the level of mere *survival*. "In a time of troubles," writes Christopher Lasch, "everyday life becomes an exercise in survival. People take one day at a time."[8] Camus's thought is still true today: "Comfortable optimism surely seems like a bad joke in today's world." From within and without, life seems to be ebbing away. We starve for meaningful relationships, yet our capacity for commitment to one another withers. We appear to be bored by our achievements and devastated by our failures.

Moral relativism has thrown our culture into confusion. Sociological trends dictate morality. Premarital sex, marital infidelity, and homosexuality are now accepted in many circles as commonplace. Virginity is an embarrassment to many teenagers, and abortion on request is designated a civil right. If the scale of our militarism and nuclear weaponry were translated into terms we could experience firsthand, we would be conscious of an overwhelming military presence. We would drive to work past tank columns, missile launchers, and fully armed GIs. The skies would be filled with bombers and choppers. In many respects our psychic survival is already strained by the tension and insecurity of a world on the edge of catastrophic confrontation. We may be at peace, but the sword of nuclear power is held by a thread. Modern men and women exude style and sophistication, thrive on image, and feed on self-gratification, but inside they are deeply troubled.

As the human predicament gnaws at us and preoccupies our moments of honest reflection, we do not know whether to ask or to suppress ultimate questions. When people can hardly get through the day, they do not want to be bothered with tomorrow. "People have lost confidence in the future," contends Lasch. "They have begun to prepare for the worst . . . by executing a kind of emotional retreat from long-term commitments that presuppose a stable, secure, and orderly world."[9] Lasch's thesis deserves consideration. He claims that psychic survival in troubled times results in a minimal self. People preserve emotional equilibrium by distorting their image of the real world. Their everyday pursuit of success and survival absorbs such intensity and energy that concerns beyond their perceived self-interests are trivialized.

Such a scenario may help to explain why Jesus' ethic, on numerous counts, is considered hopelessly idealistic by many Christians. They consider serious reflection on Jesus' teaching to be one of those loftier concerns that is expendable in troubled times, with the result that many Christians succumb to cultural seduction. They exchange religiosity and ethical passivity for Christian discipleship. Time pressures squelch our desire to know Christ, and spirituality tends to be relegated to Sunday mornings. The same may be said of pastors who are so taken up with administering programs, meeting people's expectations, and surviving another Sunday that a serious consideration of Jesus is a luxury.

The minimal self is a product of hard times. Instead of building character, it has stripped our lives of genuine creativity, community, and worship. Even family, friends, and neighbors become a burden too expensive to carry as we withdraw into ourselves. Not surprisingly, the minimal self corresponds to nominal Christianity and a minimal Jesus. In practical terms, knowing Christ is not as interesting to us as the latest trends in fashions, computer software, and music. As many Christians in Latin America, Eastern Europe, Africa, and China are struggling to know Christ more deeply, many North American Christians seem intent on their secular pursuit of success. This orientation may make knowing Christ more difficult for us, because we have substituted a knowledge of ourselves and a knowledge about Christ for a knowledge of Christ. "Salvation" and "survival," in the terms which have been used, have trivialized Christian redemption and discipleship and have made knowing Christ a theoretical matter instead of one that is practical. We need to remember that Jesus' strategy for self-fulfillment follows a road that leads right out of self. C. S. Lewis came to realize that the path to self-fulfillment was not to be found in one's self. Lewis writes, "I had tried everything in my own mind and body; as it were, asking myself, 'Is it this you want? Is it this?' " Even his noble pursuit for Joy drew him to the conclusion that he needed something other than aesthetic experience.

> I thus understood that in deepest solitude there is a road right out of the self, a commerce with something which, by refusing to identify itself with any object of the senses, or anything whereof we have biological or social need, or anything imagined, or any state of our own minds, proclaims itself sheerly objective.[10]

This book is about knowing in profound relationship the objective reality of Jesus Christ and being wonderfully and supernaturally transformed into his image. Its purpose is to provoke a passion for the knowledge of Christ which illuminates our understanding of Christ and guides us in genuine Christian action. My conviction is that the key to knowing Christ is to become like Jesus as he is presented in the Bible. For only as we expose ourselves to him and allow his accomplishments to humble us and motivate us do we begin to understand Christ. Then Jesus' life begins to transform every aspect of our lives. His spirituality becomes the model for our worship. His teaching is the ground for our ethic; his self-understanding, the pattern for our self-awareness; his self-sacrifice, the paradigm of our service; his bodily resurrection, the hope for our resurrection. His method of evangelism becomes our strategy for witnessing, and his call for justice becomes our commitment.

This picture is not meant to overwhelm and burden the Christian with the impossible task of reaching for perfection. There is a critical difference between striving to be Christlike in our own strength and turning to Christ for the power and wisdom to become like him. If we do not know the person of Christ, we cannot follow the work of Christ.

Becoming like Jesus does not evolve automatically. It is a process which allows Christ's life by the Spirit to take shape in ours. The knowledge of Christ rests on the supernatural reality of Jesus' presence in our lives to transform us into his image. "For those God foreknew he also predestined to be conformed to the likeness of his Son, that he might be the firstborn among many brothers" (Rom. 8:29). The person and work of Christ cannot be divided. Just as the Christian faith cannot be separated from the Christian life, neither can the issue of Christ's deity be understood apart from the practical questions of what it means to be Christ's disciple. Instead of patterning our lives after trends, we need to submit to the one who claims to be the way, the truth, and the life. From scaled-down expectations, we must turn to Christ, "in whom are hidden all the treasures of wisdom and knowledge" (Col. 2:3). We offer no illusions of spiritual perfection. But we do believe that popular images of success fade when the image of Christ comes into focus. The evidence of genuine spirituality is humble service and honest repentance. The more Christlike we become, the greater our sense of dependence upon God's abiding presence and the more conscious we are of our need for God's constant forgiveness and mercy.

AN ABSTRACT CHRIST

As Christians understand and reject the cultural pressures which desensitize spiritual life and depreciate the knowledge of Christ, they have the opportunity of knowing Christ as he should be known. However, believers need to be aware that there are not only cultural pressures which produce a minimal Jesus but religious pressures which produce an abstract Christ. Today people declare themselves against abstractions, especially theological abstractions, which perhaps has the positive effect of sifting our knowledge of religious jargon, clichés, and shibboleths. It exposes a doctrinaire Christ who is neatly sequestered in confessional statements and safely removed from daily practice. Surely, no amount of information about Christ is adequate if the knowledge of and obedience to Christ is missing. Sometimes a traditional emphasis on confession has obscured the need for practical obedience.

Of course, it is also possible to be ardently committed to a thoroughly misunderstood Jesus. When people complain that theology is too abstract, they usually criticize its perceived irrelevance. The complaint is justified when the knowledge of Christ degenerates into a knowledge about Christ that is high on verbal output and low on obedience and spiritual vitality. Ironically, however, dissatisfaction with seemingly irrelevant theological complexities often serves to simplify rather than challenge abstract versions of Christ. Instead of a fresh desire to know Jesus as he is revealed in God's Word, believers settled for a simplified version of an abstract Christ. They are repelled by dead orthodoxy, yet they substitute in its place a subjective and shallow understanding of Christ.

Theologians from various traditions are forcing us to reexamine our knowledge of Christ by calling attention to the disparity between our confession of Christ as Lord and the practical consequences of Christian discipleship in our lives. How has it been possible, they ask, for Christians, "in the name of Christ, to ignore or even contradict fundamental principles and values that were preached and acted upon by Jesus of Nazareth?"[11] They suspect that our view of Christ is formed independent of the actual life and teaching of Jesus and that his life has little practical impact in our lives.

The phrase *Jesus saves* can become a cliché that is cited without comprehending what Jesus saves us from and what he saves us for. People speak sincerely of knowing God's will, without any specific understanding of the claims of Christ upon their lives. For all practical purposes, they are ignorant of a consequential knowledge of Jesus' ethic. "Take up your cross" is emotive language for coping with an illness, an accident, or a difficult family situation. For others, the Cross is simply a subjective feeling of empathy with Jesus' suffering. Whether the Cross is equated with a negative circumstance or a psychological feeling, it is distanced from the definite and specific meaning of the Christian cross in the gospel.

A few years ago, *Christianity Today* produced a Christmas issue with a provocative cover.[12] Under the caption "Satan's Substitute for the Savior?" a potbellied Santa Claus was strung up to the cross by Christmas-tree lights. Beyond the heresy of preoccupation with material things is the even greater heresy that Jesus exists primarily to fulfill our wishes. As one Costa Rican student commented following an evangelistic crusade in his country,

> Certainly very pretty, but it's only a half truth. This is a "Father Christmas Christ," one who comes to give only because he's so rich. He has lots of capital. Christ becomes a commodity, and the highest bidder gets him. All we hear is, "Who wish to receive Christ as their personal Savior, and not have to go to hell? Who wish to be healed this evening? Let's see the hands." Those in need accept this gift of a witch-doctor Christ, and every time they see the minister it's "Reverend, I hurt here," or, "Reverend, please put your hand here and say a prayer." The church starts looking like Jesus the Witch Doctor's hut. Jesus, working cures? Sure he does, but cures aren't all there is—and they're certainly not supposed to be legal tender.[13]

Converts to this way of thinking are disciples of a phony Christ and are susceptible to superstitious whims and cultic teaching. The name of Jesus becomes a magic potion for solving all their problems.

When I was in university one of my professors accused the majority of Christians of understanding Jesus as an infantile projection. He argued that celebrating Christmas allowed people to reminisce about their childhood and feel close to the "babe in the manger." Sunday School inculcated the "mild" morality of Jesus, and spring was ushered in with new clothes and Easter services.

I found this caricature of Christian experience haunting and more accurate than I cared to admit. My experience as a child growing up in a Christian family, attending Sunday School and church, was very positive and provided me with an authentic exposure to Jesus, but such is not always the case. Yet even then, many areas of Jesus' life were never mentioned to me, such as his concern for justice and regard for the poor. Our traditions can impede our understanding of Jesus Christ himself.

Consider our children's Christmas programs, in which the boys and girls act out the shepherds coming to visit Mary. We strain our necks to see how cute they look and are amused as they stumble over their lines. The historical Jesus is a shadowy figure in our candlelight services. We want a feeling—the quickening of sentiment or the inspiration of a mood—rather than an encounter with Jesus Christ.

Those who have been Christians for years and have pursued highly sophisticated careers in science and industry typically know little more about Jesus' ethic than they did during their high-school years. If we pursued Jesus with the same zeal and devotion we give to fashions, homes, careers, finances, studies, sports, and cars, I imagine we would understand him better and have a greatly increased capacity for obedience and sensitivity to the Spirit. Ironically, the one who should mean so much to us has been displaced by many things which by comparison are trivial. Our abstract Christs arise as much, if not more, from our theological neglect and spiritual emptiness as they do from our overintellectualizing the faith. The attractiveness of an abstract Christ is found solely in the imagination of those who mold him into their own image. But to those who earnestly seek to know him according to the Word and Spirit of God, all abstract Christs, from a Santa Claus Christ to a guerrilla Christ, are repulsive.

We want to know Christ as he has made himself known to us. We want to take the Incarnation seriously, as a command to come to Jesus on his own terms by way of his teaching, his spirituality, his self-awareness, and his cross. Therefore we desire with God's help to resist a minimal Jesus and an abstract Christ. Abstract theologizing and superstitious imagining are equally rejected when we give ourselves humbly and passionately to Jesus Christ. As we endeavor to know him, theological thinking and practical Christian living must be bound together.

KNOWING CHRIST

Since the nineteenth century, knowledge has suffered a remarkable devaluation philosophically as well as practically. Instead of a comprehensive view of knowledge encompassing spiritual and moral dimensions, knowledge for many intelligent people has been reduced to matters of science and logic. Accordingly, the study of humanity—psychologically, physiologically, sociologically, and anthropologically—falls within the acceptable sphere of knowledge, but the knowledge of God is excluded. To know Christ in the apostolic sense is presumed by many to be impossible. Biblical revelation is evaluated as a compendium of human religious experiences and rejected as a definitive source of propositional knowledge about God. Religion within the limits of reason discounts the historicity of supernatural events and God's self-revelation and derives truth from various sources, including nature, existential self-authentication, and historical praxis.

Instead of human reason fulfilling its intended purpose as a divinely fashioned instrument for recognizing truth as theologian Carl Henry has maintained, it has artificially limited the field of knowledge and given free rein to speculative theologies. When we examine the various approaches to the study of Christ, we shall see the consequences of this new view of knowledge. Not surprisingly, the limitations imposed on knowledge by certain philosophical ideas coincide with a popular and pragmatic reductionist perspective of knowledge. Today's market for innovation, invention, and information has shaped the attitudes of modern humanity. Simply stated, knowledge and wisdom have been exchanged for information and technique, to the extent that, when people speak of knowledge, they think of data stored on computer disks or of facts easily transmitted through television and newsprint. Even for computer experts, "The assertion that all human knowledge is encodable in streams of zeros and ones [is] hard to swallow." Joseph Weizenbaum, a computer professor at the Massachusetts Institute of Technology, objects to the increasingly popular assumption that the only knowledge worth having is computerized information.

> In effect, the whole world is made to seem computable. This generates a kind of tunnel vision, where the only problems that seem legitimate are problems that can be put on a computer. There is a whole world of real problems, of human problems, which is essentially ignored.[14]

As people become more preoccupied with statistics, budgets, flow charts, and polls, they become less inclined to turn away from the computer and the newspaper and to consider seriously the fundamental questions of God, humanity, history, morality, and death. It is important for Christians not to be intimidated or compromised by reductionistic views of knowledge. It is equally important that they be aware of just how revolutionary the knowledge of Christ is in today's culture. Whoever is committed to the knowledge of Christ is really committed to much else besides. "He is committed to a view of God, to a view of man, to a view of sin, to a view of redemption, to a view of human destiny found only in Christianity."15 In short, the disciple of Jesus is committed to Jesus' world view, a conceptual framework which gives structure and meaning to all his or her convictions, relationships, and actions.

Knowing Christ sets believers apart from nonbelievers, both philosophically and practically, giving them a knowledge of God and humanity, morality and mortality, and time and eternity which is both coherent and comprehensive. When the apostle Paul expressed his passion to know Christ, he was aware of the need to distance himself from prevailing concepts of knowledge that distorted the truth. Hellenistic culture doubted "the possibility of arriving at the truth about the world and reality along rational lines." According to the spirit of the age, people experienced "the world and history more or less as an impenetrable fate" beyond their influence. They felt they were "handed over like a powerless slave" without their consent.16 Escape from the world was made possible by a secret gnosis, a magical, mystical, highly speculative knowledge emanating from divine, noncosmic sources, which was designed to free the soul from history, matter, and human experience, exactly those concerns which control our knowledge in the twentieth century. The hallmark of this emergent Gnosticism was an absolute cosmic dualism, rendering daily life and human history as meaningless. Salvation was achieved by absorption into the divine, in response to an esoteric illumination absolutely detached from historical revelation and ethical action. The apostle contended with a world view contrary to contemporary scientism and historicism but similar in its regard for speculation and self-salvation.

The meaning of "knowledge" in Paul's epistles deserves a more biblical rendering than many conservatives, liberals, or revolutionaries are inclined to give. The knowledge of Christ is not simply information about Christ, an interior reflection of one's self-awareness, or political praxis in the midst of social conflict. When considered separately, propositional content, personal awareness, and political impact are inadequate to express the biblical meaning of knowing Christ. Knowing him also involves a personal encounter, an exclusive relationship, a permanent union, and a transformed life.

The most appropriate biblical analogy for the relationship between Christ and the believer is the marriage commitment between husband and wife. Paul's comparison of a husband's responsibility to his wife with Christ's love for the church belongs to a long biblical tradition of illustrating God's intimacy and loyalty to his people through the marriage relationship.

The marriage description in Genesis parallels the Christian's relationship to Christ. "For this reason a man will leave his father and mother and be united to his wife, and they will become one flesh" (Gen. 2:24). The publicly declared, permanent relationship is consummated in sexual intercourse. By becoming "one flesh," the couple is united emotionally, intellectually, and spiritually, as well as physically. God performs a miracle, and on the profoundest level, the two become one. The analogy is helpful for several reasons. First, the intimacy of the marriage union parallels our communion with the Lord. God chooses the intensity and passion of the love between a man and a woman as a picture of his love for us and our love for him. A spouse who is treated like an employee or a roommate is exasperated because of the high expectations he or she holds for intimacy and oneness. Minimal marriages of this type are a contradiction in terms, even if they may be commonplace.

Second, there is a parallel between the exclusivity and permanency of marriage and our relationship to Jesus Christ. Adultery is a serious violation of the "one flesh" experience, robbing the marriage relationship of fidelity, love, and commitment. As there is one husband for one wife, so the believer acknowledges "one Lord, one faith, one baptism" (Eph. 4:5).

Everything which competes against the knowledge of Christ must be sacrificed by the believer. The apostle wrote, "I consider everything a loss compared to the surpassing greatness of knowing Christ Jesus my Lord, for whose sake I have lost all things" (Phil. 3:8). Cleaving to Christ meant leaving behind his former objects of trust and confidence: pride of race, religious merit, family privilege, ideological commitments, and his passion for a cause. The means of salvation was no longer in his hands. He gave up all recourse to self-salvation. He gratefully turned off the old life-support system in order to enjoy new life in Christ. "I consider them rubbish, that I may gain Christ and be found in him, not having a righteousness of my own that comes from the law, but that which is through faith in Christ" (vv. 8–9). Paul's exclusive relationship to Christ is expressed simply in his famous line, "For to me, to live is Christ and to die is gain" (1:21).

When the apostle Paul encouraged husbands to love their wives as Christ loved the church, he referred to the "one flesh" marriage relationship as a profound mystery and then added, "But I am talking about Christ and the church" (Eph. 5:32). All that can be felt and said about the relationship between a husband and wife is superseded by the relationship between Christ and his church. What ought to take place on a human scale in a husband's unconditional love and sacrificial service to his wife is transcended in Paul's example by what Christ has already accomplished for the church. If we are devoted to Christ, intimately and exclusively, it is because Christ has made this relationship possible through his love. We marvel at the deep love between a man and woman and long for an intimacy and a permanency in human companionship. However, we tend to cut off this human longing from its truest and greatest analogy—the transcendent reality of Christ's love for us.

I come to my third observation. North American culture places a great deal of stress on compatibility as a prerequisite to marriage. We are attracted to people we can share with, whose thoughts and goals we can respect and identify with. This preference does not rule out diversity. In the presence of mutual love, differences can enrich a relationship and deepen the shared commitment to one another. The exchange of wedding vows is a mutual pledge to love and commitment. We would be appalled if, in a wedding ceremony, only the bride expressed genuine love and devotion. We would feel the relationship was doomed to fail from the beginning. Marriage involves two people giving themselves to one another to become one flesh. The analogy between marriage and knowing Christ takes a dramatic twist, however, when we examine the Old Testament prophets. They graphically reveal that we bring no beauty, wisdom, or merit to our relationship with Christ. His love for us knows no human precedent. Ezekiel's account of the Lord's vivid description of the abandoned newborn is a visual portrait of Paul's words:

> When we were still powerless, Christ died for the ungodly. Very rarely will anyone die for a righteous man, though for a good man someone might possibly dare to die. But God demonstrates his own love for us in this: while we were still sinners, Christ died for us (Rom. 5:6–8).

God's description of the human condition is as appropriate for modern men and women as it was for Israel:

> On the day you were born your cord was not cut, nor were you washed with water to make you clean. . . . No one looked on you with pity or had compassion enough to do any of these things for you. Rather, you were thrown out into the open field, for on the day you were born you were despised.
>
> Then I passed by and saw you kicking about in your blood, and as you lay there in your blood I said to you, "Live!" I made you grow like a plant of the field. . . .
>
> Later I passed by, and when I looked at you and saw that you were old enough for love, . . . I gave you my solemn oath and entered into a covenant with you, declares the Sovereign LORD and you became mine (Ezek. 16:4–8).

By virtue of our powerlessness and destitution, we have nothing to bring to a relationship with God. We are harassed and helpless, like sheep without a shepherd (Matt. 9:36). All of our confidence in the flesh is rubbish (Phil. 3:4–8; Isa. 64:6). Therefore, apart from God's own initiative, there is no christological starting point. Our first response must always be to acknowledge gratefully what God has done for us and to confess that to know Christ is to be known by him (1 Cor. 13:12; Gal. 4:9). If we have any relationship with Christ at all, it is because of Christ's prevailing love. No amount of ingenuity or provocation can stimulate a passion for Christ among those who have not felt Christ's passion for them.

Throughout this first chapter I have called Christians to know Christ. We have examined the social trends and religious pressures which produce a minimal Jesus and an abstract Christ. We have observed the devaluation of knowledge, philosophically and practically, leading to a crippling reductionism in the capacity of modern men and women to comprehend the full range of truth. We wish to overcome these barriers so that we can say with the apostle, "I want to know Christ and the power of his resurrection and the fellowship of sharing in his sufferings" (Phil. 3:10). Our desire is to know Christ personally and passionately, without fanaticism or hypocrisy. Christ alone can save us from ourselves, propel us forward in a life of service to others, and transform our destiny.[17]

2

the scripture principle

Whatever freshness or creativity is to be found in our study of Jesus must be guided and shaped by the Spirit-inspired witness of the early church. We want to know Christ as he has made himself known—an obvious conviction, to be sure, but not one automatically followed. Classical Christianity rests on this principle, and the thesis of this study requires it. We believe that Jesus Christ is God's ultimate medium of communication to man. As the author of Hebrews writes, "In these last days he has spoken to us by his Son, whom he appointed heir of all things, and through whom he made the universe. The Son is the radiance of God's glory and the exact representation of his being, sustaining all things by his powerful word" (Heb. 1:2–3). Along with the writer of Hebrews, I accept the Scripture principle. I believe in God's historical revelation, expressed in the Old and New Testaments, which conveys to humankind the message of the prophets and the witness of the Son. Apart from the Scripture principle, I have no solid basis upon which to build a christology.

The passions of this age within much of contemporary theology have robbed some of Christendom's most brilliant scholars of a passion for Christ. Instead of using their skills to present Christ to a fallen culture in the wilderness of moral relativism and agnosticism, many theologians have exchanged the Scripture principle for the modernity principle. They have recast Christianity into a highly unstable compound possessing little appeal to the non-Christian, who has little interest in a scaled-down version of Jesus. They deceive themselves into thinking that they have the authority to construct an authentic christology after discrediting the biblical witness. It is important that we weigh the impact of the spirit of this age on the study of Jesus.

WHO DO YOU SAY I AM?

This chapter distinguishes between the Scripture principle and the modernity principle, a necessary exercise if we are to divide humanistic opinion from Spirit-inspired confession. When Jesus asked the disciples, "Who do people say the Son of Man is?" (Matt. 16:13), he clearly meant to establish a distinction between popular opinion and the personal conviction of his disciples. He desired to bring the disciples into a greater spiritual understanding of the identity of the Son of Man. Matthew develops the dialogue between Jesus and his disciples by building on an earlier confession (14:33), first by contrasting the disciples' confession with popular opinion about Jesus, then by defining the role of the Son of Man in terms of suffering and death (16:21–27).

From this key text we learn two important truths from the perspective of the historical Jesus. In the popular opinion of Jesus' day, the greatest compliment was to be compared to the Old Testament prophets. The prophets at that time were revered, respected, and, in some cases, feared as powerful men who were used of God. There was no higher ideal to the religiously minded than to be like Elijah or Jeremiah. Yet Jesus contrasts the peoples' complimentary conclusion about him with the disciples' confession. He makes a distinction between the point of view of spectators and those who have been encountered by God.

"But what about you?" Jesus asked. "Who do you say I am?" Speaking on behalf of the disciples, Peter responded emphatically, "You are the Christ, the Son of the living God" (Matt. 16:15–16). Peter's confession and Jesus' response demonstrate that the difference between the highest human ideal (being like one of the prophets) and the Son of the living God was a difference not only in degree but in kind. Jesus was perceived by Peter as being on an altogether different plane than the prophets, even though much of Jesus' ministry was in continuity with the prophets. There is an obvious contrast between an opinion reached by human insight and analogy and a confession based on God's revelation and personal encounter.

Moreover, we learn that true insight into the identity of Jesus must be revealed by God. "Blessed are you, Simon son of Jonah, for this was not revealed to you by man, but by my Father in heaven" (Matt. 16:17). Our openness to the living God is predicated on the self-revelation of God to us. Apart from Christ's passion for us (see Gal. 2:20—he "loved me and gave himself for me"), we cannot know Christ. As Jesus said, "No one can come to me unless the Father who sent me draws him"

(John 6:44). If we take this statement seriously, our study of Christ will lead us along a path that is wholly different from the one commonly followed today.

Submitting to Christ as he is revealed in Scripture by the power of the Holy Spirit is very different from speculating on a christology acceptable to contemporary thought. As Peter wrote,

> We did not follow cleverly invented stories when we told you about the power and coming of our Lord Jesus Christ, but we were eyewitnesses of his majesty. For he received honor and glory from God the Father when the voice came to him from the Majestic Glory, saying, "This is my Son, whom I love; with him I am well pleased." (2 Peter 1:16–17).

Unless we affirm that our perspective of Jesus does not originate in the will of man but through the revelation of God, we will be seeing Jesus from a "worldly" point of view. An authentic christology begins with a dogmatic disavowal of a minimal Jesus. A humanistic reduction is exposed. A believer can no longer know Christ from a worldly point of view (2 Cor. 5:16). Knowing Christ is a matter of contemplating and obeying what God has revealed through wisdom and power of the Spirit rather than accepting speculative new versions of Jesus compatible with modern views.

Our starting point is quite different from those who seek to abstract Jesus from the obscurity of ancient creeds and the New Testament accounts of his life. We need to keep in mind the apostolic norm presented to us in Scripture as we explore how today's scholars are refashioning Jesus. Their motivation is to make Jesus intelligible to the modern world; their procedures, unfortunately, are faulty.

As we explore the influence of modernity in shaping theological perspective, I seek to identify the motives behind the new christologies and the significance of their interpretation. I am concerned not with individual theologians but with the presuppositions shaping many of today's approaches to Christ. Compliance with the so-called modern outlook is incompatible with the Scripture principle and with classical Christianity.

CREATIVE LICENSE

We have a great many fictional accounts of Jesus' life, from the "infancy Gospels," ancient tabloids sensationalizing Jesus as a boy wonder, to modern creations recasting the biblical account in style and substance suitable for popular consumption. One of the first to exercise unrestrained creative license with the life of Jesus was Ernest Renan, professor of Hebrew and Semitic languages at the Collège de France, who published *Vie de Jesus* in 1863. Renan portrayed Jesus as a young Galilean romantic in love with nature and indifferent to the houses and clothes more necessary in a European culture than in the "sweet and simple life" of Palestine. With a soft voice, a gentle touch, and a mind in tune with the peasant's life, Renan's Jesus extolled a contemplative existence and individual freedom.

In time, however, Jesus' exalted morality nurtured in the "free life of Galilee," degenerated under the pressure of his daily teaching in Jerusalem. He became prone to "fits of severity" and "excessive self-abnegation." Obsessed by his own message, Jesus went too far in demanding of his followers a fanatical detachment from the world and a cultic allegiance to himself.

> Carried away by this fearful progression of enthusiasm, and governed by the necessities of a preaching becoming daily more exalted, Jesus was no longer free; he belonged to his mission, and, in one sense, to mankind. . . . Urgent and imperative, he suffered no opposition: Men must be converted, nothing less would satisfy him. His natural gentleness seemed to have abandoned him; he was sometimes harsh and capricious.[1]

Sadly, the passion of Jesus' own life and ideals was no match for the real world of pressure and greed. In an effort to silence his opposition, Jesus—according to Renan—accepted the wild scheming of his disciples, who contrived, with Lazarus, to put on a show for a gullible public. Having allowed himself to be wrapped in bandages and shut up in the grave, Lazarus stumbled from the tomb at the climactic moment, convincing the superstitious crowd that Jesus had the kind of wonder-working power they expected him to have.

Renan's treatment of the life of Jesus was a sensation in France, selling sixty thousand copies in the first six months and upsetting enough people that he lost his teaching post. Ironically, the romantic-turned-eccentric motif governing Renan's fiction ends not with a disavowal of Jesus but with an eloquent tribute to him. Renan concludes, "Jesus is the one who has caused his fellow man to make the greatest step towards the divine. . . . In him was condensed all that is good and elevated in our nature. . . . All the ages will proclaim that among the sons of men there is none born who is greater than Jesus."[2] Renan's approach to christology marked the onset of a mentality that is still in vogue today.

Behind the captivating style and entertaining fiction is a serious rebellion against the "tyranny of dogma." Renan was committed to a philosophical rejection of the miraculous and complete freedom in a speculative reshaping of what the Bible says about Jesus. His biography illustrates creativity unchecked by the Scripture principle.

ORTHODOXY: THE NEW HERESY

Today's speculative approaches to christology are more sophisticated than Renan's, but they illustrate the same fascination with novel and ingenious creations. Modernity has overtaken the study of Christ, producing inventive new portraits of Jesus and revolutionary ideological agendas. The Logos of God has become a logo exploited for all its worth by people who coopt Jesus for their own purposes. Many contemporary studies on the person and work of Christ seem spurious. I do not blame the student whose first impulse is to reject exposure to these contemporary studies of Christ in favor of a simple biblical study.

Classical Christianity, however, must clarify its teaching in the face of the prevailing heresies of our day. The sheer magnitude of the revolt against orthodoxy requires a critique of the "new" approaches to christology. "Today heresy and orthodoxy have changed roles. It is fashionable, not dangerous, to be a heretic, and dull if unsafe to be orthodox."[3] What began as an open affront to classical Christianity has become the *modus operandi* for doing theology. The evaluation of heresy and orthodoxy has shifted to such an extent that those who hold to classical christology, replete with the Chalcedonian Creed, a literal Incarnation, heaven and hell, the vicarious atonement, and other perceived anachronisms, may soon be labeled heretics.

Truth is an exceedingly precious commodity in any era. Have we become indifferent and cavalier to the distinction between what is false and what is true? Do we revel in relativism and apathetically ask, "What is truth?" knowing full well that the answer has no bearing on our practice? There is indeed a need today for Christians to respond with fresh passion for the truth.

Directly involved in the revolt against orthodoxy is a rejection of the Scripture principle. Does the Bible critique me, or do I critique the Bible? Do I pass judgment on what I find acceptable in the Bible? Do I accept what I want and reject what does not conform to my philosophical ideas, ideological convictions, or personal preferences? True Christians have been convinced that there is a finality about the gospel message. As Jude put it, "I felt I had to write and urge you to

contend for the faith that was once for all entrusted to the saints"
(Jude 3). Genuine believers acknowledge that there is a great deal about
Christ that they do not know. The apostle Paul expressed it well when
he wrote, "Now we see but a poor reflection as in a mirror; then we
shall see face to face. Now I know in part; then I shall know fully, even
as I am fully known" (1 Cor. 13:12). This limitation should always
humble us, but it is a humility derived from a firm conviction in a
definitive revelation from God.

The faith we are challenged to contend for is a body of truth set
down for us. The apostle Paul wrote to Timothy: "What you heard from
me, keep as the pattern of sound teaching, with faith and love in Christ
Jesus. Guard the good deposit that was entrusted to you—guard it with
the help of the Holy Spirit who lives in us" (2 Tim. 1:13–14). The
apostle's warning about a person who "teaches false doctrines and does
not agree to the sound instruction of our Lord Jesus Christ" (1 Tim.
6:3) continues to remind Christians of their responsibility to guard the
gospel of Christ. The Word of God may still have great power among
theologians who methodologically reject the Scripture principle. Their
christologies may still convey profound truths about Jesus Christ that
are ignored or obscured by those who accept the Scripture principle.
But when the unchanging truths revealed in Scripture are downplayed
to make the gospel more compatible with the modern outlook, then the
strength and authenticity of their christology is weakened.

THE MODERNITY PRINCIPLE

Much of modern theology has a compelling concern to make the
gospel intelligible for modern men and women. Changes have to be
made, it is argued, if Jesus is going to have any significance for
generations raised on the hypotheses of modern science, the tenets of
contemporary philosophy, and the comparative studies of sociology and
anthropology. According to John Hick, Christian discipleship will be
possible for our children's children only if Christianity can "remain
honestly believable by being continuously open to the truth."[4]

In 1799, Friedrich Schleiermacher published *On Religion: Speeches
Addressed to Its Cultured Despisers*, in which he developed a thesis which
has remained with modern theology ever since. Schleiermacher argued
that the educated and cultured people of his day were justified in
rejecting the external trappings of religion. They had worn out their
usefulness with the passage of time. They were nothing more than
culture-bound expressions of Christianity that were built up around

genuine expressions of religious experience. According to Schleiermacher, these vestiges of religious consciousness required dismantling to make room for new expressions prompted by contemporary religious feeling. The essence of religion is found not in an ancient biblical revelation of God's self-disclosure in the past but "in the immediate feeling of the Infinite and Eternal." Schleiermacher's principal legacy to contemporary theology was not his intuitive and abstract theology of immediate self-consciousness but his relativizing of religion according to the spirit of the times. Christianity could be stripped of all events and beliefs that a modern thinker perceived to be offensive or anachronistic.

In less abstract language the well-known church historian Adolf Harnack justified reinterpreting the Gospels according to the spirit of the age by claiming that Jesus was a product of his times.

> Jesus Christ and his disciples were situated in their day just as we are situated in ours; that is to say, their feelings, their thoughts, their judgments and their efforts were bounded by the horizon and the framework in which their own nation was set and by its condition at the time.

According to Harnack, the cultural setting determined the substance of the gospel. Jesus was a product of his time, he reasoned, just as we are a product of our time. Consequently, Harnack challenges us to determine what is of permanent value for us today and "not to cleave to words but to find out what is essential."[5]

Either we accept the gospel "in all respects identical with its earliest form, in which case it came with its time and has departed with it," or we sift through its various historical forms for what is of permanent validity. Harnack warns us to be prepared for "one metamorphosis followed by another." The answer Harnack gave to his question "What is Christianity?" includes the key themes for twentieth-century liberalism: the fatherhood of God, the brotherhood of man, and the kingdom of God expounded in the simple, powerful style of Jesus, the moral teacher *par excellence*. Harnack's comment regarding miracles might just as well have been said about the Atonement and the high christology in the Gospel of John: "If there is anything here that you find unintelligible, put it quietly aside. Perhaps you will have to leave it there forever."[6]

Possibly the most famous New Testament exegete of this century carried the modernity principle to an even greater extreme than Harnack. Rudolf Bultmann popularized the concept of *demythologizing,* a term he used to refer to the necessary task of stripping the gospel of its various layers of myth and cultural traditions. Bultmann included much

more in his definition of the mythical view of the world than the
cosmology of a prescientific age. Before he was finished demythologizing, he had eliminated virtually every tenet of the Christian faith.[7]
His dogmatic style of writing gives the reader the impression that
the views expressed are so self-evident and beyond dispute that only a
simpleton would disagree.

> For modern man the mythological conception of the world, the
> conceptions of eschatology, of redeemer and of redemption, are over
> and done with. Is it possible to expect that we shall make a sacrifice of
> understanding, *sacrificium intellectus,* in order to accept what we
> cannot sincerely consider true—merely because such conceptions are
> suggested by the Bible?[8]

The extent of his radical exegesis of the New Testament, prompted by
his loyalty to the modern science of interpretation, becomes evident
when he concludes, "I do indeed think that we can now know almost
nothing concerning the life and personality of Jesus." As a result,
"Attention is entirely limited to what he *purposed,* and hence to what in
his purpose as a part of history makes a present demand on us."[9] For
Bultmann, the modernity principle allows us to salvage from the New
Testament only an existential Jesus who calls men and women in their
moment of crisis to a self-authenticating freedom. As Norman Perrin
said of Bultmann's influential book *Jesus and the Word,* "Socrates the
philosopher or even Attila the Hun" might have appeared as readily as
Jesus the Christ as the critical subject for Bultmann's existentialism.[10]

"I am convinced," writes the late John A. T. Robinson, for many
years one of Britain's leading advocates of the modernity principle, "that
there is a growing gulf between the traditional orthodox supernaturalism in which our Faith has been framed and the categories which the
'lay' world . . . finds meaningful today." Supernaturalism has become
less and less credible to modern humanity. According to Robinson,
theology is encultured with outdated superstitious notions. "The whole
schema of a supernatural Being coming down from heaven to 'save'
mankind from sin, in the way that a man might put his finger into a
glass of water to rescue a struggling insect, is frankly incredible to man
'come of age.' "[11]

Robinson has intended to strike a middle course between natural-
ism and supernaturalism, producing a new theism relevant and
acceptable to modern men and women. He has argued that we can
protect Christianity from its eroding influence in the world only by
recasting the mold, throwing everything into the melting process.[12]

Robinson has flatly stated, "Our image of Christ must change," and has expounded the thesis that "all that Christianity has meant by seeing in Jesus the human face of God can be expressed without its being tied to an image of supernatural intervention." He assures us that he has no intention of denying or depreciating the reality of Christ: "For Christ remains for me the deepest clue to all life and all living." His concern, however, is to release the reality of Christ, "to become more transformingly a part of our twentieth century secular existence."[13]

To accomplish such an objective, Robinson argues, three things must change. First, Jesus must be seen as a product of the evolutionary process like everyone else. The biblical tradition of the Virgin Birth should be taken symbolically or metaphorically. Second, our image of Christ needs to undergo a change from the "idealized portrait" of the Gospels to a more realistic appraisal of his life. We cannot prove his moral perfection, argues Robinson. "The only honest answer is that we do not know." But we can recognize that Jesus was a model of psychological wholeness, able to achieve a fully integrated personality through temptation and suffering. Third, we need to describe the identity of Jesus from a relational and functional point of view rather than from an ontological perspective. "He is not a supernatural figure from the other side. He is a human figure born and raised from among his brothers to be the instrument of God's decisive work and to stand in a relationship to him to which no other man is called."[14] Along with many others, Robinson contends that how we speak of Jesus is governed by what the modern mind finds intelligible. His preoccupation with the spirit of the age and with making the gospel relevant runs counter to the apostolic concern to defend the gospel of Jesus Christ.

A TRUE NORM

In the mystery cults, Judaism, and early forms of Gnosticism, the apostles saw contemporary world views opposed to the gospel of Christ. The apostle Paul expected to be in conflict with the mentality of the age: "Has not God made foolish the wisdom of the world?" (1 Cor. 1:20). He was prepared to "demolish arguments and every pretension that sets itself up against the knowledge of God" (2 Cor. 10:5). There can be no passion for Christ as long as modern men and women are embarrassed about what the Bible says about Jesus. It is not the Spirit of God that prompts this endeavor but the spirit of fear, coupled with pride and arrogance.

Conforming the gospel to the spirit of the age under the guise of contemporizing Christ to secular people is heretical. Furthermore, it is impossible to commend a reduced version of Christianity convincingly. "The idea that the less you take it on you, as a Christian, to affirm and defend, the easier it will be to affirm and defend it, is totally mistaken." James Packer explains:

> Versions of Christianity that have been de-supernaturalized, de-doctrinalized and de-absolutized get torpedoed by the following dilemma: if you believe as much as this, why do you not believe more? But if you believe no more than this, why do you not believe less? This dilemma exposes their arbitrariness, and the realization of that arbitrariness annuls the authority to which they laid claim; for it exposes them as so many private ideas of what Christianity ought to be, in contrast to what it actually is in its biblical and historical form.[15]

If, as we have argued, modernity produced a reduced version of Christianity, then not only is the arbitrariness of the contemporary "authenticating" process revealed but Christian passion is severed from its true source in the apostolic witness. A passion for Christ depends upon a Spirit-inspired life response to the Scripture principle. The modernity principle is but one threat to an authentic, biblically based experience of Jesus Christ. Dead orthodoxy and empty pietism, as we will see, can produce the same effect by squelching a genuine passion for Christ. Neither sterile, clinical exegesis nor a shallow, sentimental experience does justice to the Bible's witness to Jesus Christ. However, those who are exposed to christologies based on the modernity principle should understand more specifically the impact of the spirit of the age on theology. Before we can proceed with a biblically based christology, we need to clear away the confusion and disorientation of the modernity principle.

3

tRuth anÒ Relevance

Making Jesus newsworthy again should concern every Christian. But how contemporary should we be? Truth and relevance drive us to find ways of presenting the gospel with fresh authenticity and challenge. Don Posterski of Inter-Varsity Christian Fellowship has commented, "People outside Christian circles have stopped listening to the voices proclaiming Christ in our culture. . . . For the majority, Jesus is another item of cultural folklore."[1]

Many attribute the passé status of Christianity to the church's inability to change with the times. With twisted logic, some condemn fidelity to the Scripture principle as a pharisaic reaction to change. They argue that, in his own day, Jesus was a liberal and a revolutionary, breaking fresh ground for a new and progressive movement. They add that we should not attempt to capture a static or timeless portrait of Jesus but should follow his dynamic example of change and development in order to meet the needs of contemporary human experience.

Certainly there is some validity in the attack against empty confessionalism, static theologizing, and critical legalism. We acknowledge the need to expose the "heresies" of orthodoxy. But Jesus Christ is not served by reconstructing the gospel according to the arbitrary spirit of modern consciousness. This chapter highlights the tenets of the so-called modern approach to theology and shows their significance for christology.

A WORLD-VIEW SHIFT

The Copernican revolution in the sixteenth century serves as a model for the colossal change in twentieth-century theology. The discovery of the earth's rotation around the sun radically altered the discipline of astronomy. Just as the earth was no longer a fixed point of reference, neither was the Bible and its world view a fixed point of reference for theology. Obviously, the discovery of the earth's orbit had no bearing on planetary motion itself. It was simply a new and more accurate understanding of material reality. Likewise, many modern theologians advocate a reinterpretation of theology in light of current world-view thinking. The definitive and straightforward confessional quality of biblical revelation is relativized, demythologized, and historicized. The Bible is seen solely as a product of its numerous and diverse cultures.[2]

The pervasiveness and popularity of pre-Copernican science and the resistance to change, especially by the institutional church, perhaps encourages contemporary theologians to think that, sooner or later, Christendom will acknowledge this profound world-view shift and accept the hypothesis that the supernaturalism of the Bible is simply a primitive way of speaking. The clarity of the biblical message, which the writers of Scripture themselves have assumed, has been reappraised by modern scholars, who, through scientific criticism of the biblical message, expose its sources, accentuate its diversity, and reduce its truth to the flux of existential experience and cultural modes of expression. Naturalistic assumptions surround biblical interpretation, precluding Scripture's internal claim to authenticity.

Is the world view of Jesus outmoded? On the basis of its supposed lack of relevance, intelligibility, and credibility, many contemporary theologians answer with an unqualified yes. Even those who warn that the gospel must not be shaped by the contemporary thinking maintain that theology faces the task of constructing a new world view consistent with the modern outlook.[3]

THEOLOGICAL DOUBLETHINK

In George Orwell's *1984,* the state is involved in a continuous process of altering historical records and daily news to bring every perspective into conformity with the current thinking of the political party. "Day by day and almost minute by minute the past was brought up to date. . . . All history was a palimpsest, scraped clean and reinscribed exactly as often as was necessary." The image of Winston Smith, tucked away in his small computerized cubicle, rewriting history to suit the purposes of Big Brother, is frighteningly similar to theologians' recasting the gospel in the mold of modernity. Orwell's description of "the labyrinthine world of doublethink" sounds strangely similar to the "newspeak" of modern theology when it comes to redefining the Resurrection and the Atonement: "to know and not to know, to be conscious of complete truthfulness while telling carefully constructed lies."[4]

Theological doublethink is best illustrated by the apparent need for two sets of language: one that is natural, scientific, and descriptive, and another that is supernatural, mythological, and interpretive. "The former views the cause of events in the categories of an evolutionary cosmology, the later in terms of 'moments' like the Creation, the Fall, the Incarnation, the Parousia." These moments, says John Robinson, "are not particular events in the historical past, but ways of giving theological expression to processes and experiences that are going on all the time."[5] Many contemporary theologians work with two stores, or models: historical events are appropriate for the scientific model, whereas theological statements belong to the mythological, or symbolic, model.[6] The symbolic, or metaphorical, language of theology enables the theologian to speak of God, Christ, and salvation as pointers to a transcendent reality that belongs to a single cosmic process but that, in the words of Frances Young, a New Testament scholar in England, "cannot be fitted together in a literal way" with history and science.

> So I find myself able to say: "I see God in Jesus," and "God was in Christ reconciling the world to himself," and other such traditional statements, without necessarily having to spell it out in terms of a literal incarnation.[7]

Latin American theologian Jon Sobrino relies on a similar bifurcation of reality to clarify the confession "Jesus is God." According to Sobrino, this sentence is not to be understood as a *historical* statement commenting directly on Jesus' essence. "Jesus is God," he claims, is a *doxological* statement symbolizing Jesus' unique historical relationship with the Father. He advises us to give up the usual understanding of the copula *is* and to think of the confession relationally rather than ontologically.[8] Sobrino separates the reality of doxology from the realm of history and ontology.

For one unfamiliar with theological doublethink, the use of one set of words with two sets of meanings is confusing. By driving a wedge between the "doxological" and the "historical," Sobrino dehistoricizes the Incarnation and rejects a tenet that the Christian faith has always affirmed, namely, the historicity of the Incarnation. "The Word became flesh and made his dwelling among us" (John 1:14).

Although Orwell did not have theology in mind when he wrote *1984,* his description of doublethink is certainly apropos. "To know and not to know" may be a suitable slogan for much of contemporary theology. Borne along by a legacy of orthodoxy, ecclesiastical establishment, or academic professionalism, many contemporary theologians have moved to the modernity pole. Their confessions are stripped of historic content. Well-intentioned affirmations become little more than denials. Everything is still said, in one form or another, but nothing is proposed that is hard for a secular person to swallow. Is it any wonder that theology has lost credibility? Much of what the world hears from theology only echoes a worldly point of view.

A PSEUDOSCIENCE

Insofar as true exegesis follows principles and procedures designed to recover accurately what the biblical text meant to its original hearers, we are justified in calling biblical interpretation a science. I do not mean to imply, however, that the study of Scripture is reserved for scholars. Rather, we must read the Bible as it was meant to be read, with an eye toward its original historical situation, literary form, grammatical structure, theological context, and contemporary application.

Modern consciousness, however, poses a far greater danger to the science of biblical exegesis than does the ignorance of conservative Christians. Contemporary New Testament scholarship has become in many quarters a pseudoscience that is incompatible with Christian faith because of its presupposition that much of the New Testament is simply inaccurate in describing what actually happened in the life of Jesus.

It is assumed that fiction and history are blended together by first-century writers who are indifferent to the insights which modern historiography holds as essential. Numerous hypotheses have been proposed to suggest a criterion of authenticity which will enable the modern scholar to see behind the various layers of tradition and discover the irreducible historical core. The most famous one was proposed by Bultmann and is still popular today, although few take it to the radical extreme he did. His criterion of dissimilarity identified as authentic those sayings of Jesus which "opposed Jewish morality and piety," exhibited "no specifically Christian traits," and reflected "the eschatological temper characteristic of Jesus' proclamation."[9] In other words, historical authenticity is determined entirely on the basis of Jesus' originality. Therefore, what Jesus actually said must have run contrary to Judaism and have been foreign to the thinking of the early church. Even then Bultmann remained skeptical.

By means of this critical analysis an oldest layer is determined, though it can be marked off with only relative exactness. Naturally we have no absolute assurance that the exact words of this oldest layer were really spoken by Jesus. There is a possibility that the contents of this oldest layer are also the result of a complicated historical process which we can no longer trace.[10]

Although Bultmann's criterion has been criticized and qualified, his legacy continues. Along with other early New Testament radical critics, he has endowed New Testament scholarship with a "minimalistic" mentality toward the Bible. Reginald Fuller, professor of New Testament at Virginia Theological Seminary, commends the criterion of dissimilarity as "the best tool we have if what we want is a critically assured minimum, rather than a maximum that appears excessively vulnerable to skepticism and doubt."[11]

Others who seriously question the criterion and point to its obvious weaknesses still encourage its use because "an insight into a critically guaranteed minimum . . . is indeed a gain in understanding."[12] The scholarly reserve and tentative conclusions that much of modern New Testament scholarship displays has created its own professional ethos that is out of touch with the larger Christian community and seemingly oblivious to the contradiction between Christian confession and the tenets they find compatible with their minimalistic criteria.

Such scholarship is a pseudoscience because its modern bias against supernaturalism precludes a genuine openness to biblical reality. Christian theism is reinterpreted by means of a code of intelligibility accepted by the reigning trends of Western cultural thought, resulting in an a priori falsification of history as it is recorded in the New Testament. History and theology are divorced, under the necessity of having two sets of language. The Dutch Dominican theologian Edward Schillebeeckx states his position clearly regarding the authenticity of the New Testament.

> In the historical quest for Jesus of Nazareth the picture of Jesus afforded by the primitive local churches is precisely what cannot be taken as a criterion, as those kerygmatic interpretations of Jesus were the driving force behind creative tradition. . . . Critically reconstructed details, which bit by bit help to build up a complete picture of the earthly Jesus, are a safer starting-point for further investigation than is a priori acceptance of broad historical reliability.[13]

A passion for Christ is not inimical to the true science of biblical interpretation, but within the hermetically sealed confines of the pseudoscience of modern criticism, theology is left with no reliable criterion for knowing the Christ confessed by the early church.

HUMANIZATION

Orthodox Christians have always believed that Jesus in his very being was God incarnate. This conviction has necessitated reflection on a paradox that ultimately remains a mystery to us. I intend to use mystery not as a way to conceal the absurd but rather as an occasion to acknowledge that the truth of God exceeds our human ability to fully understand and explain.

Since its earliest days the church has resisted the temptation to solve the mystery of the Incarnation through a docetic reinterpretation of the life of Christ. The Greek word *dokeō,* "seem; appear," described the view of some that the humanity of Jesus was a mere appearance. "Psychological Docetism" is a suitable contemporary term to describe the tendency among Christians, especially conservative Christians, to emphasize the deity of Christ and minimize or trivialize his genuine humanity. Norman Anderson, a leading Christian thinker in England, describes his own docetic inclination. "Indeed, as I look back at my own youth and early middle age, I am conscious that I thought of Jesus in such a way that his humanity was largely swallowed up in his deity." Anderson continues,

> However much we may disagree with some of their conclusions, we owe a real debt to those of our contemporaries who have forced us to think much more radically and seriously of "the *man* Christ Jesus," and to ponder anew the mystery of how the Word could, in very fact, "*become* flesh."[14]

No matter how crucial the deity of Jesus of Nazareth becomes in contemporary christology, Christians cannot afford to minimize the genuinely human character of Jesus' life. A docetic defense of the deity of Christ destroys the biblical testimony of Jesus' own growth and development, the humanness of his spirituality, the practical relevance of his ethic, and the pattern of his discipleship. In short, Docetism destroys the significance of the Incarnation.

By dehumanizing the Incarnation, God's purpose for becoming human is concealed, and the apostolic witness is tacitly denied. Classical Christianity, however, challenges the contemporary process of humanizing the figure of Jesus, more by what it denies than by what it affirms. The modern outlook has developed a strategy for humanizing Jesus by emphasizing three interrelated themes: (1) a new understanding of human personhood, (2) the absolutizing of contemporary human experience, and (3) a relativizing of Jesus' own history. Existentialism, combined with an evolutionary understanding of human development, has redefined the way many philosophers and theologians define the human self. Personhood is thought to be a product of what we become through the changes and crises of human existence. We do not begin with a real "essence" or a "substantial self." Self-authentication comes through actualizing our own existence and developing our unique identity. Selfhood is not assumed but is achieved by change and development. Consequently, we come to know who we are in relationship with others and in the context of our own social situation.

The application of this new interpretation to the personhood of Christ results in a functional and relational view of Jesus. Who he is, is determined by his actions. Questions pertaining to his ontological existence are seen as obsolete. Comprehending who Jesus is in himself as a foundation for the meaning and interpretation of what he did is no longer the task of christology. Early church fathers used metaphysical or ontological terms in their christology simply because they were most familiar with these categories of thought. Theology, in accord with the modern world-view shift, presently limits itself to a functional and relational approach. "Essentialism" is abandoned for the sake of modernizing Christianity. If we insist on speaking of Christ as being "one substance with the Father as regards his Godhead, and at the same time of one substance with us in regard to his manhood" (Chalcedon), we run the risk, according to many modern theologians, of speaking in meaningless categories. We must transpose these ideas into relational categories. Therefore, the theory continues, when we speak of the deity of Jesus, we mean that God acted *in* and *through* him in a way different in degree but not in kind from the way God works through us. These theologians, mainly Europeans with an existentialist, phenomenological philosophical orientation, argue that they are not denying that Jesus is God. They are simply denying the concept of the substantive self and the language of essence.

Limiting christology to functional and relational categories, however, relativizes the Incarnation and changes the meaning of Jesus' uniqueness. As Norman Pittenger, a process theologian, comments:

> Indeed, I should be prepared to argue that if we attempt to confine Incarnation to that individual in his supposed discreteness (Jesus), we

shall find ourselves in the end in a position where we are in effect denying his genuine humanity and thus making of the Incarnation a docetic exception to conditions, circumstances, and situations.[15]

By "modernizing" the concept of personhood, Pittinger has significantly redefined the uniqueness of the incarnation of Jesus Christ. If we continue to affirm the absolute uniqueness of the Incarnation, as classical Christianity and the apostolic witness have always done, we will be charged with Docetism.

Humanization has also resulted in the relativizing of Jesus' own history. Since Jesus is seen as a product of his own time and place, with his teachings and actions suited to his particular situation, we are instructed to discover what is normative for our unique situation today. Liberation Theology has made a great deal of the humanity of Jesus, finding in him a paradigm for radical social engagement. Gustavo Gutiérrez, Jon Sobrino, Leonardo Boff, among many others, have challenged Christians to reread the Bible in the light of today's pressing social issues. There is, however, a curious twist to their emphasis on the humanity of Jesus. For these theologians, the significant feature is not Jesus' specific ethical teaching or pattern of political action but his break with Judaism and his openness to the future. Overcoming today's situation of conflict and oppression cannot be accomplished by adhering to yesterday's orthodoxy.

According to this theory, Jesus does not show us one path that is absolute for all time, for his teaching and specific actions were relative to his own unique situation. Liberationists choose the praxis of Jesus over his teaching, thereby distinguishing between Jesus' approach to ethics and the specific content of his ethic. Only a "mature faith," writes Juan Segundo, "can relativize Christ's historical context." He argues that the promise of the Spirit, who "will guide you into all truth" (John 16:13), "points not towards a better understanding of what has already been spoken but towards the learning of new things." These new things may be in conflict with what Jesus has said in the past. As a true man of his times, Jesus was open to the future. He did not live in the past. Liberation theologians encourage us to read the direction of Jesus' life rather than the specific content of his message. Segundo summarizes:

Jesus is not an historical monument. If he were alive and active today, he would say many things that would differ greatly from what he said twenty centuries ago. Without him, but not without his Spirit, we must find out what he would say to free us if he were alive today.[16]

Closely related to the relativizing of Jesus' history is the *absolutizing* of our own experience. Since "Jesus reveals not so much the mystery of God himself as something to be *known cognitively* but rather the way to God that now can and should be travelled by humanity," our own history becomes normative for the *content* of faith. For Jon Sobrino, the Latin American situation supplies much more than the context for meaningful discipleship:

> We realize that our history has absolute importance and that it is only through history that we can envision and arrive at the absolute. The most obvious practical consequences of this realization are bound up with our essential obligation to seek out, here and now, those historical mediations that most clearly seem to point out the way to what is authentically absolute.[17]

Humanization poses some serious problems for classical christology, for theology cannot shrink from admitting human growth, human ignorance, human mutability, and human struggle and temptation in the biblical concept of the Incarnate One.[18] Jesus is not an eternal principle, a pattern for life, a timeless truth, or a divine force.[19] Jesus is not an abstraction. He is a real man with a real history. The Bible affirms that it is impossible to understand christology apart from the concrete history of Jesus. The person of Christ cannot be known directly, in isolation from his words and deeds. The question of Jesus' identity arises from the biblical witness to his life. But starting with the man Jesus does not guarantee a true christology.

How we start with the man Jesus is absolutely crucial in the formulation of christology. If we interpret his history according to the ordinary limitations of our own situation, we dismiss automatically a large portion of his reported history. When his uniqueness becomes subject to our ordinariness, we not only control the evidence which can be legitimately submitted but also shape the remaining evidence according to our purposes.

Approaching the history of Jesus in this way will not adequately account for the uniqueness and significance of the man Jesus, either in his day or our own. If his history is controlled by our history, then we have determined from the start that, regardless of the superlatives we use to describe the historical Jesus, he is not normative in any absolute and lasting sense. This conclusion would be true, precisely because contemporary theological theory has severed the relational from the ontological and the absolute from the historical. Are we willing to let the history of Jesus shape our understanding of his humanity? The only record we have of Jesus' life leads us beyond "functional uniqueness," which puts Jesus on the same level as everyone else except that, for some inexplicable reason, he obeyed the will of the Father more completely than anyone else! It is difficult to imagine why anyone would be seriously concerned to make a case for the absolute relational uniqueness of a man who lived in the first century, apart from the history of conviction that Jesus is in fact God incarnate. Would Jesus still be newsworthy in contemporary theological circles if there had been no legacy of belief in his deity?

Far from doing justice to the full humanity of Christ, the process of humanization, which denies the "substantive self," relativizes the life of Jesus, and absolutizes contemporary experience, shows a conceptual affinity with second-century Ebionites. Like the ancient Ebionites, modern theology wishes to delete the early history of Jesus (Matthew 1 and 2), deny the Virgin Birth, reject the sonship of Christ, dismiss his preexistence, and negate the Atonement. "There can be no doubt," writes Aloys Grillmeier, "that the Ebionites to some extent recognize a transcendence of Jesus and do not simply regard him as a 'mere man'. For them, Christ is the 'elect of God' and above all the 'true prophet.' "[20] Even so, argues Grillmeier, this remarkable presence of God in Jesus was not to be confused with the churches' confession of the Incarnate One. As ancient Ebionism was shaped by the Jewish-gnostic world view of its day, today's version of humanization conforms readily to the modernity principle. In either case we find many commendable insights into the life of Jesus, but historic Christianity judges all versions of Ebionism contrary to the eternal truth of the apostolic witness.

BEING CONSERVATIVE AND CONTEMPORARY

We have argued that the quest to make Jesus relevant again through a reinterpretation of his life according to a modern world view quenches a passion for Christ. Without the norm of Scripture and an openness to a biblical perspective, the simple, clear confession "My Lord and my God!" becomes meaningless and irrelevant. Christology shaped by the modernity principle deprives Jesus of his distinctiveness and turns his name into a logo for an ideology instead of into the Logos of theology. Probably one of the reasons for the popularity of contemporary christologies is the linkage between the known symbols of Christendom and current ideological passions. Many theologians have succeeded in making Jesus popular again in some quarters, but he is not the same Jesus who was worshiped by the apostles.

Obviously, parroting the ancient creeds does not inspire a passion for Christ either. Cold, doctrinaire orthodoxy is rightfully unappealing. By arguing against the modernity principle, we are not making a case for an abstract, irrelevant Jesus. Classical Christians have a twofold task. "On the one hand, we need to face the negative task of overcoming modernity, while on the other hand we need to grow into a more mature and historic expression of the faith."[21]

Orthodox Christians widely agree that theology requires continuous reformulation. Their concern is "to be faithful to historic Christian beliefs taught in Scripture, and *at the same time* to be authentic and responsible to the contemporary hearers." Theology should be both conservative and contemporary, the former pole indicating "that there are limits to adaptation that we ought not to transgress because they represent essential elements of the apostolic proclamation" and the latter pole indicating "our proper *responsibility* to the contemporary hearers of the Gospel whereby we seek to communicate the message meaningfully to them and apply it creatively to the modern situation."[22]

Classical Christians ought to be both conservative and radical. For Donald Bloesch this stance involves going to the roots of the original faith, dispelling the clichés of any particular theological tradition, and subjecting "all traditions to the scrutiny of the original gospel message." It also means conserving "the authentic spiritual values in all theological traditions" and resisting "the way of reaction and repristination, for this road leads to obscurantism and fanaticism."[23] Missiologist Charles Kraft writes,

> If I am to be truly Christian I dare not be simply conservative, especially in a day when people are turning from and misunderstanding Christianity because they fail to see the dynamic of this truth that once "turned the world upside down" (Acts 17:6). [24]

The present Evangelical climate is ripe for an in-depth examination of who Jesus is, what he purposed to do, and what he bids us to do. Latin American Evangelicals such as Samuel Escobar are calling us not only to right thinking but to right action.

> Every cost in terms of sweat and blood, sacrifice and humiliation or persecution for the cause of right and justice will demonstrate that we are crucified with Christ and that we are not just experts on the doctrine of crucifixion.[25]

We need a christology which will overcome the nonbiblical divorce "between evangelization and theology, between preaching and teaching, between conversion and discipleship."[26]

Christologies shaped by modernity may serve the useful purpose of shaking us out of our dogmatic slumbers and our ethnocentrism, but one fact remains: although Evangelicals stress the ongoing need for reformulating the gospel in order to maximize its holistic import, they are convinced that the essential meaning of biblical truth remains unchanged. Admittedly, cultural sensitivity and theological contextualization are necessary if we are to interpret the words of Scripture in their historical and linguistic context. Doctrines, as well, need to be explored from a variety of vantage points if a comprehensive and integrative perspective is to be maintained. Contextualization also plays a vital role in the presentation of the gospel. Receptor-oriented proclamation involves a sensitivity to those emphases within the gospel that will lead its hearers to a full apprehension and appropriation of the biblical message.[27]

Orthodox theology differs from all theologies because it sees a great need to limit relativism. Classical Christians have historically refused to extend the principle of relativity to the essence of faith itself. The truths of the Gospels, quite frankly, are understood in a manner conceptually consistent with the precritical, pre-Enlightenment, historic Christian faith. "The gospel is a non-negotiable revelation from God and we have no liberty to sit in judgment on it, or to tamper with its substance," writes Anglican Evangelical John Stott.

> It is the search for a combination of truth and relevance which is exacting, yet nothing else can save us from an insensitive loyalty to formulae and shibboleths on the one hand, and from a treasonable disloyalty to the revelation of God on the other.[28]

We have frequently erred by not being both faithful to "the apostolic deposit as the essential deposit of faith" and relevant in its application.[29]

We are like the apostle Peter. We get the confession right, but we do not understand its implications. We freely confess, "You are the Christ, the Son of the living God," but a few moments later we take the Lord aside, as Peter did, and rebuke him. Dogmatically we whisper, "Never, Lord!" to the path of discipleship that Jesus himself laid down. We stand between Jesus and the Cross, slow to understand the meaning of the gospel and resistant to the practical realities inherent in confessing Christ as Lord. It is not only the principle of modernity that stands in the way of knowing Christ and becoming like Jesus.

4

the imitation of christ

Jesus had just commended Peter's admiring confession of his deity when he had to rebuke him harshly: "Get behind me, Satan! You are a stumbling block to me; you do not have in mind the things of God, but the things of men" (Matt. 16:23). Although Peter had confessed boldly, "You are the Christ, the Son of the living God," he quickly expressed a cultural opinion about the Messiah, eagerly counseling Jesus on the basis of his preconceived notions of the Messiah's work.

Peter's positive confession, followed by a response negating the words of Jesus, is a vivid picture of culture-bound Christians who proclaim the deity of Christ but who are sinfully resistant to the practical meaning of a true confession. Peter lacks the humility and openness to hear correctly what Jesus has to say. His enthusiasm cannot tolerate Jesus' explanation of the Messiah's suffering and death. Ironically Peter boldly contradicts the one whom he confessed to be the Son of the living God. Instead of permitting Jesus' explanation to shape his expectations, which were self-conceived illusions of success and triumph, Peter readily rebuked Jesus. He was willing to follow Jesus on his own terms and according to his own expectations, which meant rejecting the concrete realities of true discipleship.

Getting the confession right is only half the battle. Like Peter, we may hear the Spirit but still end up in Satan's camp. For this reason, I have emphasized the truth that knowing Christ means becoming like Jesus. Christlikeness is the key for christology. The great Pauline theme of union with Christ is consistent with the emphasis in the Gospels on following Jesus. Biblical christology holds together two essential and inseparable dimensions which we tend to separate in our traditional approaches to christology: the person of Christ and the life of Jesus. If we limit the scope of our study to the nature of Christ alone, we unwittingly distort the relationship between theology and ethics, spirituality and doctrine, salvation and sanctification. We convey the false impression that christology involves a theoretical and abstract discussion on the relationship between the divine and human in Jesus Christ.

This approach is inadequate because it divorces serious reflection on the person of Christ from an equally profound consideration of the teaching and action of Jesus. We cannot know Christ apart from understanding Jesus. To admit otherwise is to render the Incarnation superfluous. We need to comprehend the nature of Jesus' spirituality, the impact of his ethic, and the meaning of his salvation. If we achieve this understanding, we will discover, as Peter did, that confession can never stand without commitment, no matter how correct.

CONFESSION AND COMMITMENT

Some people preach Christ, although their actions and motives are alien to the ways of Christ. Through God's mercy and in spite of them, others may at times genuinely benefit from their preaching. We do not therefore condone hypocrisy (Phil. 1:15–18). Similarly, we cannot critique the modernity principle for undermining the historic confession of Christ without acknowledging that conservative Christians have often been guilty of a heretical divorce between confession and commitment. Instead of a passion for Christ, well-meaning but misguided Christians have frequently cultivated a false enthusiasm based on a preconceived notion of Christ and the Christian life. They assume the validity of a certain understanding of Jesus Christ without testing their assumptions or scrutinizing their easily acquired convictions. It is time we develop a constructive suspicion of our popular notions about Jesus and subject them to a careful examination by God's Word.[1]

Jesus emphasized to his followers that a life of discipleship was the true follow-up to confession: "If anyone would come after me, he must deny himself and take up his cross and follow me" (Matt. 16:24). Insight means action, and action results in understanding. There is a lively exchange between confession and commitment which authenticates confession and purifies commitment. We cannot follow Jesus authentically any way we please. We must follow him according to his example through the power of his Spirit.

Christians must realize that this double task is not easy. We do not naturally adopt a pattern of life which reflects Christ. We have too many preconceived notions of what life should be like to readily transform our thinking and change our actions according to the will of Christ. Sin is too deeply ingrained within and too manifest without for anyone to assume an automatic Christian maturity.

Earlier I argued that the supernatural incarnation is incredible to modern men and women. But is not costly discipleship incredible to many conservatives? The language of losing one's life for Christ's sake may be as symbolic and mythical to conservatives as the Virgin Birth and substitutionary atonement are to liberals. Yet precisely because conservative Christians have been willing to risk their intellects in order to discover the truth disclosed in Christ, they now need to risk their lives in order to discover the fullness of life in Christ. "If you hold to my teaching," said Jesus, "you are really my disciples. Then you will know the truth, and the truth will set you free" (John 8:31–32). Knowing the truth and living obediently are always bound together. Becoming like Jesus is the only way to do christology authentically.

A BIBLICAL PATTERN

I will establish the biblical precedent for understanding Christ by exploring the apostolic witness. Can we find support within Scripture for our emphasis on becoming like Jesus as the key to christology? Around the turn of the century, William Wrede proposed the thesis that the apostle Paul's vision of Christ and the Synoptics' portrait of the historical Jesus were so different as to be unrelated. He argued that there was an "enormous gulf" between the "historical human personality" of Jesus and the supernatural Christ of Paul. According to Wrede, Paul simply transferred his previous conception of the Messiah to Jesus.[2] If the great Pauline theme of union with Christ has nothing to do with the historical Jesus, Paul's christology was simply a personal recounting of his own religious experience and vision.

If we read only Paul's letters, we would never know that Jesus taught in parables and healed the sick or that he was baptized by John and tempted by Satan. Nor would we know of Peter's confession at Caesarea Philippi or of the Transfiguration. Paul repeatedly interpreted the Crucifixion theologically, but he did not describe the events leading up to Jesus' death.[3] Do these omissions mean that Paul considered Jesus' life and teaching unimportant? Was Paul's understanding of being in Christ different from Jesus' meaning when he commanded his followers to take up their cross and follow him? Several observations may be made.

First, Paul chose a natural literary form for his dialogue with the churches. His epistles were an extension of his ministry, building on his previous teaching, correcting misinterpretations, and developing doctrinal and ethical implications. He never implied that he was saying all there was to say about Christ. It seems more reasonable to assume that he left the task of portraying the historical Jesus in written form to those who were closely associated with Jesus' earthly ministry than it does to conclude that he discounted the historical Jesus.

Second, the differences between Paul's writings and the Gospel accounts are similar to the differences between the other Epistles and the Gospels. The writers assume that the readers have either an oral or a literary source for the life of Jesus. They make no attempt to reconstruct the historical Jesus, but in their teaching and theologizing they assume it. For example, the Book of James makes only two specific references to Jesus Christ, and it does not mention the Cross or the Resurrection. Yet it is filled with allusions to Jesus' ethical teaching. Although James never explicitly quotes Jesus or recounts his actions, we hear the historical Jesus in every line, and his parables and teachings come readily to mind. Evidently the writer assumes the reader's knowledge of the life of Jesus. I. Howard Marshall argues that the Gospel tradition and the material appropriate to the Epistles were deliberately kept separate. Evidence for this "lies in the fact that the Epistles of John are free from the type of historical material found in the Gospel of John." Marshall adds, "It would seem legitimate to conclude that the Gospel tradition was a distinct stream in the early church with its own special channel of transmission."[4] We do not have to conclude that Paul's proclamation of Christ was without historical content. The evidence suggests two streams of tradition which were distinct but compatible.

Third, the difference between Paul's christology and the Gospel accounts is exaggerated when the close affinity between Jesus' ethical teaching and that of the apostles is ignored.

> In particular, we ought to compare the ethical section of the Epistle to the Romans (12:1–15:7), where Paul summarizes the practical implications of the gospel for the lives of believers, with the Sermon on the Mount, to see how thoroughly imbued the apostle was with the teaching of his Master.[5]

Furthermore, Paul's description of Christ's character and example fits well with the Gospel portrait of Jesus (2 Cor. 10:1 with Matt. 11:29; Rom. 15:3 with Mark 8:34; Rom. 15:1 with Luke 22:27; Phil. 2:7 with John 13:4–15).

Finally, the apostle Paul's christological starting point was Christ's resurrection. Paul's life and theology were dramatically shaped by his Damascus-road encounter with the risen Christ. Blinded by a light from heaven, Saul fell to the ground and heard a voice say to him, "Saul, Saul, why do you persecute me?" "Who are you, Lord?" Saul asked. "I am Jesus," was the response, "whom you are persecuting" (Acts 9:4–5). The idea that the risen, historical Jesus was one with the lowly Nazarene he was fiercely persecuting must have haunted Saul. Paul's theology of union with Christ gives no cause for the charge that he minimized the historical Jesus. We know that he had no inclination to form his own sect (1 Cor. 1:10–13) and that he emphasized that his message was basically the same as the other apostles (15:11).

Many modern scholars are skeptical of Paul's appreciation for the historical Jesus. For them, the division between the Jesus of history and the Christ of faith remains sharp. This view is reflected in Bultmann's rather odd exegesis of 2 Corinthians 5:16. Bultmann equated the recognition of Christ "from a worldly point of view" with the history of Jesus, which allowed him to affirm that Paul rejected Jesus' self-understanding and messianic consciousness.[6] The evidence, however, indicates that Paul intended to contrast his former attitude with his present view of Christ and the world. "In Christ" Paul was not only a new being but profoundly interested in the historical Jesus. Like the Epistles, the Gospel accounts were written with the Resurrection in view, but unlike the Epistles, the Synoptic writers endeavored to present the revelation of God in Jesus of Nazareth as it developed and unfolded. Paul viewed the Gospel tradition as a reality undergirding his christology. His bold proclamation of the historical, bodily resurrection of Jesus coincides with his emphasis on being in Christ. Christ's atoning sacrificial death and bodily resurrection make the believer's present experience with the risen Christ possible (1 Cor. 15). For Paul, the believer's present relationship with Christ looks back to the historical Jesus and forward to the risen Christ. This dual thrust is inseparable in the mind of Paul.

A brief examination of the apostle's famous christological statements reveals a conscious dependence upon the example of Jesus. "Your attitude should be the same as that of Christ Jesus," writes Paul in his preface to the Christ-hymn of Philippians 2. Through this hymn Paul presents Jesus as the supreme example of the "humble, sacrificing, self-denying, self-giving service" that he has been urging believers to practice. Especially important for our purposes is the apparent parallel with the Gospel account of Jesus' washing his disciples' feet (John

13:3–17). According to Hawthorne, "The parallels in thought and in the progression of action are startling. So precise in fact are these parallels that it is difficult to consider them the result of mere coincidence." "Perhaps," adds Hawthorne, "this act and saying of Jesus became the basis for deep insights into the nature of Christ for both John and Paul."[7]

This possibility is significant for our thesis. If the hymn is the result of meditating on this particular event in Jesus' life, it reinforces the conclusion that Paul's christology is derived from the historical Jesus. It is also important to realize that, for Paul, ethics and theology were not divorced. Understanding the nature of Christ coincides with living out the ethics of Jesus. Paul saw fit to use the unique reality of the Incarnation with its humiliation and exaltation of Christ for the purpose of teaching ethics.[8] He is not compelled to inform the believers of the differences between Christ and themselves. He does not qualify his stress on Christlikeness by stating the obvious. Although Paul often considers the uniqueness of Christ's substitutionary death on our behalf, he frequently uses the life and death of Jesus as a pattern for Christians to follow (Rom. 15:1–7; 1 Cor. 10:31–11:1; 2 Cor. 8:6–9; 1 Thess. 1:6). The apostle Peter stressed the ethical implications of Christ's sacrificial death as well: "If you suffer for doing good and you endure it, this is commendable before God. To this you were called, because Christ suffered for you, leaving you an example, that you should follow in his steps" (1 Peter 2:20–21).

The apostles assumed the unity of salvation and sanctification to a degree uncommon in conservative as well as modern theological reflection. Conformity "to the likeness of his Son" is an accomplishment wrought by the predestinating, justifying, glorifying work of God (Rom. 8:29–30). Because "we are God's workmanship, created in Christ Jesus to do good works" (Eph. 2:10), we are reminded by Paul to become like Jesus. Paul ties the spiritual, supernatural experience of knowing Christ to a tradition he expected his readers to be fully aware of and governed by: "Surely you heard of him and were taught in him in accordance with the truth that is in Jesus" (4:21). The apostle Paul's obedience to the pattern of Christ gave Paul confidence in calling believers to imitate his own life. As he followed Christ, believers were to follow him (Phil. 3:17).

If we desire, as Paul did, to reflect the Lord's glory and be "transformed into his likeness with ever-increasing glory" (2 Cor. 3:18), we will root our spiritual experience in the finished work of Christ on the cross *and* in the powerful example of Jesus' life. The Spirit of God has always impressed believers with both dimensions. Gratitude for salvation will result in true spirituality and moral action.

The biblical precedent for uniting discipleship and christology is also found in 1 John, where we read, "This is how we know we are in him: Whoever claims to live in him must walk as Jesus did" (1 John 2:5–6). As in Paul's epistles, salvation and sanctification, theology and ethics, are combined. "He is the atoning sacrifice for our sins," writes John, and then adds, "we know that we have come to know him if we obey his commands" (vv. 2–3).

The writer of Hebrews follows a similar pattern. Christology involves conviction and challenge. He combines the high christology of his introduction—"The Son is the radiance of God's glory and the exact representation of his being, sustaining all things by his powerful word" (Heb. 1:3)—with the challenge to follow Jesus. His immediate vision of Christ is dependent upon the history of Jesus. "But we see Jesus, who was made a little lower than the angels, now crowned with glory and honor because he suffered death, so that by the grace of God he might taste death for everyone" (2:9). Growth and maturity in Christian understanding results in moral action and ethical sensitivity. "Let us leave the elementary teachings about Christ and go on to maturity" (6:1) is as much a plea for belief in the supremacy of Christ as it is a challenge to Christian discipleship. The believer's existential experience of Christ today must be rooted in the historical Jesus.

> Let us fix our eyes on Jesus, the author and perfecter of our faith, who for the joy set before him endured the cross, scorning its shame, and sat down at the right hand of the throne of God. Consider him who endured such opposition from sinful men, so that you will not grow weary and lose heart. (12:2–3)

The biblical pattern in the Epistles that assumes and develops the Gospel tradition of the historical Jesus is evident within the Gospel accounts as well. Understanding Christ is invariably tied to following Jesus. For example, the saying of Jesus, "It is enough for the student to be like his teacher, and the servant like his master" (Matt. 10:25), bears far greater significance in the context than the simple analogy might suggest. Obedience to Jesus, or becoming like the teacher, is equated with obedience to the Son of Man (v. 23), a title used by Jesus which bears significance for his self-understanding as the Messiah. Furthermore, becoming like Jesus involves the disciples in rejection and persecution. "If the head of the house has been called Beelzebub, how much more the members of his household!" (v. 25). Nothing less than salvation itself is at stake if we fail to acknowledge Jesus before other people (v. 33). Becoming like Jesus thus assumes the authority of the Son of Man, the cost of discipleship, and the acknowledgment that Jesus is decisive for salvation. Commitment entails understanding and confession.

A similar pattern is found in the christologically charged context of Jesus' invitation, "Come to me, all you who are weary and burdened, and I will give you rest. Take my yoke upon you and learn from me, for I am gentle and humble in heart, and you will find rest for your souls" (Matt. 11:28–29). Those who come to Jesus do so because of the Father's revelation of the Son: "No one knows the Son except the Father, and no one knows the Father except the Son" (v. 27). Jesus' simple invitation rests on divine revelation and the absolute uniqueness of the Son. God himself must call us and enable us to come, in order for us to become like Jesus. Matthew's Gospel closes with a final exhortation to adhere to the teaching of the historical Jesus within the context of Jesus' full authority in heaven and on earth and the promise of his abiding presence (28:19–20). His commissioning of the disciples assumes the unity of confession and commitment, salvation and sanctification, theology and ethics. There is no reason to break with this biblical pattern.

By relying on this biblical pattern in developing a christology, we hold these two focuses in tension in a way that many theologies relinquish, and we realize several distinct advantages. First, creedal orthodoxy sometimes leans toward an unbiblical abstraction of the absolute uniqueness of the incarnation of Jesus Christ in a way that separates it from a practical application to Christian living. Perhaps some are surprised to learn that Paul used the christological hymn in Philippians 2 to underscore the need for Christians to show humility. We can determine from the context that his main concern was not the ontological, metaphysical reality of the Incarnation but putting to shame the selfish ambition and vain conceit of certain believers. Paul used the profound truth of the Incarnation to make his point.

Another example is Jesus' High Priestly Prayer in John 17. Jesus compares his own essential relationship with the Father with the unity that should be evident among believers. Through a series of comparisons Jesus freely illustrates that what is true of his own person and work applies to his followers. Just as the Son is the recipient of the Father's word, unique identity, special protection, and divine glory, so the believer becomes a beneficiary of these same privileges. The apostles were convinced that the very relationship between God the Father and

God the Son could be used analogically to apply to believers in relationship to God and one another. They made this analogy without feeling compelled to explain what was for them an obvious difference in kind between Christ and themselves. As we follow their pattern, we hold together the absolute uniqueness of Jesus Christ and the absolute relevance of everything about Jesus for our lives.

Perhaps creedal orthodoxy is overly cautious at times in safeguarding the uniqueness of Jesus at the expense of his relevance. It is a terrible irony when Christians excuse their failure to become like Jesus by using the docetic excuse that his deity makes him exceptional. Actually, just the opposite is true. Because God was in Christ reconciling the world until himself, we have the requisite spiritual power and forgiveness of sin to become like Jesus (Phil. 4:13).

Second, when we unite christology with discipleship and sanctification, we give to Christ's earthly life the attention it deserves. Becoming like Jesus underscores the continuity between the Gospel tradition and the Epistles. It unites history and doctrine after the manner of the apostles. "The evangelical wing of Christianity," writes Howard Marshall, "has a strong temptation to concentrate its attention on the crucified and risen Lord Jesus and to ignore his earthly life." "There is a temptation," he warns, "to ignore the religion of the Gospels and to concentrate on the Epistles."⁹ Many Christians have only a Christmas-and-Easter christology. They jump from the manger to the cross without giving serious consideration to the life of their Lord. Our emphasis on the historical Jesus is true to what the apostles assumed and developed when they wrote their letters to the churches.

Third, an authentic confession of Jesus Christ depends upon a genuine commitment to the ethic and example of Jesus, which is the only way people will find our christology credible. A theoretical theology is no match for the realities of human existence. Skeptics will be proven right if all our talk about "spiritual reality" has no concrete meaning in daily life. If we do not share in the compassion and justice of Jesus, it will become painfully obvious that we do not know the person of Christ. This fact helps to explain the tremendous disparity among Christians who share the same verbal confession but differ radically over very serious matters of ethics and lifestyle.

Can we share the same christology and yet fundamentally disagree over the life and example of the historical Jesus? Effective evangelism and Christian unity depend upon true confession and costly commitment. The apostle Peter said as much when he challenged believers to set apart Christ as Lord (1 Peter 3:15). Whether or not the world believes our confession depends upon our commitment to the example of Jesus and obedience to his commands (John 13:35; 17:23). In fact, we can say further that whether or not *we* believe *our own* confession depends upon commitment and obedience (1 John 3:16–24). Apart from doing what Jesus did through the power and wisdom of the Spirit of God, we lack assurance of our confession of Christ.

Finally, we must not equate becoming like Jesus with a humanistic achievement. Christ's life takes shape in ours through the grace and power of God. All attempts to follow Jesus through legalistic attachment, self-generated mysticism, or shallow sentimentality are bound to fail. Without the supernatural power of God working in us, the "imitation of Christ" overwhelms the individual as an impossible burden to bear, leading to the excesses of self-righteousness. In order to be properly understood, the imitation of Christ must be considered within a comprehensive view of spirituality that affirms the sovereign grace of God and the power of the Spirit of God to transform us into his image (Rom. 8:29).[10] Just as we have sought to define *Christlikeness* by the specific example of the historical Jesus, we also need to affirm the supernatural character of discipleship. For only through the Spirit of God can we be "transformed into his likeness with ever-increasing glory" (2 Cor. 3:18).

A UNIFIED CHRISTOLOGY

The passion for Christ I seek to nurture and stimulate is rooted in an undivided Jesus, whose life is disclosed comprehensively through the apostolic witness. I desire to hold together what the biblical testimony unites. Therefore I seek to take seriously both the historical example of Jesus' earthly ministry and the apostolic testimony to the preexistent Logos. I believe that Christ has accomplished for us our eternal salvation through his atoning sacrifice and glorious resurrection. But I also believe that his life and teaching have always been the concrete model for Christian discipleship. He is coexistent with the Father, even as we gratefully accept his identification with us through the changes and development inherent in human existence.

We want the benefit of appreciating Jesus Christ both relationally and ontologically, learning from his spirituality and self-understanding, even as we are drawn to worship him in the mystery of his being. We are not embarrassed by his miracles and impressed only with his ethics. We accept them both as authentic and foundational for our study of Christ. We need to learn from Jesus' identification with the downtrodden and the poor, even as we need to preach salvation in Christ alone. By the power of his Spirit we want to have faith *in* Jesus as well as the faith *of* Jesus. We believe he is not only the object of our worship but the example of how we are to worship. Our unified approach to christology takes seriously the classical Christian conviction that Jesus was truly God and truly man.

But the imitation of Christ is not easily accomplished, as any quick survey of famous Christian personalities will indicate. Perhaps we assume too quickly that our understanding of Jesus captures the essence of Christian living. We need to ask ourselves if genuine confession and costly commitment actually forge our passion for Christ and if our understanding of Christ is shaped by the Spirit of God and the historical Jesus.

A HISTORY OF IMITATION

Like a musical theme uniting the various movements of a great symphony, the "imitation of Christ" is a powerful theme resounding through the history of Christianity. The frequent use of the word *imitation* in today's vernacular may imply a cheap copy of the real thing, but in the church the term has been used to describe serious discipleship.

Five hundred years ago Thomas à Kempis wrote *The Imitation of Christ,* a devotional classic which has not ceased to stimulate genuine spirituality in the lives of Christians world-wide. He awakened earnest believers to the rigors of discipleship, the deceptiveness of self, and the lusts of the world and challenged them to cultivate a deeply personal awareness of Christ. "Our chief pursuit," wrote Kempis, "is to meditate upon the life of Jesus Christ." Whoever "would fully and feelingly understand the words of Christ must endeavor to conform his whole life to Him."[11] *The Imitation of Christ* proved to be a catalyst for spiritual renewal, calling Christians "to a simple conformity to Christ" and "to a more realistic view of the demands of Christian life."[12] We may wish that Kempis had set forth the great Reformation themes of justification by faith and the imputed righteousness of Christ, but his work has had lasting significance nevertheless.

Humble submission to the work of God was honored by Thomas à Kempis above the extremes of speculation and intellectualism. Although he wrote for fifteenth-century Christians who were contemplating monastic vows, Thomas appears to have envisioned a spiritual life accessible to everyone.[13] He claimed that true piety for all believers finds its source in a Spirit-inspired imitation of Christ. Twentieth-century believers can still learn much about the cultivation of the inner life from him.

But the imitation of Christ involves not only our devotional life but our professional life as well. The solitude of the monastery which was so much a part of Thomas à Kempis's vision of spirituality has given way to the activism of today's church. There is a growing sense that we need to become like Jesus not only when we pray but also when we vote. We need Jesus' example both in our solitude and in our social action. If we aspire to an ever-deepening spirituality, we must follow Jesus into the world.

We have seen that the controlling factor in the apostolic understanding of the imitation of Christ was the historical Jesus. In their experience, the imitation of Christ was a passionate commitment which radically transformed their world-and-life view. Jesus' concrete life was the model for their lives. Sadly this standard has not always been followed in the history of the church. At times the life and teaching of Jesus have become obscured and distorted.

Certain monastic models of imitation illustrate this distortion. Reacting to worldliness, political power, and the corrupting influences of culture, elements within the monastic movement equated Christlikeness with specific vows of poverty, chastity, and submission. Spiritual perfectionism prohibited private ownership and marriage, since property and belongings prevented complete reliance upon Christ and family life distracted from single-minded devotion to Christ. In some orders, rigorous asceticism became the only path to spirituality. Severe privations were enforced in the routine activities of eating, sleeping, and conversation.

Monastic imitation identified features of the life of Jesus—his chastity, poverty, and fasting—as important qualities of Christlikeness and held these out as the marks of true spirituality. Unfortunately they often obscured the meaning of the Incarnation, the humanness of spirituality, the social impact of Jesus' teaching on culture, and the freedom to be found in the experience of God's grace in Christ. Justification by faith in the finished work of Christ was overshadowed by a highly selective appropriation of Christlike qualities. The tension between the two was spoiled. The totality of Jesus' life and teaching was fragmented into a code of spirituality designed to compensate for past sin and heighten sensitivity to the austerities of Jesus.

Moving beyond the Galilean example, the mystics stressed the immediate mystical relation of the soul to Christ. By divesting themselves of all temporal concerns and shunning society, they devoted themselves to an intuitive and imaginative comprehension of Christ. They dwelt for long periods on the suffering of Jesus in order to evoke a oneness with the Savior. Although the imitation of Christ was their passion, they failed to hold the grace and example of Jesus' life in Spirit-directed tension. Spirituality collapsed under the burden of self-effort, separation, and self-afflicted suffering.

In the tradition of authentic monasticism represented by Bernard of Clairvaux, Francis of Assisi, and Thomas à Kempis, Martin Luther reacted against these excesses with a fresh presentation of the biblical Jesus. He held together the person and work of Christ and heralded justification by faith as the liberating ground for sanctification by grace. He struck down the notion that monastic life created a spiritual elite who followed the "counsels of perfection" unachievable by ordinary Christians who simply settled for the gospel commands. Luther's quip, "I will give myself as a sort of Christ to my neighbor," underscored his practical, other-directed spirituality. Luther's attitude was "It is better to sweep a room carefully than to fast or flog oneself in a cloister."[14]

Luther opposed those who venerated the tortured Christ in images and imaginations. After all, said Luther, "The wounds of Jesus are safe enough for us." An emotional contemplation of the cross did not necessarily result in a true understanding of Jesus' death or lead to genuine Christian crossbearing. What mattered to Luther in his "theology of the Cross" was actual solidarity with Christ in real suffering: "the mortification of the old Adam in life-long penitence; the conformity of Christians with Christ as opposed and crucified by sinful men."[15]

Along with Luther, other Reformers rooted the imitation of Christ in justification by faith, the priesthood of all believers, and obedience to Christ in the culture at large. Years later John Wesley said, "I take religion to be . . . a constant ruling habit of soul, a renewal of our minds in the image of God, a recovery of divine likeness, a still increasing conformity of heart and life to the pattern of our most holy Redeemer."[16] We cannot introduce the subject of the imitation of Christ without acknowledging the very different conceptions of Christlikeness to be found in the history of the church. Disagreements have existed that are still with us today. For example, should we renounce the world or change the world? Should we emphasize outward action or inward contemplation? Should we admonish conformity to standards or encourage freedom from rules? Should we stress austerity or settle for legitimate accumulation? Should we live in community or focus on individuality? In short, how do we become like Jesus?

MODELS OF IMITATION

The meanings of the "imitation of Christ" today vary so widely that some versions seem completely alien to the apostolic witness. But if christology and discipleship take the history of Jesus seriously, then current models of imitation ought to be evaluated. In the three models I discuss here, I illustrate the tendency of many to isolate from Jesus' life an aspect of his personality or a feature of his ministry as the essence of discipleship. In all three cases the resultant "Jesus model" becomes the author's paradigm for perfection.

Myron Rush is a businessman who uses Jesus to develop a biblical approach to management. Rush congratulates Jesus for being "the best manager and developer of human resources the world has ever seen." Rush is drawn to Jesus because Jesus created "a work environment for those He trained that allowed them to start the church." Therefore "the manager interested in creating an effective and productive work environment should pattern it after the principles used by Christ."[17] The author does not identify the principles of Jesus' lordship, his call for justice on behalf of the poor and oppressed, sacrificial servanthood, or the coming of the kingdom. Instead he points to principles popular in our democratic society, noting that Jesus encouraged individual initiative and personal creativity among the disciples by allowing them to make decisions. He trusted them to think for themselves and work out their problems.

Was Jesus an ideal business manager? Unquestionably, Jesus treated the disciples with human dignity and employed principles conducive to human development. To that extent, Rush is correct. But to use Jesus to affirm general relational qualities as a special dimension of his ministry is to reduce the imitation of Christ to the implementation of managerial skills. While Rush's aim is admirable, he overshadows Jesus' specific history and unique teaching by reducing him to serve as an illustration of popular principles. Calling Jesus the best manager the world has ever seen conjures up images of salesman of the year, Rotary Club lunches, and the smooth, friendly manner of a model businessman. In fact, Jesus and his disciples were worlds apart from board rooms, production deadlines, and capitalism. Even democracy was foreign to them. Will businessmen therefore find little to imitate in Christ's life, especially when it comes to business practice? Not at all, as we shall see when we examine the ethics of Jesus. Becoming like Jesus is relevant to modern business in a distinctive and costly way.

Another "Jesus model" is heralded by popular advocates of self-esteem and possibility thinking. According to Robert Schuller, psychiatry rather than theology has exposed our deepest needs. Human beings hunger for self-esteem, self-worth, and personal dignity. For Schuller, human dignity is the ultimate human value. The church has not been able to communicate the gospel creatively because it has depended upon inappropriate starting points, namely, Scripture and the doctrine of God. This claim sounds sensational, Schuller admits, but emphasizing these points only leads to disunity. The only "theological launching point of universal agreement" is the "dignity of the Person." He concedes, however, that "we cannot simply anoint self-esteem as our philosophical supreme authority unless it is in fact the centrifugal force in the mind and heart of Christ."[18]

Laying aside "salvation from sin" and what he sees as an overemphasis on the theology of Paul, Schuller turns to Jesus as the paradigm of perfection. Jesus is the Ideal One, the Ultimate Person, the Universal Human Standard.[19] Historically, theologians have dealt with humanity's willful rebellion from God and the power of sin and the devil, but Schuller concentrates on people's negative self-image, their inability to trust, and their sense of inferiority and anxiety.

In one sense Schuller is right. Jesus appealed to the dignity of the person, raised people's self-esteem, and fellowshiped with those struggling with depression and guilt. Becoming like Jesus, counsels Schuller, means using your positive attitude the way Jesus did to allow negative situations to make you a more sensitive, understanding, compassionate human being. Jesus' "only achievement," says Schuller, "was the building of a personal character and reputation that would be an inspiration to millions yet unborn. How did he become this kind of person? By specializing in the building of self-worth in persons that appeared worthless."[20] But does this emphasis represent the essence of the imitation of Christ?

It may sound overly critical to condemn Schuller's approach, because so many people do suffer from low self-esteem, loneliness, inferiority, and anxiety. Nonetheless Schuller does use Jesus as a model for contemporary notions of the ideal self and ends up Christianizing the popular self-help movement. Nowhere do we find Jesus saying "think positive," "believe in yourself," or "dare to love yourself." Schuller reduces the imitation of Christ to a technique of self-affirmation, which results in a gospel susceptible to our culture's notions of success and sacrifice, self-fulfillment and self-denial. Jesus' example has much to say to the contemporary self-image, but it cannot be reduced to clever slogans gleaned from pop psychology. Becoming like Jesus means knowing the Father through a Christlike spirituality and developing self-understanding and dependence upon God's Word as Jesus did. There are no shortcuts to the true imitation of Christ.

John Alexander, editor of the *Other Side,* provides our third case study. Alexander has presented Jesus as the paradigm of perfection for the poor, contending that, because Jesus owned no possessions, neither should believers. The author reasoned that, if Mahatma Gandhi, a Hindu, could follow Jesus into poverty, then all Christians should. After describing his simple lifestyle, which included a fifteen-inch black-and-white television, a ten-thousand-dollar life-insurance policy, a ten-speed bike (instead of a car), and the lowest food budget of any American family he knew, Alexander lamented that he still had too many possessions.

> They say Gandhi could put all his possessions in a bag. I think that's the road Jesus meant. That's the gospel. Funny, isn't it? A Hindu doing what Jesus taught when Christians won't. It hardly ever occurs to us that Jesus might mean anything like that. And if it does occur to us, we immediately say that Jesus couldn't have meant that because it isn't practical. You can't sell your possessions. How would you live? And other Christians hasten to assure you that it wouldn't work to sell our possessions. But Gandhi did it.[21]

The difficulty with this particular appeal to Christlikeness is that it equates poverty with discipleship and true spirituality. Generating false guilt and polarizing the Christian community by projecting a rationale for simplicity not found in the New Testament, the article fails to turn to the historical Jesus.

Jesus was indeed poor, and his lifestyle was simple. Since he was neither controlled by his possessions nor prejudiced against those who had material things, he was free to serve poor and rich. Jesus' relationship to the poor should be of special importance to us. We cannot seek to imitate Christ without demonstrating solidarity with those in need. The lifestyle hailed in the editorial, however, is more reminiscent of Gandhi and the Bohemian portrayal of Jesus in modern movies than of the man supported by influential women (Luke 8:3) and falsely accused of being a glutton and drunkard (Matt. 11:19). Undoubtedly, Jesus will judge the materialism of the North American church and our fascination with acquisitions. Nonetheless we should not confuse the meaning of becoming like Jesus with whether we own our own homes or rent. Such a preoccupation distorts the true imitation of Christ.

These three models of Christlikeness have two similarities. In the first place, becoming like Christ is defined more by the author's perspective than by the actual life and teaching of Jesus. Each assumes to know what Jesus stands for and then bolsters his position by referring to Jesus as the paradigm of perfection. For business managers, he is the best manager the world has ever seen. Possibility thinkers look to him as the Ideal Self; athletes, as the great competitor. To radicals he is the poorest of the poor, and to success enthusiasts he is a true winner.

I realize that we cannot think about Jesus apart from our backgrounds. To some extent all interpretations reveal our cultural experience, but this limitation need not seriously interfere with discovering who Jesus Christ is and what he expects of us. To some extent the demands of discipleship are new every moment, and the question of what it means to imitate Jesus is open-ended. But such sensitivity and insight grows out of the definitive example and teaching of Jesus rather than out of our preconceptions.

In the second place, these models exhibit the natural tendency to simplify what is involved in becoming like Jesus so that discipleship is safely limited to a manageable agenda, whether it be building up someone's self-esteem or selling all one's possessions. We so often see what we want to see in Jesus' life and hear what we want to hear in his teaching that our discipleship bears only a vague resemblance to what Jesus stood for. Interpretations of the imitation of Christ show us how easy it is for Christians to go astray by selecting one of the qualities of Jesus' life as the essence of the Christian life. Jesus never wished to be identified as the best business manager that ever lived. What right do we have to say to athletes that Jesus is the great competitor or to radicals that Jesus is the poorest of the poor?

We all need to become aware of our penchant to cast Jesus as our ideal self, which does not mean that becoming like Jesus is inscrutable. The opposite of a reductive christology is not an intricate, academic christology but a profound embracing of all that Christ represents. We cannot escape responsibility by claiming that the imitation of Christ is too esoteric or abstract.

A mind cluttered by excuses may make a mystery of discipleship, or it may see it as something to be dreaded. But there is no mystery about desiring and intending to be like someone—that is a very common thing. And if we intend to be like Christ, that will be obvious to every thoughtful person around us, as well as to ourselves.[22]

If we anticipate the temptation of projecting Jesus into our traditions or of making him the product of our imagination, we may be more careful in grasping the true realities of Christlikeness and more eager to explore the meaning of Jesus for today. Above all else, we must follow the biblical pattern laid down by the apostles.

Some people would like Jesus without any of the theology of Christ. They would be satisfied with a minimal commitment to a few of Jesus' wise sayings. Others would like an otherworldly Christ who saves their soul for eternity without changing their lives today. Both are heresies. Either Jesus is the Christ, the Son of the living God, or he is nothing at all. We cannot explain his teaching and actions apart from his person, nor can we accept him apart from following his example.

5

the name of jesus

The imitation of Christ depends upon the Old Testament understanding of the knowledge of God. To know the name of Jesus in the biblical sense is to avail oneself of the fullness of divine revelation. In this chapter we explore the significant parallel between the name of the Lord God in the Old Testament and the New Testament name of Jesus Christ, our Lord and Savior.

In many ancient as well as contemporary cultures, the name of a person represents an individual's character, family history, and cultural status. As Westerners, however, we usually use names as arbitrary labels merely to differentiate people from one another. We are not in the habit of infusing a name with the history, memory, and character of a person's life. Throughout the Bible the significance of a person's name is evident. Although Adam's name is simply the Hebrew word for man, or for human being, the name assumes a significantly personal and historical reference in the first man. He is what he is called. His name is synonymous with his character. The word becomes distinctly defined in the life and personality of a single individual.

Implicit in Adam's responsibility to name the animals is his authority and wisdom. Naming the animals was a unique privilege extended to Adam by the Creator. We are told that God "brought them to the man to see what he would name them; and whatever the man called each living creature, that was its name" (Gen. 2:19). The biblical reference implies that Adam had the wisdom to recognize each creature and designate it by an appropriate name. The same is true of Eve, whose name not only distinguished her own personal identity from Adam but defined her equality with Adam. As a play on another Hebrew word for man, Adam's choice of "Eve" wisely identified her as a unique individual who was neither inferior nor superior to himself. The meaning and significance of names, as illustrated in the Genesis account, is an important biblical theme throughout both testaments, especially when it involves the name of God.

The apostles found that the expression *the name of Jesus* summarized the specific content of the life and character of the historical Jesus; it represented who he was and what he had done. Far from using Jesus' name as a convenient label to express their own perspectives, his name summoned them to a distinctively defined idea. The apostles found in his name a direct link with the reality of God, represented by the name *Yahweh* in the Old Testament. Jesus not only embodied the message of God but also revealed the character of God. His name became synonymous with God himself. Therefore, to be called by his name involved an inseparable commitment to a patterning after his life and a confession of his being. It is possible to use the name of Jesus and mean almost anything by it. When we infuse the name of Jesus with our own perspectives and passions, however, we no longer know Christ through the specific content of Jesus and in direct continuity with the historical revelation of God.

AN UNDEFINED NAME

A Bill Gaither song popular among many North American Christians is entitled, "There's Something About That Name."

> Jesus, Jesus, Jesus!
> There's just something about that name!
> Master, Saviour, Jesus!
> Like the fragrance after the rain;
> Jesus, Jesus, Jesus!
> Let all heaven and earth proclaim:
> Kings and kingdoms will all pass away,
> But there's just something about that name![1]

Every time I hear this song I think of Norberto Preiss, a thirty-seven-year-old father of two who died from cancer. During the ordeal, his wife, Elianne, sat by his bedside softly singing this chorus over and over again. The pleasing melody and reassuring lyrics were a comfort to them. In their desperation she and her husband used this chorus to cling to Jesus. During my visits I was conscious of the power of Jesus sustaining them. Ignoring the strong antiseptic smell that permeated the air, they sang of the "fragrance after the rain," and the two of them joined with "all heaven and earth" to proclaim Jesus. Whatever it was about the "name," it changed the perspective in that hospital room. For many, the name of Jesus stirs deep emotions. It is a precious name, cherished above all other names. Yet for these same people it can be a name almost void of content and meaning. The last line of the chorus ends in exclamation; perhaps it should end with a question— what *is* it about the name of Jesus? Some Christians have sentimental- ized the name of Jesus to the point that other Christians prefer to speak of Christ or Lord rather than Jesus. I have a vivid impression of one prayer meeting I attended where the leader suddenly began to shout, "Oh Jesus! Jesus! Blessed Jesus! We love you, Jesus!" Immediately he was joined by others chanting, "Oh, Jesus! Hallelujah, Jesus!" As they provided the background, he rattled off faster than a disk jockey the "blessings of Jesus." They were certainly familiar with the name of Jesus, but I wondered if they were as familiar with the ethic and spirituality of Jesus.

I am concerned that the name of Jesus may be defined by a popular mentality which substitutes emotion for theology and exchanges biblical content for positive feelings. When the Scripture principle no longer shapes the meaning and significance of Jesus, then even the name of Jesus takes on worldly power and passion. People use his name for their own ends and identify Jesus with their cause, instead of becoming identified with Jesus and his cause. He may be turned into a symbol for material success, middle-class family life, and patriotism. Somehow the cause seems greater and the case stronger if it is given in Jesus' name, regardless of whether it is consistent with the Jesus portrayed in the Bible.

Such transformation occurs not only in circles that emotionalize or sentimentalize Jesus but also in theological circles. The name of Jesus can be psychologized or politicized to the point where it bears only faint resemblance to the testimony of the apostles. His name is tampered with and made to represent what Jesus opposed.

In 1982, McNEILAB, makers of Tylenol, faced one of the worst disasters a pharmaceutical firm could experience. Their name became associated with death. For weeks the nightly newscasts carried reports on the "Tylenol Murders." Someone had laced Tylenol extra-strength pain capsules with a lethal dose of cyanide and had returned the product to drugstore shelves where it was bought by unsuspecting victims. As the story broke, the Tylenol product was pulled from drugstore shelves and medicine cabinets across the nation. The company spent millions in repackaging their product to make it tamperproof and millions more to convince the public that their name and product were reliable.

In similar fashion, the name of Jesus has been tampered with to such an extent that the reality of Jesus has been lost to those who define the name of Jesus according to their own ideas and practice. Countless individuals have rejected the biblical witness because they have been turned off by christologies that echo false philosophies and practice. Some profane the name of Jesus by conscious deception, but the majority do so perhaps unwittingly, out of apathy and self-centeredness. Some are so zealous for their cause that they simply assume they are speaking for Jesus. Still others are so immersed in certain cultural forms of religion that they cannot be provoked to question the authenticity of their understanding of Jesus.

After debunking the liberal lives of Jesus, fabricated in the nineteenth century, Albert Schweitzer concluded that the disciples never came to a clearly defined understanding of Jesus. In his view, Jesus remained an enigma to the disciples right up to the end, resulting in frustration for anyone who would grasp the specific meaning of his name today. Schweitzer concluded *The Quest of the Historical Jesus* by suggesting that his readers not even make an attempt: "Jesus has no answer to the question, 'Tell us Thy name in our speech and for our day.' " Although Schweitzer believed Jesus calls us to follow him, Jesus remains "without a name."[2] The apostles would have found Schweitzer's pessimism unfounded because they were convinced God had revealed the meaning of Jesus' name in a very specific and understandable way.

A DESIGNATED NAME

What should Jesus' name mean to those who are intent on becoming like him? We begin with God's pronouncement, "You are to give him the name Jesus, because he will save his people from their sins" (Matt. 1:21). The naming of Jesus was part of the revelation about him. God identified this one who entered human history at a special time, through a unique birth, by the common name *Jesus*. (*Joshua* is the corresponding Hebrew form, which means "God our Savior.") Parents throughout Palestine in the first century commonly named their sons after the courageous successor of Moses. In Jesus' case, the promise of future accomplishment gave his name such profound significance: "He will save his people from their sins." Instead of looking back to an ancient hero, God looked forward to what this designated individual would accomplish.

The naming of Jesus was another instance of the extraordinary contrast between the normal pattern and God's absolutely unique self-disclosure through the Incarnation. Mary conceived through a supernatural miracle but delivered her baby through the pain and labor of a normal delivery. Jesus received a name designated by God but given by Joseph and Mary; it was an ordinary name, yet interpreted like no other name in Israel. Matthew accentuated this contrast between the divine and human when he alluded to the prophecy in Isaiah; "The virgin will be with child and will give birth to a son, and they will call him Immanuel—which means, 'God with us'" (Matt. 1:23). The one who is called by the ordinary name of Jesus is actually "Immanuel." Consequently, his name represents more than a reflection of his parents' faith in Israel's God. Parents who believed in the heritage of God's blessing and in the reality of God's salvation called their children Joshua, but in Jesus, the man to whom God gave a specific name, the individual embodied the reality in himself. *He* was to save his people from their sins. Jesus is "God with us."

As we observe the significance of the frequently repeated New Testament expression "the name of Jesus," we conclude that this name was not a vague, undefined idea with an indeterminate effect. On the contrary, we believe that the apostles intended to convey through their name-theology a specific christological concept which comprehended the total reality of the historical Jesus and the glory of the risen Christ.

The juxtaposition of the ordinary name of Jesus and the extraordinary designation of Jesus as Immanuel is seen throughout the biblical witness. When Peter was brought before the Sanhedrin on charges of proclaiming the Resurrection and performing miracles, he emphasized the continuity between his proclamation of both the risen Christ and the historical Jesus with the addition of a single word. "By what power or what name did you do this?" (Acts 4:7), the authorities challenged Peter and John. Peter's response was emphatic: "Know this, you and all the people of Israel: It is by the name of Jesus Christ of Nazareth, whom you crucified but whom God raised from the dead, that this man stands before you healed" (v. 10). Peter's choice of words is significant. By referring to Nazareth, Peter consciously drew attention to the historicity of Jesus. If Peter's desire had been to depreciate the historical Jesus, he could easily have dropped the reference to Nazareth. For Peter, the name of Jesus was a historical name, and he had no intention of ignoring Jesus' earthly life, even though reference to Jesus' hometown might have sounded trivial to his hearers. Recall that, when Philip told Nathanael that they had found the Messiah and that he hailed from an insignificant Galilean village, Nathanael exclaimed, "Nazareth! Can anything good come from there?" (John 1:46).

A similar juxtaposition is found in the christological hymn of Philippians 2. The glory of the risen Christ is preceded by the humiliation of Jesus' incarnation and crucifixion. After "he humbled himself and became obedient to death—even death on a cross" (Phil. 2:8), he was glorified.

> Therefore God exalted him to the highest place and gave him the *name* that is above every *name,* that at the *name* of Jesus every knee should bow, in heaven and on earth and under the earth, and every tongue confess that Jesus Christ is Lord, to the glory of God the Father (vv. 9–11, italics added).

Paul uses the moral and ethical dimension of Jesus' life to shape the mentality of the Philippian Christians. In the process, he affirms that the one whose name is above every name is none other than Jesus. Hence without giving any additional titles, Paul can freely say, "At the name of Jesus every knee should bow."

When the apostles used the expression *the name of Jesus,* they consciously filled that expression with the content of Jesus' life, death, and resurrection. In one phrase it encompasses everything Jesus represents. "The whole content of salvation revealed in Jesus is comprised by his name"[3] (Acts 2:17–21; 4:12; 9:14; Rom. 10:13; 1 Cor. 1:2; 6:11). Belief in Jesus' name is equivalent to believing in his messianic mission (John 3:17–18), obeying God's command (1 John 3:23), receiving forgiveness of sins (Acts 10:43; 1 John 2:12), possessing eternal life (John 20:31; 1 John 5:13), escaping judgment (John 3:18), and receiving the gift of the Spirit (Acts 2:38). The baptismal formula, "in the name of Jesus Christ," underscores the fullness of Christ's saving work contained in his name.[4]

His name means as much to us for our sanctification as it does for salvation. "Whatever you do, whether in word or deed," challenges Paul, "do it all in the name of the Lord Jesus" (Col. 3:17). We pray in his name (John 14:13; 15:16; 16:24; Eph. 5:20), suffer for his name's sake (Matt. 10:22; 24:9; 1 Peter 4:14), and proclaim his name with power (Acts 9:34). "A Christian's whole life is dominated by the name of Jesus (Col. 3:17), whose glorification is the goal of faith (2 Thess. 1:12)."[5] The apostles correctly applied the history of revelation and redemption found in Jesus to the meaning of his name, which represented the totality of Jesus' life and ministry. It was a name to live by and, if necessary, die for. What the apostles came to regard in the name of Jesus, encompassing the historical Jesus and the risen Christ, the benefit of salvation and the responsibilities of discipleship, was shaped by the truth that the name of Jesus shared the same respect and awe accorded to the name of God.

THE REALITY OF GOD

If we stopped here in our consideration of the name of Jesus, we would miss the biblical precedent for the christological significance of the expression. For profound theological reasons, the apostles linked the Old Testament concept of the name of God with the New Testament meaning of the name of Jesus. What they had believed and respected in the name of God was transferred to the name of Jesus. Our Western tendency to minimize this continuity and perceive it more as a stylistic or literary motif than as important theological truth must be overcome.

Within the Old Testament the name of God is used as a powerful expression of God's character and actions. "One of the most fundamental and essential features of the biblical revelation is the fact that God is not without a name: he has a personal name, by which he can, and is to be, invoked."[6] When God made himself known to Abraham, he identified himself: "I am God Almighty [El-Shaddai]; walk before me and be blameless" (Gen. 17:1). Contrary to the gods and myths of Abraham's culture, God disclosed himself as the powerful one whose presence required Abraham's personal loyalty and obedience. God revealed himself according to his own personal prerogative, choosing to define himself in successive stages to the people of Israel. This pattern is especially evident in God's self-disclosure to Moses: "I am the LORD. I appeared to Abraham, to Isaac and to Jacob as God Almighty, but by my name the LORD [Yahweh] I did not make myself known to them" (Exod. 6:2–3).

Out of compassion for the plight of the Israelites, God revealed more of himself. It was a matter not of Israel knowing God by a new title but of understanding the meaning of that title in a new and more historically specific way. When Moses asked for further identification to support his claim before the people that God had sent him and to lend credibility to his mission, he was seeking not a title but a description of the meaning of God's name.[7] In response, God declared his sovereign power ("I AM WHO I AM" [Exod. 3:14]), in the flow of his personal and historical relationship with Israel ("The LORD, the God of your fathers—the God of Abraham, the God of Isaac and the God of Jacob" [v. 15]). Far from being a nameless, impersonal force, the God of creation chose to be known by his covenant relationship with specific individuals who walked before him and obeyed him.

In the highest forms of Buddhist, Hindu, and Taoist thought, God is imagined to be a nameless and undifferentiated spiritual reality beyond personality. The conception of God in Islam is impersonal and deterministic. His name is associated with power and transcendence. Contrary to these various descriptions, however, the God of the Old Testament reveals himself through specific acts, propositional teaching, and personal communion. Honoring the name of the Lord God involves an exclusive relationship with him (Exod. 20:3–4; Pss. 44:20; 79:6; Isa. 42:8) and specific obedience to his commandments (Lev. 18:21; Deut. 18:20; 2 Chron. 7:14; Amos 2:7). Apart from God's own initiative, people would be unable to honor his name. He has promised his enablement to all who earnestly seek to honor his name (Exod. 20:24). He overrules wickedness and crushes oppression "for the sake of [his] name," in order to protect his own reputation among the nations (Ezek. 20:9).

The name of the Lord God represents who he is and what he has done. His name is synonymous with his righteousness (Ps. 7:17), majesty (Mic. 5:4), presence (Deut. 12:11; 14:23), power (Ps. 54:1; Prov. 18:10; Jer. 10:16), and wisdom (Amos 4:13). God did not remain nameless but disclosed himself personally and concretely in the Old Testament, which has enormous significance for our understanding of Jesus Christ. The emphasis on name-theology illustrates the continuity between the Lord God, who made himself known to the patriarchs, and Jesus of Nazareth. To define a christology in any authentically Christian manner, we must include the Old Testament understanding of the reality of God. If theology strips the meaning of God's name of its specific content, historical manifestation, and cultic significance, then Schweitzer's verdict is correct: we cannot know the meaning of Jesus' name for today. But Jesus is not theologically innovative here; he does not break with the Old Testament meaning of God, and neither can we, if we expect to understand him. However, Jesus does not simply repeat what the people already knew about God.

As we have seen, God revealed more of himself to Moses than he had to Abraham. Out of compassion and justice, in accord with his covenant relationship, God took a significant step in further disclosing his character to Israel. Similarly through the Incarnation, God once again took the initiative that is exclusively his to reveal himself more completely. This time the revelation took the form of God's ultimate medium of communication. As in the past, God's disclosure of his character was personal and historical; now through the Incarnation it reaches its climax in a single individual, who was born "when the time had fully come" (Gal. 4:4). There is a particularizing of God's covenant with Israel, which reaches its ultimate depth of hiddenness and, paradoxically, its greatest revelational impact in one Israelite—namely, Jesus Christ.[8]

As shocking as it may have seemed to the Jews, the apostles were compelled by the Spirit of God to attribute to Jesus all that was represented by the name of the Lord God. What must have appeared like a radical departure from the truth was actually the promised fulfillment of God's redemptive program (John 6:45–47). The Jewish notion of monotheistic exclusivity made it virtually impossible for the disciples to invent the theological equation between the name of Jesus and the name of the Lord God. Rather, the disciples took their lead from Jesus. Like the prophets before him, Jesus claimed to come in the name of the Lord, but unlike the prophets his name became synonymous with the name of the Lord God.

He challenged his followers to welcome little children in his name, because "whoever welcomes me does not welcome me but the one who sent me" (Mark 9:37). Simple acts of compassion such as offering a cup of cold water in his name "because you belong to Christ" were commended (v. 41). Community life, as well as miraculous power, depended on the name of Jesus. Jesus promised his presence "where two or three come together in my name" (Matt. 18:20). When the disciples returned from their preaching and healing ministry, they were excited about the power of Jesus' name: "Lord, even the demons submit to us in your name" (Luke 10:17). Jesus warned the disciples that they would be hated "because of my name" (John 15:21; see also Matt. 10:22; Mark 13:13).

Jesus consciously assumed that his name had become as crucial for obedience and salvation as the name of the Lord God. This assumption is especially evident in the Gospel of John, both in his repeated claim to come in the Father's name and in his "I am" sayings. When Jesus declared, "I have come in my Father's name," he claimed to be the very embodiment of the revelation of God (John 5:43). Through him, God's name had been made known (17:6, 26). Miracles he performed in the Father's name substantiated his claim that he represented the Father. Jesus and the Father share the same name, a name given by the Father to the Son, in direct continuity and filled with the specific content of the Old Testament revelation of God.

The status of Jesus' name in relationship to the name of the Lord

God reaches its peak in the "I am" sayings, which are reminiscent of God's self-disclosure to Moses ("I AM WHO I AM" [Exod. 3:14]). The Jewish religious leaders, having already accused Jesus of being demon-possessed, knew exactly what Jesus meant when he declared, "Before Abraham was born, I am!" (John 8:58). Without hesitation, they picked up stones to stone him for blasphemy. Together the "I am" sayings in John (6:35; 8:12; 10:7, 9, 11, 14; 11:25; 14:6; 15:1) constitute a powerful expression of Jesus' self-understanding. For the most part, Jesus' self-identification with the name-theology stresses the functional and representative nature of the continuity. As we will see in our study of Jesus' self-understanding, this is in keeping with his desire to emphasize obedience to the Father's will and the completion of his ministry before claiming for himself the full designation of Messiah.

The original as well as functional way in which Jesus commanded obedience, sacrifice, fellowship, and prayer in his name was consistent with the apostolic development that equated the name of Jesus with the very name of God (Matt. 12:21; 28:19; Luke 24:47; Heb. 1:4). The parallel is striking between the meaning of the Lord God's name in the Old Testament and the meaning of Jesus' name in the New Testament. Those who believe and obey are called by his name (cf. Num. 6:27; 2 Chron. 7:14 with Rev. 3:12–13; 14:1; 22:4). Only through his name does salvation come (cf. Ps. 79:9; Isa. 43:1–7; 54:5; 63:16; Joel 2:32 with John 20:31; Acts 4:12; Rom. 10:13). His ways are betrayed by those who claim his name but reject its true theological and ethical significance (cf. Jer. 14:15; 29:9 with Matt. 7:21–23; 24:4–5). His name alone is worthy of all praise and glory (cf. Isa. 45:23; Zech. 14:9 with Phil. 2:9–10).

In the mind of the apostles the name of Jesus was an all-encompassing expression representing the totality of Jesus' earthly ministry as well as the reality of his glorified state as the risen Christ. The "name" was shorthand for everything that Jesus meant to them—so much so that on occasion they referred simply to "the Name" (Acts 5:41; 3 John 7). They also came to see, in accord with Jesus' own words, the direct relationship between Jesus and the God of Abraham, Isaac, and Jacob. All that was attributed to the name of God in Israel's experience was carried over and applied to Jesus in the faith and practice of the early church.

THE THIRD COMMANDMENT

After nearly two thousand years the name of Jesus is more popular than it ever was. Perhaps no name is used more widely and with as many meanings as the name of Jesus. Whether out of devotion or deceit, it can stir deep emotions and evoke passion. For many others it is no more than a cliché. Some use his name to defend the status quo; others use it to inspire revolution. According to some professing Christians it holds no practical significance for daily life, yet for others his name means a costly commitment of everything they are and have. In some situations it is dangerous to speak of Jesus, but in other places his name is degraded from thoughtless overuse.

God commanded the Israelites not to profane his name. "You shall not misuse the name of the LORD your God, for the LORD will not hold anyone guiltless who misuses his name" (Exod. 20:7). The Jews rarely pronounced the Hebrew for *Yahweh* and left out the vowels when writing it because of superstitious fear that they would be guilty of misusing the name of God, thereby violating the third commandment. In spite of their sincere desire to respect the command, they missed its meaning. The purpose of the commandment went far beyond prohibiting profanity.

God's primary concern was not the verbal slander of his name but the violation of his name through misuse. God invited Israel to call him by name, but he would not tolerate people who were called by his name misrepresenting him. The third commandment challenges the people of God to do nothing that will desecrate the name of God. It warns that there is an ever-present danger that the people of God may obscure the truth about God through their persistent sin.

It is odd that the name of Jesus is such a popular swear word. People who have never been in a church punctuate their anger or sarcasm with Jesus' name. Executives and laborers alike defame the name of Jesus yet sit piously through weddings and funerals conducted in Jesus' name. However, those who use the name of Jesus as a swear word are of less concern to God than professing Christians who, though called by his name, do not do what he commands. Jesus warned, "Not everyone who says to me, 'Lord, Lord,' will enter the kingdom of heaven, but only he who does the will of my Father who is in heaven." Then he predicted, "Many will say to me on that day, 'Lord, Lord, did we not prophesy in your name, and in your name drive out demons and perform many miracles?'" But his response is decisive: "I will tell them plainly, 'I never knew you. Away from me, you evildoers!'" (Matt.

7:21–23). Although their abuse of Jesus' name was accompanied by a claim to great power, it did not change God's verdict.

Consider the tragic misrepresentation of Jesus' name by those who ignore what Jesus exemplified and accomplished, who profess his name with their mouths but profane his name with their lives. Becoming like Jesus involves knowing his name in the fullness disclosed by God through his life and teaching as well as through Spirit-inspired prophecy and the witness of his people.

6

the human spirituality of jesus

The ancient people of Babel sought to make a name for themselves. They translated their desire for human solidarity and a sense of glory into an unprecedented building project (Gen. 11). Superficially the project was innocuous, if not commendable, but spiritually it revealed a quest for transcendence through idolatrous means. "Making a name for themselves" meant much more to them than promoting their reputation. They sought within themselves, through their own ingenious technology and planning, to create transcendence. They were driven by a passion to achieve self-glory.

Modern parallels to the Babel mentality seem to abound not only in Western culture in general but also among those who profess to follow Jesus. There is plenty of evidence that we have not taken seriously the pattern of Jesus' spirituality. Even among earnest Christians there is a decline of the sacred and a ready acceptance of secularism in every aspect of life.[1] Devotion to Jesus has lost the vitality of Jesus' spirituality. There are obvious cultural reasons for this neglect, but there are also theological notions which obscure the influence of his spirituality.

SELFISM

Popular wisdom challenges us to make a name for ourselves. We are told that, to achieve our goals, we must believe in our own success. Independence, wealth, self-esteem, and power are achieved through self-confidence and self-actualization. Guilt feelings, inferiority complexes, and fits of depression are dispelled—so it goes—when we believe in ourselves, take charge of our destiny, and think positively. Psychologist

Wayne Dyer promotes an increasingly popular way of looking for self-fulfillment.

> Using yourself as a guide and not needing the approval of an outside force is the most religious experience you can have. It is a veritable religion of the self in which an individual determines his own behavior based upon his own conscience and the laws of his culture that work for him, rather than because someone has dictated how he should behave.[2]

Narrowing the quest for transcendence to the autonomous self dramatically reveals the impoverishment of modern men and women. Out of their private psychological and relational resources, people are trying to create their own transcendence, to lift their spirits above the vicissitudes of human experience. We need not elaborate on our culture's fixation with the self, but we should be aware of its impact on spirituality. We noted earlier Christopher Lasch's analysis of the preoccupation of Western culture with the "minimal self." Coping with daily life seems challenging enough for many today, much less dealing with ultimate questions of meaning. Expectations have been scaled down to an ethic of survival and a moral duty to self.

Nevertheless, human nature seeks transcendence. All of our luxury, pleasure, freedom, and self-expression cannot meet the human need for self-fulfillment. In spite of the establishment of secular humanism, the domination of scientism, and the pervasiveness of selfism, the quest for transcendence and spirituality continues. "What is lamentable," writes Theodore Roszak, "is that the human will to transcendence . . . has been left without counsel or guidance. Untutored, it runs off into many dead ends and detours. It easily mistakes the sensational for the spiritual, the merely obscure for the authentically mysterious."[3] As the inadequacy of self-centered existence becomes more apparent alongside Western culture's disillusionment with empiricism and materialism, the quest for some form of transcendence will grow. Out of quiet desperation people will continue to turn to drugs, music, sex, yoga, sports, mysticism, astrology, and even science-fiction movies to fill the spiritual vacuum and transcend their immediate feelings of loneliness. They crave a sense of ultimacy and meaning, and they will invent new ways of coping with that innate spiritual hunger.

Christians have a tremendous opportunity to reveal the meaning of God and salvation, but first they need to grasp the authentic spirituality of Jesus. Perhaps our evangelism has proven ineffective because we are tainted with the same selfishness and secularity as our culture. Roszak observes that the human will to transcendence "may reach out toward emotionally charged, born again religions," but this effort often "weakens toward smugness, intolerance, and reactionary politics." His observation is valid. The only way the church can be purified of carnality is to allow the truth and beauty of Jesus' spirituality to shine through her community life.

Culturally speaking, selfism epitomizes the secular quest for fulfillment. It deceives the world and beguiles the Christian into an impotent devotion to "self-transcendence." Jesus was driven by a different passion. His singular ambition was to know the Father and obey his will. This explains his intensity as well as his composure. It helps us understand his compassion and his fortitude. We cannot know him or become like him apart from following the example of his spirituality. Our knowledge of Christ is dependent on a personal and practical grasp of his prayer life, humility, faith, and dependence. Jesus saw no need to make a name for himself (Phil. 2:6).

HERESIES

Theological ideas may also obscure the significance of Jesus' spirituality, especially if they involve defending his deity at the expense of his humanity. Serious confusion results when the spiritual life of Jesus is viewed either as a performance for our benefit or a phenomenon unique to Christ. The spirituality of Jesus is a challenge to christology. How we understand the person of Christ must do justice to his human experience of God.

New Christians often ask perceptive questions, such as: If Jesus was God, why did he have to pray? If Christ never changes, how did Jesus grow in wisdom and in favor with God and men (Luke 2:52)? If Jesus was God and possessed the attributes of God in full measure, including omnipotence, omniscience, and omnipresence, how could he have experienced genuine humanity? These questions go to the heart of the meaning of the Incarnation and reveal a profound and paradoxical mystery. Since her earliest day, the church has wrestled with these questions, but the process has not always led to a better understanding of Jesus or a deeper spiritual life.

One of the early heresies the church faced was Docetism. A docetic approach resolves the paradox of the Incarnation by denying the humanity of Jesus. Since his humanity was only a "special effect," his spirituality was merely a performance. Docetism stresses the deity of Christ in such a way as to deny the genuineness of his humanity and the intrinsic necessity of his spiritual growth, prayer life, and dependency upon the Word of God. For Docetists it is impossible for Jesus to be truly God and at the same time experience suffering, temptation, and spiritual agony. They are unable to reconcile divinity with vulnerability and dependence, so they turn Jesus into a divine actor playing a human role. The apostle John warned believers against the incipient forms of this heresy when he wrote, "This is how you can recognize the Spirit of God: Every spirit that acknowledges that Jesus Christ has come in the flesh is from God, but every spirit that does not acknowledge Jesus is not from God" (1 John 4:2–3; cf. 2 John 7).

Apollinarius, the bishop of Laodicea, proposed a more subtle approach to the humanity of Jesus. He believed that, unless Jesus' identity as a human being was qualified significantly, an untenable dualism resulted. "If perfect God were joined to perfect man, they would be two." Since he found this man-God hybrid unthinkable, he proposed an original and speculative solution. Working within a Platonic trichotomy of body, mind, and soul, Apollinarius argued that the place of a human mind or the rational self was taken by the eternal Logos. He reasoned that, if Christ was directed by a human free will, he would be a sinner like every other person.

Apollinarius's solution gave Jesus Christ a single divine nature and a human body. Christ possessed human emotions and flesh, but the thinking, willing, directing principle in him was purely divine. According to Apollinarius, "In Christ there is a middle-being of God and man, therefore he is neither fully man nor God (alone), but a mixture of God and man."[4] He conceived this composition not as a static union of divine and human components but as a living unity of the divine Logos and human flesh. In his concern to preserve the integrity of Christ's deity and to explain the union of God and man with the help of Platonic and Stoic concepts, Apollinarius unintentionally devalued the humanity of Jesus.

A contemporary of Apollinarius, Gregory of Nazianzus, refuted Apollinarianism by exposing the implications of Christ's diminished humanity for the doctrine of salvation. He argued that, if Christ was not completely man, then our salvation is incomplete: "What he did not assume, he did not heal [or redeem]."[5] Ironically, the way in which Apollinarius defended the sinlessness of Christ and the purity of his consciousness actually jeopardized the doctrine of the Atonement. But Apollinarianism also has implications for the meaning of Jesus' spirituality. By denying a "human center of life and consciousness" in Jesus, it diminished the significance and impact of his spirituality.[6] Jesus was not subject to the same pressures and temptations as we are because his life was completely directed by the divine Logos.

It is unlikely that contemporary Christians will accept Apollinarius's Logos-flesh christology, but they are tempted, as Apollinarius was, to retreat from the completeness of Christ's humanity. Christians continue to struggle with "psychological Docetism" and "practical Apollinarianism." They are not as concerned with philosophical speculation over the union of the divine and human in Christ as they are with the practical implications of limiting the manifestation of his deity. It sounds heretical to many Christians to suggest that Jesus was not omniscient during his earthly life. From their perspective this denial is tantamount to questioning his deity. It is easier for them to accept the fact that Jesus was not omnipresent (because he assumed a human body), but they view any limitation on his knowledge and power as unacceptable.

Practical Apollinarianism commands a large following today because its implications suit the popular perception of many Christians. On the one hand, there has been a continuing tendency simply to divide up the attributes of Jesus into divine and human categories. Christ's hunger, thirst, weariness, and weeping belong in the human category, with miracles and prophecies in the divine category. Jesus' knowledge of people and his insight into their thoughts and actions are presented as proof of his omniscience (cf. John 2:24; 4:17–18; 5:6; 6:64; Matt. 9:4; 12:15; Mark 2:8). And his miracles display his omnipotence. This approach destroys the concept of Jesus as a fully integrated personality and virtually eliminates the human experience of God in Jesus. Consequently, according to this position, Jesus never experienced human ignorance, spiritual growth, or genuine dependence. The directing principle of life within Jesus was purely divine. Apparently, the only thing Jesus had to put up with on the human side was a biological body.

On the other hand, there has also been a tendency to minimize the obvious human limitations claimed by Jesus. Scripture clearly teaches that Jesus was genuinely dependent upon the Father for power and wisdom. He experienced spiritual growth, suffered temptation, learned obedience and was required to exercise faith in God. Jesus' words in Mark 13:32 are especially significant: "No one knows about that day or hour, not even the angels in heaven, nor the Son, but only the Father." In the same context in which he distinguished himself from people and the angels because he is the Son of God, he claimed to be ignorant of the time of his return. The implications for his own self-understanding are significant, especially in view of his denial of omniscience. Would the disciples find it expedient to invent the ignorance of Jesus? No theological formulation which rationalizes away the clear teaching of this passage does justice to the spirituality of Jesus.[7] What Christians have normally accepted about the physical reality of his humanity needs to be applied to the spiritual dimension. If we allow the Scripture principle, rather than our theological positions, to dictate the meaning of the Incarnation, we will seek to learn from Jesus' human experience of God.

Theological perspectives which defend the deity of Christ at the expense of his genuine humanity dehumanize the Incarnation and distort the Christian life. Unless the full value of Jesus' own spirituality becomes a personal challenge, we will be guilty of misrepresenting the imitation of Christ. Throughout Judaism and Hellenism Jesus' humanity was a liability, yet the apostles emphasized the human dimension without embarrassment or depreciation. The author of Hebrews actually built his case for Christ's supremacy over the angels on the benefits of Christ's humanity (Heb. 2:5–9).

BEING AND BECOMING

According to one speculative theory circulating in Palestine through the Qumran sect, the Messiah was a created being subordinate to the archangel Michael.[8] Understandably this theory appealed to Jewish Christians because it preserved the monotheistic transcendence of God without the doctrine of the Trinity and afforded them the opportunity of proclaiming Jesus as the Messiah in accord with popular Jewish messianic thought. But the writer of Hebrews saw the tendency to subordinate Jesus to the superiority of angels as a great threat to the meaning of the Incarnation. The prologue emphatically affirms the deity of the Son. He "is the radiance of God's glory and the exact representation of his being, sustaining all things by his powerful word" (Heb. 1:3). But when it came to proving the superiority of Jesus over the angels, the writer argued mainly from the humanity of the historical Jesus. He might have gone on to declare the essential oneness of God the Father and God the Son; instead he directly tackled the meaning of the Incarnation. He did not flinch under theological pressure and diminish the humanity of Christ. Even though the author was refuting proponents who considered the Messiah to be less than God and less than the angels, he specifically developed his argument on the basis of the benefits of Christ's humanity.

Unquestionably, Jesus is superior to the angels by virtue of his identity as the Son. But the writer of Hebrews goes beyond that truth to prove the validity of the Son's status through his suffering and death. "After he had provided purification for sins, he sat down at the right hand of the Majesty in heaven. So he became as much superior to the angels as the name he has inherited is superior to theirs" (Heb. 1:3–4). Orthodox Christians frequently have difficulty with the language of Hebrews. If Jesus was God in the first place, how did he *become* superior to the angels? In what sense does the writer apply Psalm 2:7 to Jesus, "You are my Son; today I have become your Father" (Heb. 1:5)? How can he speak of God's *firstborn* (v. 6), without suggesting that the Messiah was created? We are even told that Jesus belongs to the same family as we do (2:11), "made like his brothers in every way" (v. 17), and that he shared our humanity (v. 14) and "suffered when he was tempted" (v. 18). The author boldly admits that Jesus "was made a little lower than the angels" (v. 9). How do we reconcile these statements with Jesus' deity?

Furthermore, the writer presents Jesus as having his own spiritual experience of God. He worships and prays to his God. He is dependent upon God and exercises trust in him (Heb. 1:9; 2:12–13). These are remarkable statements to make for one who is defending the deity of Christ and his supremacy over the angels. But they are completely consistent with the apostolic understanding of the Incarnation. The apostles believed that Jesus in his essential being was God and that, through the Incarnation, he shared completely in our humanity. This involved his identification with us in the full range of human experience, especially on the negative side of life, including suffering, temptation, and death. It also involved the human experience of God, namely, trust, dependence, and faith. The writer of Hebrews made no attempt to explain the mystery of the Incarnation, but he did elucidate the meaning and benefits of that mystery. God became man for the sake of our salvation and participated fully in our human experience (vv. 9–10, 14–17; 12:2). The writer of Hebrews therefore had to use the concrete language of "becoming" to describe the human course of Jesus' life of obedience and spiritual pilgrimage.

Reference to Christ as the firstborn does not imply an ontological status below God, nor does it suggest that the Messiah had a starting point in time. New Testament scholar C. F. D. Moule has suggested that there is a twofold significance to the designation *firstborn;* Christ is both "prior to and supreme over" all creation. Thus we discover the superior rank of Christ over all creation as well as emphasizing his relationship to creation.[9] The preincarnate Christ is absolutely eternal, but he is personally involved with creation, first as our creator (Heb. 1:2–3, 10), then as the author and perfecter of our salvation (2:10–18; cf. Col. 1:15–18).

When the writer interpreted Psalm 2:7 ("You are my Son; today I have become your Father") in a messianic manner, he had no intention of implying that there was a time when the Son of God did not exist. The reference was to what Jesus had achieved through his life, death, and resurrection. As the preceding verse explains, "So he became as much superior to the angels as the name he has inherited is superior to theirs" (Heb. 1:4; cf. Acts 13:30–34; Rom. 1:4; Eph. 1:19–21; Phil. 2:9). Jesus did not have to make a name for himself because of who he was in his very being; nevertheless, through his suffering, obedience, and genuine spirituality, he achieved and retained the meaning of that name.[10] It is not surprising that Christians have had difficulty holding together doctrinally and practically the *being* and *becoming* of Jesus. But it is absolutely crucial that we hold to this revealed paradox of supernatural reality if we are to know Christ according to his self-revelation.

Arianism is one of the most significant misinterpretations of the Incarnation. It was first formulated in the early fourth century by Arius (ca. 280–ca. 336), an Alexandrian priest who taught that, if the Father "begat" the Son, there must have been a time when the Son did not exist. Arius took the facts of Jesus' humanity seriously. He believed that Jesus grew in wisdom and favor with God and man (Luke 2:52), that he was ignorant of the date of the Second Coming (Mark 13:32), that he experienced emotional anguish (John 12:27; Mark 14:34), and that, after suffering on the cross, he was abandoned by God (15:34).

Arius interpreted these facts from a philosophical and theological background, which led him to the conclusion that the Son was ontologically inferior to the Father (Prov. 8:22; John 14:28; Col. 1:15). His thinking was a product of Greek rationalism, combined with the teachings of Origen (ca. 185–ca. 254) on the subordination of the Son. Arius departed from Origen's insistence on the "eternal generation" of the Son, and instead argued that there was a time when the Son did not exist. He wanted to explicate the mystery itself and bring it into line with his concept of God. Arius asserted that God was a remote and inaccessible being, immutable, indivisible, and unique. He "felt no substance of God could in any way be communicated or shared with any other being."[11]

Ironically Arius sacrificed the doctrine of the Incarnation on the grounds that he was upholding the logical postulates of the Supreme

Being. Therefore, in spite of the apostolic testimony, Arius held that the Son was "not the eternal God himself that comes to us in Christ for our salvation, but an intermediate being, distinct from God, while God himself is left out, uncondescending, unredemptive."[12] Biblical passages which refer to Christ as God or as the Son of God are using titles that simply honor Christ's role rather than define his being. The titles are merely honorific. "Even if He is called God," wrote Arius, "He is not God truly, but by participation in grace. . . . He too is called God in name only."[13]

There are striking similarities between fourth-century Arianism and the Jehovah's Witnesses cult.[14] Anthony Hoekema believes that the Jehovah's Witnesses' view of the person of Christ is essentially a revival of Arianism. Although he is careful to recognize the differences, Hoekema observes that both movements interpret the begetting and becoming of Christ in literalistic terms. The Son is not equal to the Father and is created by the Father prior to creation. Like Arius, their ancient predecessor, Jehovah's Witnesses do not believe that the Son and the Father are of the same essence. Consequently, they must offer a new translation of many biblical passages in order to remain consistent with their theology. Perhaps the most famous textual revision is John 1:1: "In (the) beginning the Word was, and the Word was with God, and the Word was a god" (New World Translation).

There were times in the fourth century when it looked as though Arianism might triumph in the church, but in the end the Nicene Creed prevailed.[15] The creed was formulated at the first ecumenical council in the history of the church. Over three hundred bishops, mainly from the eastern provinces of the Roman Empire, where the controversy with Arianism was the greatest, met in A.D. 325. As the following sections of the creed demonstrate, the bishops strongly affirmed the deity of Christ and directly refuted the Arian position:

> We believe . . . in one Lord Jesus Christ, the Son of God, begotten from the Father, only-begotten, that is, from the substance of the Father, . . . begotten not made, of one substance with the Father. . . .

> But as for those who say, There was when He was not, and Before being born He was not, and that He came into existence out of nothing, or who assert that the Son of God is from a different . . . substance, or is created, or is subject to alteration or change—these the Catholic [i.e., universal] Church anathematizes.[16]

Since its formation, the Nicene Creed has been accepted as an important affirmation of the deity of Christ. Besides refuting the specific tenets of

Arianism, it rejected an approach which sought to explain away the mystery of the Incarnation and conform christology to philosophical speculation about God.

The creed, however, affirms the deity of Christ without at the same time explaining the language used in the Bible for Jesus' humanity. Although the bishops did not see the humanity of Jesus as the critical issue, yet it was precisely the Bible's references to Jesus' humanity that Arius used to defend his notion of a created Christ. The bishops would have benefited from following the example of the writer of Hebrews, who presented both the being and becoming of Jesus boldly and without compromise. Apart from this dual thrust, our defense of the deity of Christ obscures our sensitivity to Jesus' human experience of God.

KNOWING GOD

According to Wayne Dyer, Jesus is the preeminent example of self-reliance. He writes, "A careful look at Jesus Christ will reveal an extremely self-actualized person, an individual who preached self-reliance, and was not afraid to incur disapproval."[17] Dyer misinterprets the source of Jesus' spiritual and psychological strength. It was derived neither from self nor, as Apollinarius taught, from a divine implant. The strength of Jesus' character and personality was a consequence of his total dependence upon God. When we study the meaning of Jesus' spirituality for ourselves, we need to begin with an appreciation for his complete dependence on God. Through his humanity Jesus identifies with us, especially on the negative side of life with its temptation, suffering, and death. He assumes our humanity in order to atone for our sins. But he also shows us how we should relate to God.

Jesus' understanding and vision of God is a controversial subject in theology today, for at least three reasons: first, because theologians have concluded from Jesus' radical teaching and criticism of the religious leaders that he broke with all traditions and concepts of God; second, because the biblical doctrine of God has been dismissed as an anachronism, according to contemporary views on creation, revelation, and redemption; and third, because the orthodox doctrine of God has been associated with oppressive social and political structures. God has been invoked to legitimize evil and repressive authorities who have used religion to pacify the masses and direct their attention to otherworldly concerns.

Latin American Liberation theologian Jon Sobrino illustrates this contemporary concern to picture Jesus in utter "theological abandonment." According to Sobrino, Jesus lets God be God by allowing the Father to remain an "inpenetrable mystery," and totally "incomprehensible." In the early stage of his public life, Sobrino argues, Jesus "lived the faith of earlier Jewish tradition in its purest form." But something happened in Galilee which revolutionized his "inherited faith." "The crowds are abandoning him, the religious leaders of the Jewish people will not accept him, and God is not getting any closer with power to renovate reality." (Sobrino sees the turning point coming in Matthew 13, Mark 8, and John 6.) Consequently, Jesus abandons his previous concepts about God and thoroughly reshapes his faith. He continues to have confidence in the Father,

> But now that confidence finds nothing in which to root. It becomes a confidence or trust against trust. Jesus' prayer in the garden of Gethsemane does not presuppose the same conception of God that Jesus had at the start of his life. . . . Letting God remain God now lacks any verification; it is done in the absence of any verification at all.

Paradoxically, the one whose intimacy with the Father "is wholly different from that of other human beings" must claim "complete theological poverty."[18]

Sobrino's interpretation of Jesus' rejection of the contemporary Jewish orthodoxy dismisses Jesus' theological dependence upon Old Testament revelation. Jesus, however, is thoroughly rooted in the spiritual experience and propositional revelation of the "Law and Prophets." Jesus criticized his contemporaries for their rejection of biblical revelation and forcefully proclaimed his theological kinship with Abraham, Moses, and David. It appears that Sobrino uses Jesus' criticism of the religious leaders to justify Liberation Theology's break with orthodoxy and a biblical world view. The meaning and content of his criticism do not concern Sobrino, but simply the fact of Jesus' break with Judaism. Understandably Sobrino wishes to abandon the doctrine of God that is popular among the Roman Catholic masses. He is convinced that such doctrine has served to legitimize rather than condemn the oppressive forces of economic exploitation, political fascism, and religious superstition. It has sanctioned the power of the ruling elite and secured a place of privilege for the wealthy. Sobrino's valid concern is that the majority of Latin Americans have accepted this false and manipulated version of God and as a result have become passive in the face of injustice and superstitious in their religiosity. His conclusion, however, that Jesus lives in "theological abandonment" and dies in "theological poverty" is invalid.

Knowing God according to God's own self-revelation does not result in manipulation and abstraction. On the contrary, the only protection against misrepresentation is found in comprehending and responding to the truth about God. Jesus shows us God through his complete dependence upon the Father. We cannot pretend that his dependence upon God does not have specific content and meaning. Through his own example Jesus draws us near to God conceptually and relationally.

To become like Jesus is to share in his passion for God—to believe in God as he believed in the Father, to hold as one's own his personal belief in God's commands, prophecies, promises, and judgments. Never is Jesus' knowledge of God evaporated into mere relationalism stripped of theological content. "Letting God be God," to use Sobrino's phrase, cannot mean, in Martin Buber's words, "the conceptual letting go of God," at least not if we are going to follow Jesus. Whenever Jesus is set free to disclose, through the totality of his life and the beauty of his integrated personality, the transcendent reality of God, we see in his life the eternal Logos. In him and through him the transcendent God "creates space for our 'transcendence.'"[19] Spirituality takes on its full human significance.

7

GOĐ-CENTEREĐNESS

We cannot conform the mystery of the Incarnation to the ingenious reflections of human speculation. An explanation of *how* the Incarnation took place is beyond us, but we can discover the *meaning* of this mystery for us through biblical revelation. Like the apostles, we seek to affirm both the deity and the humanity of Jesus Christ without compromise and confusion. Jesus was and is truly God and truly human. This supernatural truth, which was materialized in history, challenges us with the reality of Jesus' human experience of God. Through his dependence upon God we learn how to be human. Jesus proved that genuine spirituality is the avenue to human self-fulfillment.

It is fitting that the writer of Hebrews should apply the great anthropological statement of Psalm 8 to Jesus. God chose to invest humanity with the dignity and personality of his own image and to entrust individuals with the unique capacities and responsibilities of stewards over creation. Jesus shows us how God intended human life to be lived. Through his capacity to love, communicate, think, and worship, he demonstrated not only what it means to be spiritual but what it means to be human. If being spiritual seems unnatural and phony to us, then the problem lies either in our understanding of how to relate to God or in our perverted love for what is actually harmful to our well-being. True spirituality belongs to those who love life (Ps. 34:11–14) and seek to live it in all its fullness (John 10:10). We were made to know God, but when we reject him we actually reject our own humanity. What is contrary to God is sin, and what is sin is contrary to human life. When evaluated by God's design for men and women, the sinful nature is unnatural, pathological, and abnormal. If we compare the apostle Paul's short list of the acts of sinful nature with his description of the fruit of the Spirit, it is readily apparent what promotes human well-being and what destroys it (Gal. 5:19–24). However, the sinful nature pathologically accepts as normal what is self-destructive and rejects as unnatural and unusual what is truly human as well as truly spiritual. People have a propensity to choose death instead of life, darkness instead of light. "This is the verdict," wrote John: "Light has come into the world, but men loved darkness instead of light because their deeds were evil" (John 3:19).

An analogy can be drawn between the habits of physical health care and patterns of spiritual well-being. Dr. Steve Befus is a medical missionary in Liberia. He leads a community health program designed to instruct people in preventive medicine, which involves instruction in hygiene, sanitation, nutrition, prenatal and infant care, immunization, and other health-care basics. Much of what he teaches is normal and natural throughout Liberia's urban population but strange and unnatural to people living in villages upcountry. What ought to be natural to effective health care and a matter of common sense does not appear that way to those who for generations have lacked instruction and concern over these matters.

Similarly, in the matter of self-fulfillment our "normal" is often humanly and spiritually self-destructive. Our goals, ambitions, and drives leave us exhausted and empty. We seem to have no other recourse than to succumb to the scaled-down expectations of our culture, substituting survival for salvation and material things for meaning. We are left without the spiritual discipline necessary for life fulfillment. We appear powerless to resist fear, boredom, peer pressure, discouragement, anxiety, lust, and the like.[1] We seem either locked into a rigid and inflexible narrow-mindedness or cut loose to follow our own self-interests.

Our embattled humanness wages war on two fronts. On the right flank, we face the self-negating pressures that convince us that we are "nobodies." We feel painfully inadequate, overly dependent, unenthusiastic, prone to anxiety, and without hope. As one bumper sticker put it, "Life is hard, then you die." With our self-esteem in tatters we limp along in self-pity, feeling detached from the real world. As these pressures mount, we are reduced to impotence and passivity.

On the left flank, humanness is threatened by overwhelming pride, egotism, and selfishness. We feel strong, attractive, and powerful. Instead of limping, we strut—proud, resourceful, confident, ready to take on the world. We are in love with our own reflection, the mirrored image of a commercialized culture that is absorbed in style and trends. The end result of both the inflated self and the negated self is the same: we are dehumanized and depersonalized.

Jesus' spirituality calls us back to our true selves by showing us the true nature of communion with God. As we become like Jesus we experience strength in weakness, freedom in dependence, and exaltation through humiliation. Through him we learn the meaning of a passion for God and true self-fulfillment.

THE FEAR OF GOD

The foremost principle of Jesus' human experience of God is his complete dependence upon the living God. Everything about him, from his compassion to his convictions, draws its strength and meaning from the Father. The rhythm of his life with its strong beats of urgency and lengthy interludes of God-centered reflection is beautifully rendered in the picture of a first-chair musician in harmony with the conductor. His self-understanding and his vocational call are inseparably linked to his passion for God. The apostolic testimony does not allow us to divorce the boldness of Jesus' thinking and the decisiveness of his actions from his intimate communion with the Father. Through his relationship with the Father, Jesus reveals the meaning of the *fear of God.*

We may be unaccustomed to associating the fear of God with Jesus' dependence upon the Father, but this attitude is the hallmark of Jesus' spirituality, as it should be of our own. Consider his response to John at his baptism, his rebuke of Satan in the wilderness, and his struggle with God in Gethsemane. Each time, Jesus declares in very personal human terms that God alone is to be feared. No one else has demonstrated more effectively that "the fear of the LORD is the beginning of wisdom" (Prov. 9:10). Jesus is profoundly aware of God's holiness and the depths of sin in the world. When confronted with the human predicament, he turns to God: "Ask the Lord of the harvest, therefore, to send out workers into his harvest field" (Matt. 9:38). His action is always predicated on God's work through him (John 5:19), and his intense involvement is interspersed with disciplined communion with God. He leaves the future to God (Mark 13:32–33) and is careful to distinguish between the Father's prerogative and his own (Matt. 20:23).

Jesus repeatedly lifts the level of discussion from a one-dimensional humanism into the realm of God and the supernatural. His dialogue with the rich young ruler, for example, begins with the religious question, "Good teacher, what must I do to inherit eternal life?" (Luke

18:18). Jesus, however, must expose the young man's humanistic self-righteousness and immediately responds, "Why do you call me good? . . . No one is good—except God alone" (v. 19). This answer attacks the wealthy ruler's presupposition that we can make ourselves more acceptable to God, and it also reveals Jesus' own preoccupation with the holiness of God.

I do not imply that Jesus minimized his own righteousness or considered himself a sinner. On the contrary, his statement is exactly what we should expect from the lips of one who was fully conscious of God's goodness. This comment, like his baptism, corresponds perfectly with true righteousness. The awesomeness of God's holiness has greater impact in Jesus' experience precisely because of his sinlessness. His unique degree of righteousness made him that much more attuned to God's holiness. Jesus appealed to the young ruler to follow him within the context of God's holiness and of God's power to make people holy. As great as the power of riches is in distracting people from the kingdom of God, God's power is greater. "What is impossible with men is possible with God" (Luke 18:27). Jesus' own spirituality makes it impossible for him to isolate the call of discipleship from the holiness and power of God.

The fear of God is also expressed in his prayer life. He prays because he must pray. True spirituality recognizes the human necessity of communion with God. He practiced the presence of the living and loving God in the same spirit as David, whose single-minded devotion to God marked his life. Though it may sound paradoxical, Jesus, who is God himself, is "a man after God's own heart." Jesus is constantly interacting with God.

From childhood to his last gasp on the cross, his earthly ministry is empowered, enlightened, and preserved through prayer. "As he was praying" after his baptism, the Spirit of God descended upon him, and a voice came from heaven, "You are my Son, whom I love; with you I am well pleased" (Luke 3:21–22). Luke tells us that "Jesus often withdrew to lonely places and prayed" (5:16). He "spent the night praying to God" before choosing twelve from among his disciples, whom he designated apostles (6:12). Three of these apostles—Peter, John, and James—were praying with him when before their eyes Jesus was temporarily transformed into a spectacular image similar to the description of the Son of Man in the book of Revelation (9:28–29; Rev. 1:12–16).

Because of his own prayer life the disciples requested his instruction, "Lord, teach us to pray, just as John taught his disciples." His counsel emphasized the responsiveness of God to our physical and spiritual needs (Luke 11:1–13). Jesus did not teach a new system or technique of prayer. Profound in its simple devotion and practical dependence upon God, Jesus' prayer offers us a model for healthy self-existence. Genuine communion with God defeats self-negation and self-inflation and renounces a pathological self-existence.

Perhaps it would be helpful to look at the prayer life of Jesus in two ways. Precisely because Jesus is God, communion between the Father and the Son during Jesus' earthly ministry is normal. His prayer life reflects his eternal oneness with the Father before the worlds were formed. Jesus' praying does not make him less than God or any less worthy of our prayers today. Recognized as the greatest theologian of the early Greek church, Origen advised believers,

> Now if we are to take prayer in its most exact sense, perhaps we should not pray to anyone begotten, not even to Christ Himself, but only to the God and Father of all, to whom even our Savior Himself prayed. For when he heard, "teach us to pray," He did not teach us to pray to Himself, but to the Father by saying, "Our Father in heaven. . . ."

> [Do not] pray to someone else who prays, but rather to the Father whom our Lord Jesus taught us to address in prayers. . . . For you must not pray *to* the High Priest appointed on your behalf by the Father (Heb. 8:3) or to the Advocate who is charged by the Father with praying to you (1 John 2:1). Rather you must pray through the Holy Spirit and Advocate.[2]

Origen created an artificial distinction between Jesus' human experience of God and the eternal Son's communion with the Father. Because Jesus prayed to the Father and counseled others to pray to the Father, Origen drew the unwarranted conclusion that Jesus' prayer life was indicative of his eternal subordination. He argued that prayer should be addressed to the Father alone through the Son. The significance of Origen's point is lost, however, when we realize that Jesus is essentially one with the Father. His prayer life was "not merely a necessity of communication occasioned by the flesh" but a demonstration of the "intimacy of communion brought into the flesh."[3] In this first sense Jesus' prayer life demonstrated the eternal interdependence between God the Father and God the Son.

A second way to understand Jesus' prayer life complements the first and takes seriously the Incarnation. Jesus prays out of human necessity. The prayer life of Jesus shows us his full dependence upon the Father as a human being and his interdependence with the Father as God the Son.[4] Through prayer Jesus resisted spiritual egocentrism.

One of the most difficult problems we face as Christians is maintaining God's perspective. At times, sincere, well-meaning Christians seem oblivious to the difference between their view and God's. In business ethics, lifestyle priorities, and strategies for evangelism, we seldom subject our own ideas to serious spiritual scrutiny. Even though we may have been Christians for years, we are like children who are unconscious of being self-absorbed and immature. Becoming like Jesus means that we will earnestly desire God's will.

Gethsemane stands out as the extreme example of what Jesus experienced throughout his life. Through prayer Jesus maintained the perspective of God in his own self-identity and calling. He was enabled to resist the popular and satanic pressure that would have subverted his redemptive mission. In Gethsemane we see just how real Jesus' spirituality was. Instead of producing tranquility, his deep, human experience of God resulted in profound emotional pain and spiritual anguish as he wrestled with God's will. Do we grasp the significance of Jesus' honestly declaring, "Not my will but yours be done"? Jesus himself was faced with choices, decisions, and risks. His prayer became an active form of Christian resistance against sin. The counsel to "watch and pray so that you will not fall into temptation" (Matt. 26:41), which he gave to his emotionally and physically exhausted disciples on the Mount of Olives, was obeyed first by himself. Jesus knew the fear of God, for "he offered up prayers and petitions with loud cries and tears to the one who could save him from death, and he was heard because of his reverent submission" (Heb. 5:7).

The nature of Jesus' spirituality leads us to conclude that his overriding consideration was not so much the success of his messiahship but his passionate devotion to the Holy Father. Jesus rejected spiritual egocentrism in all its forms, even in its subtle yet common tendency to exalt the personal achievement of one's ministry over one's relationship with God. As Jesus neared the cross his experience of God intensified, rendering the finished work of the Cross and all its redemptive significance the fruit of his relationship with the Father. Does not this heightened relation account for the pathos of Jesus' final words on the cross, "My God, my God, why have you forsaken me?" The ultimate proof that Jesus shared the Father's perspective completely was his willingness to experience rejection on our behalf. If he feared human beings more than he feared God, he would have saved himself from the physical torture of the cross. But for the fear of God he submitted his own will to the Father's will and sacrificed everything—even his communion with the Father. We can genuinely appreciate Jesus' experience on the cross for *us* only as we understand his passion for *God*.

THE WORD OF GOD

Jesus' consciousness of God was defined and shaped by the Word and Spirit of God. The God of Jesus is the God of Abraham, Isaac, and Jacob. He is the Holy One, who has made himself known personally, historically, and objectively in the history of Abraham's descendents for the sake of all humanity. Jesus' spirituality and theology depended upon his reflection of biblical revelation. Apart from Old Testament Scripture we cannot understand his knowledge and fear of God. Jesus' relationship to the Bible is important. Classical Christianity has stressed submission to the authority of God's Word. Divine inspiration of the Bible is crucial for Christian theology, as we have already stressed in our advocacy for the Scripture principle. However, Christians have not always appreciated the significance of Jesus' dependency upon the Word of God.

According to our docetic inclinations we have imagined that Jesus was born with complete theological understanding. We have not taken seriously Jesus' spiritual growth and development through his intellectual and emotional submission to the Hebrew Bible. Consequently, believers tend to see the gospel message apart from its source in Old Testament theology, and they minimize the personal and spiritual discipline of scriptural study and meditation. Because it is possible to have a high view of Scripture theoretically yet a shallow grasp of biblical truth theologically and ethically, it is a practical challenge for us to realize that Jesus' spirituality was thoroughly molded by his reflection on and memorization of the biblical text.

Jesus' growth in wisdom and stature and favor with God and man (Luke 2:52) undoubtedly involved the study of God's Old Testament revelation, as was the custom for young children in God-fearing households throughout Israel. Luke's account of Jesus' experience in the temple at the age of twelve demonstrates the unusual degree of intensity and wisdom with which Jesus approached and learned from the Scriptures. The young boy's spiritual illumination and insight reflected his focus on Scripture rather than on apocryphal fantasies and "new revelations." His dialogue with the biblical scholars at Jerusalem amazed the people because they were able to learn from his insights into the Law and the Prophets. They found surprising the spiritual depth and theological understanding of one so young.

Doing his Father's will and understanding his Word preoccupied Jesus from the beginning and resulted in his responding naturally to life's situations from a biblically oriented world view. His use of Scripture to resist satanic temptation early in his ministry evidenced his dependency upon God's Word, not in terms of quotable pat answers to repel Satan, but as the basic reference point for his life and character. Scripture was not an excuse for thoughtlessness, nor did he imply that quoting Scripture automatically resulted in Satan's defeat. His biblical knowledge was useful and spiritually potent because his character and actions were fully formed by biblical wisdom. If all we had to do to ward off temptation was to cite appropriate passages, a computerized concordance would assure trouble-free existence. Jesus, on the contrary, lived on the basis of what the Word of God said, and thus his use of Scripture defeated demonic forces.

As we will see in subsequent chapters, Jesus' self-understanding and teaching were dependent upon Old Testament revelation. From Jesus' first public sermon in Nazareth to his Upper Room Discourse, he revealed a mind and heart filled with the knowledge of God revealed in Scripture. New Testament scholar R. T. France writes,

> Jesus was second to none in his reverence for the Scriptures, his diligent study of them and his acceptance of their teaching, and while employing an exegesis which differed from that of his contemporaries generally only in a closer adherence to the original sense where misunderstanding or misuse was the rule, he yet applied the Old Testament in a way which was quite unparalleled.[5]

If Jesus' experience of God is guided and inspired by the content of Scripture, should not those who follow Jesus and seek to become like him discipline themselves through the power of the Spirit of God to be molded mentally, emotionally, and spiritually by the Word of God? We will fail to understand Jesus' distinctive interpretation and application of the Old Testament revelation if we do not understand the continuity and consistency between Jesus and the God of Abraham, Moses, and David. All that we see and hear in Jesus, including the imagery of parables, the terms of divine judgment, the meaning of redemption, his vision of the kingdom, his compassion for the needy, and his prophetic ethic, shows conclusively that Jesus was immersed in the biblical point of view. Jesus neither cut himself off from the Old Testament nor used it out of convenience as a cultural starting point to convey his distinctive ideas. Jesus' spirituality was not the encultured product of his religious environment but the free and joyful response flowing from a personal knowledge of the God who had made himself known. The impact of the knowledge and fear of God in Jesus' spirituality exposed the false paths to spirituality in the lives of many sincere people around him.

ABNORMAL SPIRITUALITY

Sometimes the more earnest a Christian is, the more distorted is his or her spiritual life. How easy it is to accept the gospel theoretically and verbally but to reject the disciplines of true spirituality. Frequently, those who deliberately reject Jesus' spirituality as a practical model for their own spirituality do so because their lives contradict his example. However, others are actually convinced that their self-styled spirituality is compatible with the Christian life. One of the ways of exposing abnormal spirituality is to examine Jesus' criticism of the superspirituality of the Pharisees and in turn the Pharisaic criticism of Jesus. This double-edged critique exposes the difference between a life-negating religiosity and a life-fulfilling spirituality.

"Pharisaic spirituality" has come to mean hypocrisy, even though in Jesus' own day the populace considered it a bulwark of spiritual strength. To be a Pharisee was to lead an exemplary life that was marked by precise observance of the Old Testament law, rigid standards of conduct, and loyalty to Hebrew nationalism. Why, then, did Jesus criticize them so severely (e.g., Matt. 23)? The answer lies in the Pharisaic perception of spirituality as a self-righteous achievement instead of a self-fulfilling relationship with God. Jesus criticized the self-centeredness and pride of their pseudospirituality.

Throughout the Gospel narrative we are presented with an exceedingly unattractive picture of their self-absorbed religiosity. The Pharisees loved the self-recognition and acclaim that accompanied their show of piety and the austerity of their religious commitment. Jesus therefore railed against them, calling them hypocrites, blind fools, and sons of hell. He likened them to whitewashed tombs, "which look beautiful on the outside but on the inside are full of dead men's bones" (Matt. 23:27). Jesus reserved his sharpest criticism for the Pharisees because their religious practices were more threatening to genuine spirituality than any form of atheism or political zealotism could ever be. They had succeeded in institutionalizing religion as a means of self-gratification and self-deception by coopting God and his Word for their own purposes. Their false spirituality became a source of pride (Luke 18:11), perverting the fear of God into a deification of their own traditions and subjecting the Word of God to a casuistic method of interpretation that focused on technical compliance rather than on spiritual meaning and heart righteousness. Jesus thus condemned the formality and emptiness of their pseudospirituality.

Instead of submitting to the authority of God's Word, the Pharisees argued over the technicalities of its tithing laws and neglected "justice, mercy and faithfulness" (Matt. 23:23). Although they spent considerable time praying and exhorting others to pray, Jesus condemned their prayers as only so much babbling. We should remember that the example and content of Jesus' prayer life, emphasizing personal communion with God through simple dependence and straightforward communion, was offered at a time when prayer, at least ritualized prayer, was popular. The Pharisees had already made prayer popular and public; Jesus made prayer real.

If the essence of relating to and obeying God has been lost, the purpose of going through the motions of spirituality can be only to glorify oneself. Precisely because true spirituality is radically contrary to the religion of self, Jesus condemned categorically the pathological spirituality of the Pharisees.

There is, however, another dimension to the contrast between Jesus' devotion to God and the outward piety of the Pharisees. Not only was Jesus critical of the Pharisees; the Pharisees were critical of him. Two major contentions repeatedly surfaced in their confrontation with him: that Jesus was worldly and that he compromised in his interpretation of the Word of God. Those who pride themselves on their self-righteous separation from the world and their conservative interpretation of Scripture still level these criticisms against those who truly follow the example of Jesus. Because Jesus befriended known sinners and socialized with individuals commonly associated with greed, extortion, prostitution, and other forms of immorality, the Pharisees despised him and suspected his moral integrity. They accused Jesus of being a glutton and a drunkard, a friend of tax collectors and "sinners" (Matt. 11:19). They went beyond guilt by association to accuse Jesus of legitimizing these evil people and practices.

Thankfully, Jesus shared God's perspective on human need rather than the spiritual egocentrism of the Pharisees. The integrity of his spirituality, with its moral strength and sensitivity to the multifaceted nature of human need, led Jesus to reach out sacrificially to those in need. The Pharisees refused to see in Jesus' spirituality the quality of openness to those in need, something that is inherent in God's love. They lost sight of the necessity of depending on God not only for their own needs but also for the needs of others. They were like "over-churched" Christians who venture from their religious ghetto to condemn and complain.

Jesus was also criticized for compromising the Word of God. A simple illustration of this charge can be seen in the Pharisees' rejection of Jesus' use of the Sabbath. Their hearts were so cold and rigid that they condemned Jesus for healing on the Sabbath. Consider the irony of Jesus' question to them, "Is it lawful to heal on the Sabbath?" (Matt. 12:10). They were so accustomed to reading the Old Testament law through a grid of superimposed regulations and concessions that they could not understand the humanness of a day of rest offered to God for worship (Mark 2:27). For the Pharisees the value of the Sabbath had been reduced to the observance of a regulation.

In their false allegations that Jesus was worldly and liberal, the Pharisees reflected a dehumanized and depersonalized spirituality. They replaced devotion to God with a passionate allegiance to their acquired traditions and religious rituals. Through their asceticism and legalism they twisted the true picture of what it meant to be related to God. They refused to see the life-fulfilling quality of genuine spirituality in Jesus and focused their intensity and passion inward upon themselves instead of outward toward God and others.

BEING HUMAN

If obedience to Jesus' spirituality is as life-fulfilling as I have claimed, why does discipleship demand self-denial and a willingness on our part to give up life itself for the sake of Christ? How do we reconcile the cost of discipleship with the humanness of Jesus' spirituality? A passion for Christ doubtless impressed many people in his day as fanatical and self-destructive.

Certain pronouncements from Jesus seem to call his followers to deny their very humanity: "If anyone would come after me, he must deny himself and take up his cross daily and follow me" (Luke 9:23); "if anyone comes to me and does not hate his father and mother, his wife and children, his brothers and sisters—yes, even his own life—he cannot be my disciple" (14:26). The apostle Paul's famous words, "For to me, to live is Christ and to die is gain" (Phil. 1:21), suggest the same extreme commitment. The apostle John commands renunciation of the world; "Do not love the world or anything in the world. If anyone loves the world, the love of the Father is not in him" (1 John 2:15). How do we reconcile these seemingly fanatical demands with generous offers of abundant life (John 10:10) and genuine peace (14:27)? How does the cost of discipleship balance with Jesus' attractive invitation, "Come to me, all you who are weary and burdened, and I will give you rest. Take my yoke upon you and learn from me, for I am gentle and humble in heart, and you will find rest for your souls. For my yoke is easy and my burden is light" (Matt. 11:28–30)?

The answer lies in our understanding of healthy human existence. As mentioned above, sinful human experience reverses the Creator's design for our humanity and redefines personal fulfillment in terms of self-gratification. Consequently, the world promotes an agenda for life which is actually self-destructive. Jesus therefore calls for self-denial, and Paul condemns the "natural man" driven by the impulse to sin, because the "normal" way of living life has become morally, physically, and spiritually bankrupt. The apostle John identifies specifically what he is renouncing: "for everything in the world—the cravings of sinful man, the lust of his eyes and the boasting of what he has and does—comes not from the Father but from the world" (1 John 2:16).

True spirituality frees the soul from guilt and from the self-destructive and evil impulses that rob humanity of its true individuality and self-esteem. The call of discipleship demands that we reject the burden of evil with its habits that lead to death and that we accept the responsibility of being made in God's image. Hating the world really means loving God's creation in all of its beauty and wisdom. Despising greed, lust, and pride frees us for befriending the needy and loving the unlovely. Denying oneself calls for rejecting the sinfulness of self with all of its vain ambitions, lies, and indulgences. By the grace and mercy of God, discipleship means joy.[6] It pulsates with the liberating energy of people free from the tyranny of sin and evil.

For their own peace of mind, Christians need to take seriously the practical implications of the humanness of Jesus' spirituality. For example, Jesus' ability to cope with stress provides a working model for living life under pressure. Jesus had no illusions about the negative repercussions of Christian spirituality and obedience. He warned the disciples, "All men will hate you because of me" (Matt. 10:22). Jesus anticipated tremendous interpersonal stress because of the gospel.

> Do not suppose that I have come to bring peace to the earth. I did not come to bring peace, but a sword. For I have come to turn a man against his father, a daughter against her mother, a daughter-in-law against her mother-in-law—a man's enemies will be the members of his own household (Matt. 10:34–36).

Jesus knew the stress of demonic opposition, false allegations, the human suffering of others, and the limitations of his own energy. He had to cope with disciples who were, judging from the Gospel narrative, frequently more hindrance than help. He persevered in a vocation that increasingly became more demanding and threatening. Because Jesus was acutely aware of the spiritual realities around him and filled with compassion for those in need, he was under intense stress. How did he maintain his personal equilibrium without yielding to anxiety?

Jesus cultivated the discipline of turning to God. His strength and self-control flowed out of a passionate personal relationship with the Father. As a result of his intense awareness of God, his practical grasp of Scripture, and his commitment to God's mission, he frequently turned stress to his advantage. Jesus' spirituality illustrates the power of accepting weakness, confronting accusations, and overcoming demonic temptations through a life perspective that is shaped by the fear of God and the Word of God.

He coped with stress with the same capacities that we have at our disposal.

> When he reached the point of exhaustion from teaching and healing, he had the freedom to stop and to spend time alone or with his disciples, with an instinct which told him that his freedom from the claims upon him was upheld by the same gracious Father who gave him the freedom and power to teach and heal.

"Jesus," insists Ray Anderson, "had a better theology than his critics, not to mention his disciples. . . . It is bad theology to have to love the world more than God."[7] Jesus' ministry was an extension of his spirituality. He was driven neither by the expectations of others nor by the adrenalin of success. He made choices on the basis of his knowledge of God—otherwise he would have succumbed to debilitating stress. He humbly acknowledged the limits of his own existence and lived fully for God in a world that he knew all too well was perverted.

TRUE SPIRITUALITY

Contemplating the rich resources of Jesus' human experiences of God awakens within the believer a desire to follow Jesus' spiritual example, which transforms routine daily life and sets human existence on the plane of God-centered living. True spirituality neither sensationalizes life nor trivializes the mundane. Instead, it provides the emotional and spiritual assets God intended for our self-fulfillment. A fresh look at the spirituality of Jesus renews our passion for righteousness and reminds us again of who we are before God.

By God's grace our spirituality ought to reflect itself in our emotional oneness with Jesus. As Jesus shared the perspective of the Father, so we ought to feel the emotions of Jesus. As he experienced anger against sin, love for the lost, trust in God's provision, compassion for the downtrodden, calm before danger, and determination in obeying the Father's will, so should we. It is obviously futile to try to create these emotions out of a religious piety that is disconnected from the fear and knowledge of God. Jesus reflected these emotions because his whole life and thought were rooted in God. To our emotional kinship with Jesus should be added the indispensable corollary of action. If true spirituality is not the driving force for obedience, then obedience will soon lose its direction and motivation. True spirituality cannot survive without response and engagement. Jesus' whole life was marked by deliberate action and encounter. As we read the Gospel narrative we sense that Jesus was constantly prepared to take the initiative. Those who follow Jesus need to experience his passion for accomplishing the Father's will.

Becoming like Jesus and sharing in his spirituality require that we experience his sense of confidence and self-esteem. From his communion with the Father, Jesus developed dignity and spiritual boldness, befitting creatures made in God's image. We see this in Jesus' public teaching and in his private interaction with the disciples. In spite of repeated attacks from the Pharisees, he maintained his trust in God and never failed to authoritatively represent God's Word and purpose. The best antidote to passivity and a false sense of inadequacy is a reappraisal of Jesus' personal dignity, for in this respect too we ought to be like him. His God-given sense of self-worth undergirded his ability to affirm people and challenge them with God's power to heal and forgive. He taught his disciples to pray boldly and expectantly, confident that their heavenly Father would hear and answer (Matt. 7:7).

As we look at the life of Jesus through the convicting, illuminating power of the Spirit of God, we begin to understand who we are and how we were meant to relate to God. Jesus gives us a new consciousness of God and ourselves. In the process of his human experience of God, he revealed his own self-understanding and clearly demonstrated that victory for embattled humanity depended upon himself.

8

jesus' self-understanding

The case which has been made for Jesus' human experience of God raises the issue of his self-understanding. Why have Christians found it necessary "to talk of God becoming man and not simply of a remarkable man finding God?"[1] The fact that Jesus exemplified human dependence upon God does not in itself make him more than human. The preceding chapter explored the genuine spirituality of Jesus. But if we believe that Jesus was only a man, we deny the church's confession of his Incarnation. Furthermore, if the historic Jesus was unaware of his true identity as the Incarnation of God, the early church was either startled with a new revelation or creative in its doctrinal development.

According to the apostolic testimony the imitation of Christ was rooted in the conviction that Christ is Lord. The apostles believed that the meaning of his person was absolutely crucial for the significance of his example. The apostolic vision of a passion for Christ cannot be reduced to a humanistic impersonation of an exemplary personality, even of one who performed great deeds. Becoming like Jesus is a supernatural work of grace through the power of Christ. Apart from this conviction about the deity of Jesus, Christian faith has no biblical appeal to discipleship. Therefore, it is important to see what part Jesus' self-understanding played in leading others to this unprecedented commitment to the meaning of his person.

SELF-DISCLOSURE

Since we have taken seriously the historical example of Jesus' life, we should examine Jesus' self-awareness. Normally, what we say and do effectively indicates who we think we are. There is no reason to believe that Jesus was an exception to this common rule of human nature. The genuineness of his humanity implies at least a partial disclosure of his self-awareness. Our understanding of Jesus presupposes a relationship between his outward behavior and "the processes of his mind and the characteristic direction of his thought."[2] He does not become completely transparent to our understanding, however, any more than any human being can be understood fully by another. To some degree mystery remains in even the most intimate and open of human relationships, but insight into one's self-consciousness is especially characteristic of secure and confident individuals.

The dignity and poise reflected in Jesus' life, issuing from his relationship with the Father, suggests a meaningful self-disclosure. If Jesus was truly human, we can legitimately anticipate an unfolding of his self-identity through his conversations and actions. Furthermore, the value of his self-disclosure is enhanced by the nature and integrity of his actions. Consistent, significant action on behalf of others, combined with the widespread recognition of his wisdom, adds credence to the authenticity of his self-disclosure, as it would for anyone. Nevertheless, it should be admitted that Jesus' self-disclosure in certain situations provoked a great deal of animosity. We are told that "many" thought he was "demon-possessed and raving mad." Others disagreed on grounds that his compassionate healing was hardly consistent with insanity (John 10:19–21). They did not argue over his miraculous act of healing, but they did disagree over the way he presented himself in the light of the miracle. On numerous occasions it appears that the nature of Jesus' own self-disclosure became the critical factor and that circumstantial concerns became secondary.

Although many modern scholars imply otherwise, we cannot deal with the biblical portrait of Jesus without wrestling with the testimony of his own self-consciousness. Believers should not impose upon Jesus an identity he never claimed for himself. On the other hand, they should not obscure the meaning of his person by ignoring the evidence of his self-consciousness. When we speak of Jesus' self-consciousness, we are not looking for a purely personal portrait of Jesus. "Jesus' self-consciousness of being the Messiah is not for us an inaccessible feeling he had inside him but the demonstration of that intention in public through words and bodily activity."[3]

On the other hand, a richer view of Jesus' self-understanding heightens our appreciation for his identification with us in our humanity. The same process through which we come to know ourselves is reflected in the biblical portrait of Jesus' self-understanding. He had a developing self-awareness that was derived through relationships and experiences as well as through intuition, reason, and revelation. In other words, there is a correspondence between the mystery of our own personhood and the mystery of Christ's incarnation. The inherently human process of developing self-awareness, universally experienced, is analogous to Jesus' unique comprehension of his divine identity. Even though we cannot fully explore Jesus' consciousness, the meaning of the Incarnation, which we deduce through his own self-disclosure, implies a dependence upon the Father for his self-identity. This process of self-awareness proved effective within his own consciousness and is essential for our understanding of him.

Besides guarding the integrity of Jesus' self-understanding and exploring the implications of his developing self-concept, a proper reflection on Jesus' self-disclosure clarifies the nature of his uniqueness. Truths about the life of Jesus, including the historicity of his miracles, the authority of his teaching, and the eternal validity of his propitiating sacrifice on the cross, ultimately depend upon a conviction about his person. Is he the Christ, the Son of the living God and worthy of worship and praise, or is he a great man on the order of Confucius, Buddha, or Muhammad? Knowing the human tendency to worship those who dramatically exceed ordinary human experience and to endow their remembrance with myths and legends of superhuman feats, believers cannot dismiss lightly the issue of Jesus' self-awareness. Great personalities may be taken seriously, without ever wrestling with the uniqueness of their personal identity. They are what they are by virtue of their commanding ways, superior intelligence, and powerful charisma.

Nehru, the late prime minister of India, is reported to have said to Richard Attenborough, the producer of a film on the life of Gandhi, "Whatever you do, don't deify Gandhi; he was too great a man." Unfortunately, many people feel this way about Jesus. They argue that Jesus never claimed to be the Messiah—much less, God! Early Christians, they say, were overwhelmed by Jesus' impressive accomplishments and made him into a god to be worshiped instead of a man to be respected. Upon reflection, however, this explanation is difficult to substantiate because the criteria we use to measure greatness do not fit Jesus as they do other world-renowned personalities. Apart from the meaning of his person, it is difficult if not impossible to understand the history of Jesus. In first-century literary sources outside of the Bible, Jesus surfaces as a footnote. If we eliminate from his life what the apostolic testimony sees as the concrete expression of his personal identity, all that remains is a nonconformist rabbi.

Gandhi's greatness does not rest on the conclusion that he was more than a man, but Jesus' greatness does. If the issue of Jesus' self-identity is dismissed, it is difficult to explain his significance. Placed alongside other great figures of world history, Jesus becomes an enigma. Judging from a modern, secular point of view, we would consider Jesus a second-rate historical personality whose life was described with more legend than fact. For every point of Jesus' teaching that makes sense to the modern reader, another point appears as either anachronistic or nonsense. Virtually all of his miraculous acts are written off as fictional elaborations that embellish his record of good deeds. Taken literally, the reports of his miracles are considered by many as unbelievable in the modern age.

Throughout his public life his followers remained confused, prone to panic, and embarrassingly unaware of what seemed to matter most to him. Politically speaking, Jesus did not come close to the world's greatest statesmen. He did not evidence the political savvy and organizational skill to lead a social revolution. At critical stages he appeared to suffer from a failure of nerve. He seemed timid and uncomfortable with his role as a potential leader in a popular crusade. In the end, his cross was more likely a political accident arranged for convenience than a necessary thwarting of a serious threat to Roman control. In comparison with today's media figures, Jesus spoke to very small audiences.

Any analysis of Jesus' life that dismisses his self-understanding as a fabrication of the early church and then assesses his life from the modernity principle will have a difficult time explaining his impact. These strained explanations invariably take one of two lines of thought: either the fame of Jesus was the product of human imagination and invention, or a particular dimension of his life, such as his political impact, is blown out of proportion and made to account for his significance. Neither attempt does justice to the biblical record because each obscures the meaning of Jesus' self-disclosure.

A criterion of greatness used to explain his historical impact cannot be superimposed upon Jesus; it must arise from within his own consciousness and actions. Apart from the meaning of his person, the authority of Jesus' teaching, the power of his miracles, and the success of his redemptive accomplishment have nothing in which to take root. In other words, the meaning of the Christ-event cannot be separated from Jesus' personal disclosure of his self-identity.

SUPPRESSING JESUS' SELF-DISCLOSURE

Classical Christianity developed an understanding of Christ on the basis of the fact—undisputed within Christian circles—that Jesus claimed to be the Messiah. The focus of attention was the relationship between the divine and human in Jesus. Today, however, the debate centers on whether Jesus ever claimed to be the Incarnate One. Many contemporary theologians have held that orthodox christology rests on a mistake. They have argued that the meaning and significance of Jesus' person lies outside his "imaginary" claim to deity.

Critical presuppositions have filtered down from scholars to pastors and laity, making it acceptable to dismiss Jesus' messianic self-consciousness. Under the constraints of "traditio-historical" criticism, references to Jesus' self-disclosure are eliminated that are either paralleled in Jewish tradition or reflect the faith, practice, and situations of the post-Easter church as we know them from outside the Gospels.[4] In a pseudoscientific way this approach implies what popular disbelief has historically held, namely, that Jesus was mistakenly deified by the early church. The only difference today is that some consider a denial of Christ's deity to be compatible with Christian discipleship.

The following quotation from a letter written by a pastor in an Evangelical congregation to his deacons (reprinted here with his permission) captures the spirit and conveys the meaning of this new version of denial and disbelief.

> My growing conviction is that those scholars are correct who say that the church's teaching far exceeded anything that Jesus claimed for himself. . . . My position at the moment is that it makes nonsense of language and theology to say Jesus is God. Jesus was a man, a man sent by God, a man with a special mission and a special anointing by God (the Messiah). I will agree too that the title Son of God may well speak to His uniqueness but not, of necessity, to his deity.

> The significance of Jesus for those of us within the Hebrew/Christian tradition is that he has caught the imagination of all those who are searching for a noble meaning to human existence. The power of the ideas at the heart of Jesus' message (unconditional love and justice) are still the most civilizing ideas abroad in the world. For us, the person of Jesus is the most powerful and appealing of all religious figures. .

> However, to elevate Jesus to God is in my opinion blasphemy and represents the gravest error the Church ever made. I know that sounds pretentious on my part but believe me when I say that it is absolutely important for me to say it at this point in my journey.

Because of this theological mistake it has been difficult to come to terms with the real Jesus.

My personal quandary in all of this is that I am a committed disciple of Jesus Christ. But I also believe that I have a responsibility to follow a Jesus who enlarges my humanity. For me that means the delicate discipline of refining the gold out of the dross that has accumulated around Jesus. I believe we have a responsibility to test and challenge every statement Jesus is recorded as saying. We must be courageous enough to recognize that not everything Jesus is recorded as having said has been a useful contribution to human understanding. Indeed we must say that some of the things he said have been the source of incredible misery. By the same token we have a responsibility to affirm those of his teachings which truly enrich and enlarge our humanity. No one proclaimed the ethic of unconditional love more credibly than Jesus.

As shocking as it may seem, the above position makes good sense to many professing Christians who have followed certain critical presuppositions to their logical conclusion. By accepting the modernity principle and disregarding the apostolic testimony, they have eliminated the disclosure of Jesus' self-identity. Ironically, the biblical record is still held to be important for revealing Jesus as a man of his times and as a provocative leader among his contemporaries, but they reject the biblical record of Jesus' self-disclosure. The nature of Jesus' uniqueness is historicized to meet modern intellectual expectations.

American New Testament scholar John Knox frankly admits his bias against the biblical rendering of Jesus' self-disclosure: "I, for one, simply cannot imagine a sane human being, of any historical period or culture, entertaining the thoughts about himself which the Gospels, as they stand, often attribute to him."[5] Like those in Jesus' day who found it easier to judge Jesus mad than to believe the implications of his teaching, John Knox dogmatically rejects the *possibility* of the Incarnation. According to the bias of unbelief, some of what Jesus is reported to have said about himself is unacceptable, and those who believe it are naive and misguided.

Along with critical presuppositions and a prejudice against the credibility of the text, a reinterpretation of the meaning of personhood undermines Jesus' self-understanding. Latin American theologian Jon Sobrino emphasizes the importance of altering the way we look at Jesus' self-concept. He contends that we cannot know Jesus by investigating what Jesus thought about himself. According to Sobrino, the conception that Jesus' personhood can be defined by determining his self-awareness goes back to Greek philosophy and the supposition that the human being is a rational animal. To know oneself is not the key to personhood. On the contrary, the essence of personality must be determined by its relational nature. Following Hegel's definition, Sobrino holds that "the essence of person is to surrender oneself to the other and find fulfillment precisely in the other."

Not only does he, on philosophical grounds, discount the value of knowing Jesus' self-awareness; he also concludes that the Gospels "simply do not provide us with enough data to figure out what Jesus thought about himself exactly." Sobrino is not merely cautioning against overinterpreting the biblical testimony and reading into Jesus' self-disclosure more than was originally intended. He is skeptical that the Bible reveals anything at all which substantiates Jesus' messianic consciousness. A critical analysis of the text eliminates any indication that Jesus thought of himself as one with God in any ontological sense. He believes, however, that the Gospels do give us enough data to observe the relational character of Jesus, thereby permitting us to "plumb the depths" of the person of Jesus. Sobrino's interpretation illustrates the denial of the substantial self, which was discussed earlier as a major component of the modernity principle. He subsumes all that can be known of Jesus' self-identity under relationalism.⁶

The concept of *kenosis*, of Jesus' self-emptying, has been explored as an incarnational reality which supernaturally authenticates Jesus' true humanity. Sobrino reverses this approach and finds in Jesus' ignorance and vulnerability to temptation a process of maturation which divinizes as well as humanizes. Jesus' concrete personality as a human being was fashioned in the midst of choosing "true messianism." Through his "ignorance" and "mistakes," argues Sobrino, Jesus became the Son of God. The crisis and limitations experienced by Jesus were not the result of an ontological humiliation of Jesus' true self, the divine kenosis in the course of human history. They were, rather, the essential historical factors which concretely shaped Jesus' self-understanding and person-hood. Sobrino is convinced that we must understand Jesus in terms "quite distinct from himself." His words and actions pointed exclusively to the kingdom of God and refrained from speculating about his self-identity. Jesus is significant insofar as he embodies the principles of the kingdom of God. "Jesus is bold enough," writes Sobrino, "to assert that eschatological salvation is determined by the stance a person adopts toward Jesus' own person."⁷ But Jesus' views here do not suggest that he identified his own person with the coming Son of Man or that we can derive his self-awareness directly from the New Testament data. According to Sobrino, Jesus was so acutely aware of his personal relationship to the kingdom of God precisely because he was empty of himself. Consequently, the kingdom, not self-identity, was an issue for Jesus.

Leonardo Boff shares Sobrino's christological perspective and articulates his own objection to the ontological reality of Jesus' deity:

> Jesus does not possess what the Council of Chalcedon taught: He was lacking a "hypostasis," a substance, enduring in himself and for himself. He was completely emptied of himself and completely full of the reality of the other, of God the Father. He realized himself radically in the other; he was not anything for himself, but all for others and for God. . . . Emptying himself means creating interior space to be filled with the reality of the other. It is by giving out of oneself that human beings remain profoundly within their own selves; it is by giving that one receives and possesses one's being.[8]

Boff's statement amounts to a denial of the deity of Jesus—not simply a denial of a "traditional interpretation" of christology. His reinterpretation of Jesus in relational terms amounts to more than the rejection of a word such as *hypostasis*: it is a bold rejection of biblical testimony, apostolic conviction, and the church's historic confession. Boff and Sobrino summarily dismiss Jesus' self-understanding as a nonissue, raised only by those who cling to an allegedly anachronistic philosophical view of the person. According to them, whatever divinity Jesus knew was the result of achieving a relationship with the Father through a process of identification with the poor. Much of what they say about Jesus' compassion for the poor and his pursuit of justice is the result of significant reflection on the biblical record of Jesus' example. But it is indefensible to conclude from Jesus' spirituality and his concern for others that what he was *in himself* is unimportant. It defies the witness of God's Spirit and capitulates to a modern outlook which prefers to explain the meaning of the person through existentialism and evolutionism rather than through Christian theism. With them, I stress the sanctifying principle of becoming like Jesus, but against them I stress the absolute uniqueness of the Incarnate One, who is different from us not only by the degree of his ethical involvement but by his very nature.

DIMINISHED SIGNIFICANCE

As a result of certain critical presuppositions and the prevailing bias against the supernatural, some scholars have understandably chosen to disparage Jesus' self-understanding. Yet some conservative biblical scholars, faithful to the historic Christian creeds, may also be in danger of diminishing the significance of Jesus' self-disclosure. Their theological conclusions about Christ accord with classical Christian conviction, but their methodologies are significantly influenced by modern skepticism. The recent work of New Testament scholar James Dunn may be heading in this direction. He traces the origins of the doctrine of the Incarnation to the early church's response to the "Christ-event" instead of to Jesus' personal self-disclosure. Dunn is persuaded that a serious consideration of the "historical context of meaning" leads to a truer and more accurate exegesis of passages previously thought to point to Jesus' deity. On the basis of his research he argues that the language used by the biblical writers to describe Jesus' exalted status and unique authority was already used in the middle decades of the first century to describe previous heroes of the faith such as Enoch, Elijah, Abel, and Moses.[9] Did the language actually mean what we think it meant, Dunn asks, if in fact it was used to describe other men of faith? Dunn suggests that the historical link between Jesus of Nazareth and the Christ of dogma may not be as clear cut as we think it is. Nevertheless, he assures us that this position does not undermine traditional beliefs; it simply clarifies historical development. My concern is that Dunn is overly cautious in permitting the text to determine its own meaning. Does not the text itself imply something historically significant when it records that Jesus was about to be stoned for blasphemy or that a voice from heaven gave preeminence to the Son over Moses and Elijah on the Mount of Transfiguration?

"We need not despair," observes Dunn, "of getting back to Jesus' understanding of his role and mission." He confesses that Jesus was aware of the uniqueness of his sonship, of his unprecedented intimacy with the Father, and of his eschatological commissioning. "Beyond that," Dunn cautions, "we run out of firm evidence." He adds,

> Of course Jesus was much more than he ever knew himself to be during his earthly life. But if we are to submit our speculations to the text and build our theology only with the bricks provided by careful exegesis we cannot say with any confidence that Jesus knew himself to be divine, the preexistent Son of God.[10]

While I do not doubt Dunn's orthodoxy, I believe he is theologically insensitive to the relationship between Jesus' self-understanding and the development of the Christian doctrine of the Incarnation. If, as he suggests, Jesus did not think of himself as the divine Son of God, then the message of the text not only is relativized by the historical context but is clearly misleading. The biblical writers trace the concept of divine sonship to the personal testimony of Jesus himself (Matt.

11:27; 16:16–17; 28:19; Mark 12:6; 13:32; John 3:16; 5:25; 10:35–36). If Jesus did not disclose what he is reported to have said, we need an explanation for that phenomenon. The issue is not whether we have the very words of Jesus but whether we have an authentic rendering of his own thought and intention.

If we do not believe that the biblical text contains sufficient evidence to warrant confidence in Jesus' self-awareness of divine sonship, then we are required to take a theological leap as Dunn has done and base the doctrine of the Incarnation on postbiblical reflection on the "Christ-event."[11] Although he is concerned not to abstract the biblical text from its "historical context of meaning," he seems naïve about the theological repercussions of abstracting theology from the revelation of Jesus.

Why is Dunn confident that the biblical text reveals Jesus' self-understanding of his role and mission if it fails to accurately represent what Jesus thought about himself? Why does his research strategy of "maximal doubt" focus on passages dealing with divine sonship without suspecting that Jesus' mission might be a product of creative reflection as well? Dunn is convinced that authentic exegesis must interpret the text according to its historical context, but taken to an extreme this principle eliminates the very possibility of Jesus' disclosing the unique reality of the Incarnation. Dunn argues that the biblical interpretation must acknowledge Jewish usage of "divine" language. Apart from Jesus employing the language of preexistence, Dunn sees no other possibility for an explicit disclosure of divine sonship. Is Dunn justified in equating the concept of the Incarnation with a revelation of Jesus' awareness of preexistence? According to Howard Marshall, Dunn's confusing equation of the ideas of a "divine Son of God" and a "preexistent Son of God" leads to the mistaken assumption "that if the synoptic Jesus was not conscious of pre-existence, he was not conscious of divine sonship."[12]

I am not convinced that Dunn has made his exegetical case. And I believe that the theological implications of his thesis are greater than he supposes. His minimalistic approach to the biblical text gives the benefit of the doubt to a recasting of christological passages that have been interpreted for centuries by Christian theology to teach the incarnation of Christ. The evidence about to be considered emphasizes the significance of Jesus' self-disclosure and takes seriously his conscious awareness of divine sonship.

9

GOÔ INCARNATE

"Are you the one who was to come, or should we expect someone else?" (Luke 7:19), John the Baptist asked Jesus. What he had heard and seen finally prompted his direct, unambiguous question. He was prepared, if necessary, to shift his attention away from Jesus if Jesus did not claim to be the Messiah. John's message of judgment and repentance issued from his conviction that he prepared the way for the coming Messiah. He had told the crowds, "One more powerful than I will come, the thongs of whose sandals I am not worthy to untie. He will baptize you with the Holy Spirit and with fire" (3:16). For John, salvation required a Savior, and the kingdom of God meant a Messiah.

Everything about John's prophetic ministry pointed to the personal significance of the Messiah. Having preached repentance and judgment, John then made a personal introduction: "Look, the Lamb of God, who takes away the sin of the world! This is the one I meant when I said, 'A man who comes after me has surpassed me because he was before me'" (John 1:29–30). It is not surprising that John should have been concerned about who Jesus claimed to be. It *is* surprising that John still needed to be convinced. It is difficult to avoid comparing the faith of the centurion (Luke 7:1–10) and the questioning of John. Even though the centurion was a foreigner and did not have an Israelite's expectation of a Messiah, he responded to the authority and power of Jesus in a way unparalleled in Israel. John, however, whose association with Jesus was well known, doubted the messianic identity of Jesus and required more convincing proof. He wanted to hear an explicit messianic claim directly from Jesus.

Implied in John's question is the importance he attached to Jesus' self-disclosure as well as the integrity he anticipated in Jesus' answer. He was prepared to accept Jesus' unambiguous answer. John was asking bluntly: are you or are you not the Messiah? Fully aware of what John was asking, Jesus ironically chose to answer his question indirectly. "Go back and report to John what you have seen and heard," he said, and then he described what John's emissaries had most likely already observed. "The blind receive sight, the lame walk, those who have leprosy are cured, the deaf hear, the dead are raised, and the good news is preached to the poor" (Luke 7:22).

If Jesus had thought of himself as a prophet empowered by God in a manner similar to John, this would have been the time to say so. A modicum of integrity should have compelled Jesus to reject any pretentious and unwarranted messianic claim at this point. On the contrary, Jesus purposely called attention to his works, which unmistakably implied the fulfillment of messianic prophecy. His response emphasized rather than downplayed the issue of his personal identity. His final sentence makes this plain: "Blessed is the man who does not fall away on account of me" (Luke 7:23). Jesus' answer to John is consistent with two significant themes expressed throughout the Gospels. The first is the relationship between John the Baptist and Jesus. In spite of striking similarities between them, their self-understanding and goals for ministry were clearly different. Second, Jesus found it necessary to redefine the popular meaning of *messiah*. His guarded response to John expressed not only the fulfillment of messianic prophecy but also Jesus' conscious effort to avoid the political and nationalistic expectations popularly associated with the Messiah. Jesus preferred the ambiguity of an indirect answer in order to avoid a fairly predictable misinterpretation commonly made by those who equated the Messiah with the triumphal overthrow of Roman rule. It is likely that even John's messianic expectations were colored by this prevailing perspective and required change.

MORE THAN A PROPHET

The similarities between John the Baptist and Jesus are remarkable. The birth narratives describing their conceptions emphasize the necessity of divine intervention. Unusual circumstances and special praise surrounded each man's birth. Both grew up in humble, righteous families with a long, distinguished heritage. We are told that they were destined to play significant roles in the history of God's people, yet they spent their childhood years in obscurity. When they began their public ministry God's authority was evident in their teaching and attracted the attention of the crowds accustomed to the predictable content of the rabbis. Their prophetic ministry had a strong ethical impact, and both men died at the hands of the political authorities. The comparison between John and Jesus raises an important question. If Jesus was the unique Son of God, why is the tradition surrounding his life complicated by the life of another impressive individual whose unique birth, radical lifestyle, prophetic teaching, and political death closely parallel his own? Those who suspect that the birth narratives are legendary ought to consider the improbability of the early church's fabricating John's extraordinary birth and special circumstances, when it was their purpose—or so it is alleged—to deify Jesus. Does it make sense to mythologize the history of a "rival" of Jesus?

Many scholars conclude that Jesus was an eschatological prophet who drew attention to the kingdom rather than to himself. The evidence of John the Baptist indicates otherwise. Although the similarities may be striking, differences exist which reveal John's unprecedented conviction about Jesus. If these differences are ignored, Jesus can easily be characterized as a unique prophet who, like John, had an eschatological message. But if the differences are recognized and the biblical record is taken seriously, we gain insight into Jesus' unique self-understanding.

The purpose of John's ministry was to introduce the Promised One, which he did by calling people to personal repentance and social righteousness. He was well aware that the kingdom was not to come through him but through another. According to Mark's gospel, he preached this message: "After me will come one more powerful than I, the thongs of whose sandals I am not worthy to stoop down and untie" (Mark 1:7).

Unlike Jesus, John emphatically testified, "I am not the Christ but am sent ahead of him" (John 3:28). Consciously aware of the difference between himself and the Messiah, John specifically applied this distinction between himself and Jesus. John saw himself as the "friend," and he saw Jesus as the "bridegroom": "The friend who attends the bridegroom waits and listens for him, and is full of joy when he hears the bridegroom's voice. That joy is mine, and it is now complete. He must become greater; I must become less" (vv. 29–30). Jesus accepted John's introduction without reserve or embarrassment. He made no effort to dissuade John or reinterpret John's message. He accepted John's designation and then proceeded with his own mission. Furthermore, John's introduction of Jesus as the Lamb of God may have been significant not only for the audience but for Jesus' self-understanding.

Just as Elizabeth, the mother of John, had been used by the Holy Spirit to confirm Mary's understanding of the Lord's revelation to her (Luke 1:41–45), John's introduction may have contributed to Jesus' messianic consciousness.

By God's design John the Baptist was a significant link between the Old Testament covenant and the inauguration of the new age. Like Isaac and Samuel, whose lives also resulted from God's special intervention, John was a key figure in a dramatic new phase of salvation history. His birth, lifestyle, and prophetic word are like the Old Testament prophets. The only difference was the timing of his ministry. He stood on the threshold of God's final revelatory word. By the Spirit of God he opened the door of the new age (Heb. 1:1–2). Jesus confirmed John's calling, finding in him the fulfillment of Malachi's prophecy (Mal. 3:1; 4:5–6). According to Jesus, the prophet like Elijah had already come in the person of John the Baptist (Matt. 17:11–13). Therefore when Jesus intentionally drew the analogy between John and Elijah, his purpose was not only to disclose the significance of John's ministry but also to call attention to his own unique role as the messenger of the New Covenant. If John was the prophet "like Elijah" who preceded the "great and dreadful day of the Lord," then Jesus implied that he himself was the Lord. " 'See, I will send my messenger, who will prepare the way before me. Then suddenly the Lord you are seeking will come to his temple; the messenger of the covenant, whom you desire, will come,' says the LORD Almighty" (Mal. 3:1).

As we evaluate the similarities and differences between John the Baptist and Jesus, it becomes evident that the early church knew the difference between the birth of a prophet and the incarnation of God. John's life and testimony introduced Jesus and his messianic mission, without divorcing salvation from the Savior or the kingdom from the King. Nor can we take John seriously and at the same time scale down the meaning of the Messiah to that of an eschatological prophet. John's effort to exalt Jesus and minimize his own personal significance corresponds with Jesus' full acceptance of John's messianic introduction, "Look, the Lamb of God!" Every indication suggests that Jesus believed himself to be exactly what John proclaimed him to be.

"MESSIANIC· SECRET"

Although Jesus' response to John's question—"Are you the one who was to come, or should we expect someone else?"—made a clear allusion to messianic prophecy, it lacked the direct affirmation John undoubtedly sought. Why was Jesus reluctant to say boldly, "I am the Messiah!"? Actually, Jesus' elusive response fits a pattern in which he avoided direct answers to questions about his authority. He was reluctant to publicize his work. When the Jewish religious leaders confronted him, demanding to know by what authority he taught and acted, he declined to comment (Luke 20:1–8). He repeatedly demanded secrecy from those he healed (Mark 1:44; 5:43; 7:36; 8:26), and he insisted on silence when the demon-possessed cried out that he was the Son of God (1:34; Luke 4:41). Even the disciples were warned not to tell anyone that he was the Christ (Matt. 16:20) or to reveal their experience of Jesus' transfiguration (17:9).

William Wrede explained this so-called secrecy motif in the Gospel of Mark by seeking to show that the early church created these secrecy elements in order to interpret Jesus' earthly life messianically.[1] Wrede argued that the development of the Christian conviction that Jesus was the Messiah took place after the Resurrection. The "messianic secret" in Mark's Gospel was an attempt to read back into the life of Jesus allusions to his messianic identity, though they had no historical authenticity. Wrede concluded that Jesus did not think of himself as the Messiah.

Ironically, he interpreted Jesus' reticence to claim the messianic title as a literary invention used by the early church to emphasize the messianic character of his earthly life. In other words, Jesus' reticence to declare himself to be the Messiah is sufficiently consistent with the early church's conviction about the resurrected Christ to be considered by Wrede as a logical though fictional intrusion into the original history of Jesus. Other scholars see Jesus' refusal to claim the title as evidence that he did not think of himself as the Messiah. Others see it as a creative invention to interpret Jesus' life more messianically. In any case, the "secrecy motif" is inadequately interpreted as a denial of Jesus' messianic consciousness or as a literary theme used to prepare the reader for the postresurrection messianic claim.

Jesus efforts to stifle public exposure and acclaim have traditionally been interpreted as a conscious attempt to correct the prevailing cultural expectation of the Messiah. Jesus rejected the Jewish concept of political messiahship. His reticence to claim a title associated with political liberation and the promise of freedom from Roman rule is easily understandable. If he had not rejected that title, he could not have affirmed the messianic mission envisioned in his teaching and actions. Consequently, he takes every precaution to quell messianic rumors and to subdue popular adulation.

Just how difficult it was to redefine the meaning of the Messiah is clearly evident in Peter's inability to grasp the true meaning of Jesus' messiahship (Matt. 16:21–22). True messianic consciousness is disclosed by Jesus precisely in his endeavor to disassociate himself from popular appeal and power politics. Both the masses and the opposition responded to Jesus in nationalistic fervor, seeing him either as a new hero for a popular uprising or as a fresh threat to the status quo. On all fronts Jesus sought to redefine *his* messiahship according to biblical revelation. For Jesus to have allowed his role to be defined by contemporary messianic expectation would have been tantamount to yielding to the initial temptations in the wilderness. Jesus subjected himself and his followers to the painful course of messianic redefinition in terms anticipated in the Old Testament.

The Gospel accounts distinguish between a genuine and a false messianism. Jesus accepted Peter's confession, commending it for its heavenly source, even though he rejected Peter's interpretation of the title. What was true of the title was also true of his miraculous power. He commanded silence in the aftermath of miracles, not because he did not perform miracles, but because his purpose was to demonstrate the power and compassion of God. Instead of making the miracle a display of power, he sought to make people aware of his mission on a deeper, more costly, level. Not until the end did Jesus clearly and publicly admit he was the Messiah. When the high priest asked, "Are you the Christ, the Son of the Blessed One?" Jesus responded directly, "I am. . . . And you will see the Son of Man sitting at the right hand of the Mighty One and coming on the clouds of heaven" (Mark 14:61–62).

Helmut Thielicke has observed,

> It is striking that Jesus uses these predicates of majesty when he is being delivered up to death, exposed to humiliation, and plunged into the passion, so that the confession of his messiahship can no longer give a wrong impression of loftiness nor lead to a theology of glory, but engulfs us in the depths of his destiny.[2]

Perhaps there is another dimension that needs to be considered. Jesus freely uses the title of Christ only after the Resurrection, when he can point to the finished work of the Cross and the completion of the Father's will (Luke 24:26, 46). Before he claimed the title for himself, he accomplished all that the Father prepared for him to do. Only then did he employ the title of Messiah instead of his familiar self-designation as the Son of Man.

Through his humiliation and exaltation Jesus was shown to be what he knew he was, the eternal Son of God. He was "acknowledged

Messiah in fact not just *after* his passion and resurrection but *because* of his passion and resurrection—and, it must be insisted, in continuity with his own self-consciousness during the ministry."[3] (Cf. Acts 2:36; Rom. 1:4; Heb. 5:8–10.) Jesus did not clamor for a title which in itself implied a redemptive accomplishment yet to be fulfilled through the Cross and the Resurrection; nevertheless, he consistently disclosed that the kingdom of God had come through his own person and work.

KINGDOM REALITY

In no uncertain terms Jesus attributed the power of the reign of God to his personal presence and proclamation. No other interpretation of his words and actions takes the biblical description seriously. He was either the Authoritative One, through whom the kingdom had come, or he was a shrewd pretender. Jesus fulfills prophecy, the new age is begun, the lost are found, and judgment is handed down. What kind of man would claim such things for himself? Jesus began his public ministry with a deliberate identification of his work with Israel's anointed deliverer (Isa. 61:1–2).[4] His claim, "Today this scripture is fulfilled in your hearing," disclosed his messianic self-concept and raised immediate questions among his hearers as to his personal identity (Luke 4:18–22). Jesus repeatedly emphasized that salvation history had entered a new era of fulfillment and celebration. Jesus responded to the criticism that John's disciples fasted and his did not by asking, "How can the guests of the bridegroom fast while he is with them?" (Mark 2:19), implying that through him the joyous day of salvation had begun (cf. Hos. 2:16–20). He interpreted his custom of eating with outcasts and sinners along these same lines. When Zacchaeus the tax collector, Mary the prostitute, and the motley crew of disciples dined with Jesus, they were seated at the banquet table of the Lord, experiencing God's acceptance and forgiveness (Luke 7:31–50; 14:1–24; 19:1–9; 22:15).

Jesus personified the reality of the kingdom of God. He assumed the prerogatives of God. The prophets proclaimed the possibility of God's forgiveness and Jesus authoritatively bestowed it (Mark 2:6–12; Luke 7:48–49). He drove out demons "by the finger of God" and claimed it as confirmation that the kingdom of God had come (11:20; cf. Exod. 8:19). He went as far as to say that people no longer needed to look for the kingdom because the kingdom was already in their midst. He was not suggesting that the reality of the kingdom consisted of an interior disposition or subjective feeling but was boldly and radically equating his presence with the presence of God (Luke 17:20–21; Matt.

18:19–20). Consequently, responding to Jesus was crucial for one's eternal destiny (Mark 8:38; Luke 9:26), and following his prescription for entrance into the kingdom was mandatory (Mark 10:15). Jesus was undoubtedly convinced that the old had gone and the new had come (2:21–22). God's message spoken "through the prophets at many times and in various ways" was now "in the past." And Jesus, through his life and ministry, knew that in these last days God had spoken by his Son (Heb. 1:1–2). He was also aware that many would hear but not understand, see but not perceive. But for those who did understand there was blessing: "Blessed are your eyes because they see, and your ears because they hear. For I tell you the truth, many prophets and righteous men longed to see what you see but did not see it, and to hear what you hear but did not hear it" (Matt. 13:16–17).

Jesus' decisiveness for the kingdom is especially evident in his teaching ministry. "The people were amazed at his teaching, because he taught them as one who had authority, not as the teachers of the law" (Mark 1:22; see Matt. 7:28). Jesus refused to engage in the pedantic style of the rabbis, who were in the habit of supporting their teaching with a ponderous and intrinsic system of cross reference and interpretative precedent. He proclaimed the truth with such authority and wisdom that people questioned how he could be so learned without having received formal education (John 7:15).

Probably one of the most acceptable and popularly held opinions about Jesus today is that he was a great teacher. But all too often the compliment paid to Jesus as a teacher does not take seriously his claim to absolute authority. Immanuel Kant sought to decipher what he thought to be the true teachings of Jesus from the biblical record. He explained his perspective in personal correspondence in 1775:

> I distinguish the *teachings* of Christ from the report we have of those teachings. In order that the former may be seen in their purity, I seek above all to separate out the moral teachings from all the dogmas of the New Testament. . . . The apostles took the essential requirement for salvation to be not the honoring of the holy teacher's religious doctrine of conduct but rather the veneration of this teacher himself and a sort of wooing of favor by means of ingratiation and encomium—the very things against which that teacher had so explicitly and repeatedly preached.[5]

Kant assumed that Jesus did not consider himself as the decisive factor for his teaching. He believed in the value of Jesus' teaching because of its appeal to a universal sense of common morality. But the only report we have of Jesus teaching will not allow us to separate artificially the Teacher from his teaching. We cannot divorce Jesus' ethic from Jesus' theology.

Unlike the prophets, who claimed to speak *for* God, Jesus claimed to speak *as* God, which is the dramatic significance of his authoritative pronouncement: "You have heard that it was said. . . . But I tell you . . . " (Matt. 5:21–48). The prophets invoked the authority of God when they prefaced their words with "thus saith the Lord" and testified that "the word of the Lord came to me." Jesus, however, prophesied on his own authority, claiming to need no outside justification for his teaching.[6] He boldly equated the Word and work of God with his teaching and actions (John 5:36–40; 7:16–18). Furthermore, he distinguished himself from the prophets by relating his message to himself and the work of God in him.[7] He was conscious of being the one about whom the prophets spoke (Matt. 11:9, 13; 13:17).

As the Lord of the Sabbath, Jesus assumed his superiority to the temple: "I tell you that one greater than the temple is here" (Matt. 12:6). He saw himself transcending the prophetic impact of Jonah (v. 41), revealing a greater wisdom than Solomon (v. 42), and claiming implicitly a status above David (vv. 3–8; 22:41–46). There can be little doubt that the claim of Jesus to absolute teaching authority and provocative interpretation of the Old Testament disclose his messianic self-understanding. He saw himself and his teaching as decisive for the destiny of individuals (John 8:31–32). Jesus began to fulfill the prophecy of Isaiah, who foretold that a fruitful "branch" of Jesse would "strike the earth with the rod of his mouth" (Isa. 11:4). Accordingly, Jesus promised destruction to those who did not hear and obey his words. He likened them to a house built on the sand, ready to collapse with the first storm, and to a house which could withstand the fiercest storm because it was built on the rock (Matt. 7:24–27).

One of Jesus' favorite forms of communication was parables, which first-century rabbis also used. But there is a dramatic twist to Jesus' parables that reveals his messianic self-consciousness. Such a self-portrayal in parables appears to be unique to Jesus, who depicted himself "through images which in the Old Testament and later Jewish literature are used to depict God." Through the parables Jesus designated himself as the sower, the director of the harvest, the rock, the shepherd, the bridegroom, the father, the giver of forgiveness, the vineyard owner, the lord, and the king. Each of these images represents a significant association with God and his work which is clearly evident in the Old Testament and in all likelihood familiar to many of Jesus' listeners. For example, when Jesus drew an analogy between obedience to his words and building on the rock in the parable of the two houses, he used one of the most common pictures of God in the Old Testament. The parable implies that "response to Jesus and his words is tantamount to response to God."[8] Other biblical allusions are also obvious (Isa. 28:16; Ps. 118:22; cf. Matt. 21:42), leaving the distinct impression that Jesus is purposefully selecting an image which reflects his messianic consciousness.

Philip Payne concludes that, "out of Jesus' fifty-two recorded narrative parables, twenty depict him in imagery which in the Old Testament typically refers to God." It is reasonable to argue that Jesus was naturally drawn to Old Testament symbols for God as a means of communicating his own messianic self-understanding. According to Payne,

> Here in the parables, the most assuredly authentic of all the traditions about Jesus, is a clear, implicit affirmation of Jesus' self-understanding as deity. His sense of identification with God was so deep that to depict himself he consistently gravitated to imagery and symbols which in the Old Testament typically depict God.[9]

From whatever angle we choose to examine Jesus' teaching, we come to the unavoidable conclusion that he saw himself as more than a teacher. Through his word the kingdom was announced with authority and power. His teaching was accompanied by the kingdom reality of supernatural power. Jesus anticipated in his signs and wonders the future eschatological kingdom. He not only spoke the very words of God, he displayed the power of God. As the man of the Spirit, he embodied the wisdom and power of the kingdom. The Old Testament linked the messianic age with fresh displays of God's power over creation. Through his Spirit God promised to provide the righteous with physical abundance and spiritual wisdom. Jesus began his public ministry by claiming for himself the messianic expectation in Isaiah 61:1—"The Spirit of the Lord is on me, because he has anointed me to preach good news to the poor" (Luke 4:18)—which reveals his own consciousness of receiving "the Spirit without limit" (John 3:34). Jesus manifested the full range of the gifts of the Spirit. His life beautifully demonstrated the gifts of knowledge, wisdom, faith, and healing as signs of the kingdom.

Miraculous, supernatural power is problematic in contemporary Western thought. The more that modern men and women pride themselves on their technological prowess and mastery of the universe, the more narrow the acceptable perimeters of divine activity become. Paradoxically, insight into the wonders and intricacies of creation have resulted in the arrogant refusal to let God be God. The people of Jesus' day were astonished by his miraculous power to cast out demons (Mark 5:20). In amazement they exclaimed, "Nothing like this has ever been seen in Israel" (Matt. 9:33). When Jesus calmed the storm the disciples were terrified, asking among themselves, "Who is this? Even the wind and the waves obey him!" (Mark 4:41).

The Gospels are marked with a definite reserve about Jesus' miracles. He declined the use of miraculous power to rescue himself (Matt. 4:1–11; Luke 23:35) or to punish others (9:51–56). He rejected those who sought a sign from heaven to test him (Matt. 16:1–14), and he strictly warned those whom he healed to remain silent (Mark 5:43; 7:36). He spurned the curiosity of the Pharisees and the teachers of the law, saying, "A wicked and adulterous generation asks for a miraculous sign!" (Matt. 12:39).

The nature and power of Jesus' miracles proved to be a further attestation to his messianic self-understanding. His works signaled the beginning of a new age. In and through him God had invaded the realm of Satan—casting out demons, raising the dead, healing the sick, feeding the hungry, and restoring sight to the blind. His response to John the Baptist indicated that he was aware of fulfilling the Old Testament messianic promises (Matt. 11:5–6; see Isa. 29:18–19; 35:5–6; 61:1–2). If Jesus lacked any plan to improve the world by healing *all* the sick and casting out *all* the demons, it was because he was interested not in a better world but in a new world.[10] Besides showing God's compassion and the first sign of the kingdom age, Jesus used miraculous power to commend the faith of those who believed (Mark 2:5; 5:34; 7:29; 10:52) and to provoke others to belief (4:41; Matt. 12:23). His miracles left a spiritual impact in lives of individuals who were liberated for discipleship (Mark 5:18–20; Luke 13:13; 17:11–19; 18:43; John 5:14; 9:30).

The kingdom of God cannot be abstracted from Jesus' self-concept. There is no easy way around Jesus' messianic self-disclosure, either through radical textual criticism or through a contemporary version of the social gospel. We cannot justifiably separate what we know about the kingdom from what Jesus disclosed about himself. The two revelations are inseparable. The proclaimer cannot be divorced from his proclamation. Apart from him there is no forgiveness of sin or healing of disease. Jesus demonstrated his own conviction that knowing God depended upon his sonship and obeying God required obedience to his teaching. Thus, we are left with either the audacity of a messianic pretender or the genuine self-portrait of the Messiah.

SONSHIP

Jesus revealed an unheard-of intimacy with the Father. Through his prayer life, fellowship with the disciples, and his teaching, he disclosed a self-concept without precedent. We begin, however, with the response to Jesus from supernatural sources. Confirmation of Jesus' divine sonship was revealed to him by the Father as well as from satanic evil forces.

Linked with Jesus' personal disclosure of unique sonship is the equally significant revelation by God of Jesus' divine sonship. At his baptism "a voice came from heaven," declaring to Jesus, "You are my Son, whom I love; with you I am well pleased" (Mark 1:11). Mark's Gospel underscores the nature of this communication as *direct address* to Jesus himself. The revelation is not only for the sake of the audience but for the sake of Jesus. The Father chose the occasion of Jesus' obedient submission to baptism, an act which reflected Jesus' dual solidarity with humanity in its sin and with God in his redemptive purposes, to confirm Jesus' self-understanding. Not only is the divine pronouncement a revelation to us, but it was a revelation to Jesus. Jesus was not an actor moving through a well-rehearsed script with prearranged cues. His history reflects God's unique affirmation of his person and work, and I believe that Jesus personally benefited from this confirmation of his self-concept. The issue is not whether Jesus needed this specific pronouncement to convince him that he was the divine Son. Jesus grew in his self-understanding through a variety of means, but the significance of God the Father's personal and direct address to the Son should not be ignored. Only a docetic christology would argue that the Father's communication to the Son was redundant.

Jesus' transfiguration appears as a similar supernatural attestation of his divine sonship, significant not only for the disciples but also for Jesus (Matt. 17:1–9). The event implies a meaning and purpose which transcends whatever impact it had on the three disciples. The scene is not staged for their sake, even though they received a powerful testimony to Jesus' divine sonship. Jesus experienced the ecstasy of his glorified existence, a foreshadowing of his resurrection and eschatological fulfillment. The events on that mountaintop were primarily for Jesus' sake. The Father provided an experience of glory and communion in order to reaffirm in Jesus both his mission and his identity. It is important for Christians to know that Jesus, like all true believers, lived by faith. He believed in the Father's testimony about him. His self-concept was shaped by those significant experiences of God's revelation to him.

Supernatural confirmation of Jesus' identity came not only from God but from Satan as well. Ironically, the strong opposition from demonic personalities, who repeatedly interfered with Jesus' public ministry, ended up testifying to his divine sonship. The forces of evil found it necessary to admit the identity of their opponent. This meant, of course, profaning Jesus' identity in mocking derision or attempting to seduce him into violating himself (Mark 1:34; Matt. 4:1–11). But through their efforts to discredit him, they revealed an awareness of who they were contending against (8:29; Mark 5:7). Although it is obvious, it is still interesting to note that demonic personalities responded directly to Jesus by referring to his identity as the Son of God. Their reaction is primarily to Jesus himself rather than to an impersonal abstraction of the kingdom or righteousness. Demons had no difficulty in recognizing Jesus as the personification of kingdom righteousness and the embodiment of God's personal rule.

The way Jesus responded to Satan and the demonic is also significant. He never questioned their assumption that he was the Son of God. He did not refute Satan's premise, "if you are the Son of God," but he adamantly resisted Satan's perversion of his mission (Matt. 4:1–11). It is reasonable to assume that, if Jesus saw himself as only a unique representative of God's kingdom or as an eschatological prophet, he would have attacked the assumption as well as the proposal. If he was not in fact the Son of God, then his response was inadequate and allowed a false assumption to stand.

The external testimony to Jesus' divine sonship corresponds to his personal disclosure of intimacy with the Father. There is some debate as to whether Jesus' use of the Aramaic word "*Abba*," "Father," in his direct address to God was completely foreign to his Jewish contemporaries (Mark 14:36).[11] In any case, this extremely personal way of praying to God was highly unusual and surpassed Old Testament precedent.[12] The fact that Jesus distinguished between his own relationship with the Father and that of the disciples is probably more significant for disclosing Jesus' unique relationship with the Father (cf. 13:32; John 20:17). Jesus claimed to be the only saving way to the Father.[13]

In Matthew's Gospel, Jesus' explicit disclosure of divine sonship is accompanied by his consciousness of the Father's role in making him known. Implicit in his praise to the Father for divine revelation to "little children" is his gratitude to God for drawing the disciples to himself (Matt. 11:25–26). He acknowledged that his kingdom invitation, "Come to me, all you who are weary and burdened, and I will give you rest" (v. 28), depended upon his authority as the Son. In the context of gratitude and messianic invitation, his unequivocal declaration to be the ultimate revelation of the Father and the recipient of his full authority makes perfect sense: "All things have been committed to me by my Father. No one knows the Son except the Father, and no one knows the Father except the Son and those to whom the Son chooses to reveal him," (Matt. 11:27; cf. Luke 10:21–22; John 3:35–36; 13:3; 14:6–10).

Jesus interpreted the meaning of his sonship through his familiar self-designation as the Son of Man. He chose this title apparently because it was least likely to be misunderstood and afforded the best opportunity to reshape the popular concept of the Messiah. F. F. Bruce has shown that *the Son of Man* was not a current title for the Messiah or any other eschatological figure.[14] Therefore, Jesus' unique use of the expression reflected his understanding of his life and mission and resulted in an original fusion of Old Testament themes. Without exception, all of the occurrences of the designation *Son of Man* are attributed to Jesus himself or a direct reference to his usage (Luke 24:7; John 12:34).[15]

While the phrase may have been ambiguously understood in his day, Jesus gave it a distinctive meaning. He "saw the fulfillment of the predictions and foreshadowings of the Old Testament in himself and his work." This understanding is especially evident in his prophetic application of the eschatological figure in Daniel and the Suffering Servant in Isaiah to himself and his mission. Jesus deliberately put aside the nationalistic connotations of Daniel's Son of Man and saw in Daniel 7:13–14 "a prediction of the ultimate goal and combination of his Messianic work."[16] Unexpectedly, however, the means to accomplish this ultimate vindication and triumph were spelled out in Isaiah's prophecies of the Suffering Servant. Jesus, therefore, combined as never before two significant Old Testament themes. Eschatological fulfillment on the universal and eternal scale envisioned by Daniel was to be accomplished through suffering, humiliation, and death. According to Jesus, salvation was to come not through political triumph but through God's gracious acceptance of the redemptive sacrifice provided by a "man of sorrows" who was "led like a lamb to the slaughter."

Jesus combined these two figures into a unified and coherent self-portrait (Mark 8:31, 38; 10:45; 13:26; 14:21–62). For him the Son of Man designation represented a "creative synthesis" of Old Testament prophecies which he authoritatively applied to himself.[17] Previously separate traditions were suddenly brought together in the person and actions of a single messianic figure whose originality did not violate biblical revelation but rather illuminated and integrated it.

Understandably, this position led to opposition among those who rejected Jesus' interpretation and found in his self-disclosure an extremely provocative and controversial messianic claim. They recognized what Jesus was claiming for himself and condemned him as a blasphemer. When Jesus assumed the divine prerogative to forgive sin, the religious leaders were shocked. They exclaimed among themselves, "This fellow is blaspheming!" But Jesus refused to correct their interpretation by giving a nonmessianic qualification to his actions. Instead he intentionally emphasized his messianic prerogative by adding, "So that you may know that the Son of Man has authority on earth to forgive sins" (Matt. 9:1–8). On one occasion the Jews asked Jesus directly, "How long will you keep us in suspense? If you are the Christ, tell us plainly." For reasons discussed earlier, Jesus refrained from a direct response. He preferred to emphasize his miracles and his relationship with the Father. Nevertheless, his response left no doubt in the mind of his accusers. They were prepared to stone him for blasphemy, not for his miracles, but because Jesus, "a mere man," claimed "to be God" (John 10:24–33).

One of the clearest associations of the Son of Man title with Daniel 7:13 occurs appropriately in a situation of humiliation. Jesus was a master of indirect response and had consistently forestalled identification with the popular messianic label, which can be seen in his trial when a frustrated high priest found it necessary to press Jesus for a direct answer: "Are you the Christ, the Son of the Blessed One?" Knowing the consequences of such a confession, Jesus answered, "I am," adding, "and you will see the Son of Man sitting at the right hand of the Mighty One and coming on the clouds of heaven" (Mark 14:61–62). His response brought to a climax a carefully developed reinterpretation of the Messiah which placed hope and glory in tension with redemptive suffering. The religious leaders clearly believed they were about to crucify one who claimed to be God's own Son. And Jesus did not deny it.

MARTYR OR MESSIAH?

Jesus' preoccupation with death is difficult to explain, apart from his messianic self-understanding. Anyone else who talked about death—especially his own—as much as Jesus did would probably be judged mentally unstable. The disciples were naturally grieved and confused by Jesus' insistence on his death, which he endeavored to describe for them in detail (Matt. 16:22; 17:23; Mark 9:32). On at least three separate occasions Jesus told his disciples plainly that he was going to die violently (Matt. 16:21; 17:22–23; 20:17–19).

In addition, however, he clearly alluded to his death in his daily discourse. He predicted that "the time will come when the bridegroom will be taken from them [his disciples], and on that day they will fast" (Mark 2:20). When James and John requested positions of honor in the kingdom, he responded with the command to serve one another, adding, "For even the Son of Man did not come to be served, but to serve, and to give his life as a ransom for many" (10:45). On another occasion Jesus said, "Just as Moses lifted up the snake in the desert, so the Son of Man must be lifted up" (John 3:14; cf. 12:32–33). And again, "For as Jonah was three days and three nights in the belly of a huge fish, so the Son of Man will be three days and three nights in the heart of the earth" (Matt. 12:40).

Even his parables and figures of speech reveal a preoccupation with death: the good shepherd who lays down his life for the sheep (John 10:11), the kernel of wheat that falls to the ground and dies (12:24), and the beloved son who is murdered by the wicked tenants and whose body is thrown out of the vineyard (Mark 12:1–12). Throughout his ministry he evidences an unusual awareness of his death. Jesus even asked the crowd on one occasion, "Why are you trying to kill me?" Although the question exposed Jesus' awareness that the religious establishment had murderous intentions, it baffled the crowd and was used by the Jews to make Jesus look paranoid. "You are demon-possessed," the crowd answered. "Who is trying to kill you?" (John 7:20).

Are we to conclude that Jesus feared martyrdom? From the example of his cousin John the Baptist, he was well aware that a prophetic ministry might end in death. He knew vested interests could not be challenged without suffering and persecution. But does a fear of death account for the terrible dread he experienced in Gethsemane or explain the mystical and redemptive language he used at the Last Supper to describe his death?

It is more reasonable to conclude that Jesus' messianic self-concept caused him to reflect on the theological meaning of his death. Instead of expressing a morbid preoccupation with failure and death, he prepared his disciples for the inevitable consequences of his messianic mission. The way he spoke of his death revealed the Savior's mind, not a martyr's fear. His understanding was shaped by Isaiah's Suffering Servant (Isa. 52:13–53:12), Zechariah's prophecy (Zech. 9–14), and the psalmist's meditation (Pss. 22, 41–43, 118). Jesus interpreted the Old Testament in a way that necessitated his death. He saw his death in terms of a divine imperative: "the Son of Man *must* suffer . . . he *must* be killed" (Mark 8:31–32; italics added; see also 9:12; 14:21, 49; Luke 24:26–27). He also saw his death as a willing act of obedience: "No one takes it from me, but I lay it down of my own accord" (John 10:18). At his arrest he willingly gave himself up, saying, "Do you think I cannot call on my Father, and he will at once put at my disposal more than twelve legions of angels? But how then would the Scriptures be fulfilled that say it must happen in this way?" (Matt. 26:53–54). Jesus interpreted his death theologically and redemptively. He deliberately alluded to the role of the servant in Isaiah 53 as his own.[18] He gave his life as a ransom for many, knowing that salvation and resurrection were on the other side of human rejection and spiritual abandonment. What Jesus thought about his death only makes sense if we accept what Jesus disclosed about himself. Both dimensions need to be considered together in order to form a coherent portrait of Jesus.

RESPONSE

It may seem easier to believe that the early church invented Jesus' messianic consciousness than to believe that God became a man and lived among us. But such a conclusion is much more than a simple denial of Jesus' self-understanding. It amounts to a sweeping denial of his kingdom ethic, his salvific significance, and his filial relationship with God. Accepting Jesus' revelation about himself is central to accepting his revelation about anything. If he is not who he claimed to be, then his teaching and actions lose their integrity, his death is stripped of theological significance, and his resurrection is mythologized. As we have seen, the evidence supports the conviction that Jesus considered himself to be the Son of God. Implicitly and explicitly Jesus made outrageous claims that, if false, discredit his ministry. His messianic consciousness sufficiently pervades the Gospels that to attribute it to the ingenuity and inventiveness of the early church raises grave doubt as to whether anything Jesus said or did is authentic. The most rigid critical barriers fail to eliminate Jesus' conviction that he was the Messiah.

The process by which Jesus came to the conviction that he was the Messiah is prototypal for the believer's comprehension of new life in Christ. It is legitimate to presuppose that Jesus had an innate awareness of his messianic identity, in a manner similar to our intuitive belief that we are spiritual beings made in the image of God. Through his study of Old Testament Scripture, he gained confirmation and understanding. He choose to commit himself to the rigorous path of messianic obedience. He submitted to the Father's will and became not only what he was meant to be but what he already was in his very essence. All of the factors considered above, such as the difference between himself and John the Baptist, his embodiment of the kingdom of God, his assumptions of God's prerogative, and his unique experiences of special revelation, represent a powerful testimony to Jesus' self-understanding. Besides that, however, they provide a glimpse into Jesus' personal process of self-awareness. Even though he is the incarnate Son of God, he models for us the path to true self-awareness. If we are to become like him, we need to live by faith, entrust ourselves to the will of the Father, risk our lives in fulfillment of God's mission, and depend upon God's Word and Spirit for insight and action. As we likewise follow Jesus' principle of self-awareness by becoming spiritually sensitive, dependent on revelation, and sacrificially obedient, we disclose our true identity as his disciples.

The very same distinctive elements in Jesus' life which enhance the credibility of his messianic claim and reinforce the believer's conviction about Jesus' self-disclosure are signs of new life in Christ. We have argued that Jesus is greater than John. He is the fulfillment of John's prophecies. But Jesus promised that the one who is least in the kingdom of God is greater than John (Luke 7:28). Jesus found it necessary to redefine messianic expectation. He had to remove nationalistic fervor and political triumphalism from it. He boldly and creatively articulated a new and more biblical vision of the Messiah and his work. As we have seen, his own life reflected this vision. And Jesus applied this new messianic pattern to his followers: "Whoever wants to become great among you must be your servant, and whoever wants to be first must be slave of all. For even the Son of Man did not come to be served, but to serve, and to give his life as a ransom for many" (Mark 10:43–45; see Matt. 5:11–12; 10:25; 1 Peter 2:21).

Jesus embodied the kingdom and fulfilled its agenda (Luke 4:18–19). He personified the rule of God. He did what only God could do: he forgave sins, performed miracles, and claimed absolute authority in his teaching. But surprisingly, everything he claimed for himself he gave to his disciples. He gave to Peter, the representative disciple, "the keys of the kingdom of heaven" and with it the redemptive and judgmental significance of the gospel (Matt. 16:19; cf. Luke 22:29). He called his disciples to be "fishers of men" (Mark 1:17). He gave them authority to preach, cast out demons (3:14–15), and "make disciples of all nations" (Matt. 28:19). The one who received the Spirit without limit promised that "anyone who has faith in me will do what I have been doing. He will do even greater things than these, because I am going to the Father" (John 14:12; see Joel 2:28–29). More important than power, however, is familial intimacy with the Father (Luke 10:20). He who called God "*Abba*" gives us "the Spirit of sonship," by whom we cry, "*Abba*, Father" (Rom. 8:15).

This dynamic parallel runs throughout the New Testament. Those who follow Jesus are in the process of disclosing who they really are by their Spirit-inspired affinity with the distinguishing marks of Jesus' life. Their lives are supernaturally conceived and ethically relevant. Only those who follow in this way raise a credible witness to Jesus as the Son of God (John 17:23).

10

kingôom righteousness

Perhaps the least controversial fact about Jesus is that he was a teacher. From the earliest days of his public ministry, he was greeted by friend and foe alike as a teacher. Like the rabbis he was asked to give rulings on disputed questions of the law (Luke 12:13–14), and people sought his insight on doctrinal disputes (Mark 12:18–27). He was accompanied by a band of disciples who looked to him for instruction on theological themes popular in first-century Judaism. Throughout the Gospels we see that Jesus respected the Jewish context in which he was born, lived, and died. He supported the synagogue and the temple; he celebrated the Passover along with other special religious days. Much of his teaching was related thematically to special events on the Jewish calendar. He recognized the role of the priests and acknowledged the teaching authority of the scribes and Pharisees. But the similarities between Jesus and other itinerant teachers quickly fade in significance when the nature and content of his teaching is considered. Then everything about Jesus becomes provocative and controversial.

PARADOX

Unlike the rabbis, Jesus taught with absolute authority. As we have seen, he repeatedly made his own identity the issue of his teaching. People's response to him and his words indicated their response to God and his kingdom. Right from his first public address in Nazareth, Jesus initiated an entirely original stance toward the law which implied a highly disputed, if not blasphemous, conclusion. The more he taught, the more obvious it became to the Jewish religious experts that Jesus saw himself fulfilling and transcending the Old Testament law. Yet all along Jesus claimed total loyalty to the law. The two assertions were boldly contradictory according to the religious leaders, and the former required righteous condemnation. How could he uphold the law and at the same time claim to fulfill and transcend the law?

Another unsettling paradox in Jesus' teaching was his harsh condemnation of the Pharisees. Many contemporary Jewish scholars argue that the description in the Gospels of Jesus' interaction with the Pharisees is seriously distorted by the anti-Semitism of the Gentile church. They argue that it is difficult to justify Jesus' seemingly harsh and unbalanced caricature of the Pharisees when other groups, such as the Sadducees and Zealots, who were much less concerned with righteousness, escaped similar condemnation. Of all groups, the Pharisees were by far the most closely associated with Jesus' concerns, yet they come under his strongest criticism and sharpest rebuke.

Within the Gospels various indicators point to the close affinity between Jesus and the Pharisees. The Pharisee Nicodemus, for example, approached Jesus respectfully, if not secretly, and said, "Rabbi, we know you are a teacher who has come from God. For no one could perform the miraculous signs you are doing if God were not with him" (John 3:2). Whenever Jesus spoke publicly, the Pharisees were apparently present, debating with him and among themselves about his teaching. He was invited into their homes for table fellowship, in spite of their objection to his eating with the ceremonially unclean, another positive indication of their close connection. Although there was considerable animosity between Jesus and the Pharisees, both parties constantly interacted. Ironically, the intensity of their conflict evidenced their mutual preoccupation with the same issues. They were united insofar as they both reflected zeal for righteousness and the law. On the other hand, Jesus and the Pharisees assessed each other's righteousness on altogether different grounds.

A third paradox emerges from the tension between the style and the content of Jesus' teaching. Jesus demonstrated a profound ability to communicate. Everything about his style was intended to strike a responsive chord in the hearer. His bold claim to authority engaged people's attention. There were no predictable formulas or clichés. He cut through the perfunctory rhetoric of "safe" teaching and abstract debates and penetrated people's thoughts. Contributing to his mystique was his uncanny ability to draw powerful and insightful conclusions about issues without speaking to them directly. He left people thinking, as in the parable of the wicked tenants who killed the son. Without stating it, Jesus made his point infuriatingly obvious to the chief priests and the Pharisees. He was a master of unexpected endings, creatively adding a new twist at the end of a parable that served to sharpen its focus or expand its meaning. By introducing the grumbling elder son in the parable of the prodigal son or the inappropriately dressed guest in the parable of the wedding banquet, Jesus suddenly directed the thrust of the story against the self-righteous.

Jesus chose a style of communication which made his teaching accessible and relevant to the common person. He drew his illustrations from ordinary daily experience. Because he talked on their level when he spoke sarcastically or with hyperbole, the people understood him. They identified with his stories about sheep and farmers, wedding banquets, and rich landowners.

Certainly one of the chief features of Jesus' communication was its dialogic nature. A great deal of his teaching took place in response to people's questions. He repeatedly demonstrated the art of diverting attention from secondary issues and going to the heart of the matter. He skillfully cut through the introductory question of Nicodemus, the divisionary religious perplexity of the Samaritan woman, and the verbal tricks of the Pharisees. His passion for the truth came through in every encounter which sought to obscure the central issue somehow. Whether it was with the rich young ruler or with Peter, Jesus brought people face to face with the truth about themselves.

Jesus continually appealed to ordinary human experience for confirmation that what he said was true. He embodied in himself and expressed through his teaching the divine principle of personal encounter between God and human beings. "Come now, let us reason together" (Isa. 1:18) was an explicit pedagogical commitment evident in Jesus' communication. His teaching addressed the common moral sense of his hearers (cf. Luke 10:36).[1] "Why don't you judge for yourselves what is right?" (12:57). He often connected natural human reactions to spiritual reality. "What do you think? If a man owns a hundred sheep, and one of them wanders away, will he not leave the ninety-nine on the hills and go to look for the one that wandered off?" (Matt. 18:12). He taught them about God by appealing to a common sense of decency. "Which of you, if his son asks for bread, will give him a stone?" (7:9).

Jesus customarily involved people in the thinking process, allowing them to reach the obvious conclusions based on their own sense of right and wrong. Frequently he began a parable with "What do you think?" "He believed in the capacity of the general popular moral judgment to discern truth when presented with it."[2] Even when popular sentiment may not have been right, he had a way of posing the question to provoke a deeper moral awareness. Commenting on Pilate's particularly repugnant killing of some Jews in Galilee, Jesus asked, "Do you think that these Galileans were worse sinners than all the other Galileans because they suffered this way?" As far as Jesus was concerned the answer was obvious. His emphatic "I tell you, no!" anticipated the agreement of the crowd (Luke 13:1–5). By appealing to the conscience of his audience, as well as to their hopes and fears, Jesus showed his commitment to genuine communication, free from manipulation. He had no interest in talking above the heads of people or in obscuring truth by eloquence. They were moved by his presentation of the truth. His authoritative grasp of the relevance of God's truth to the human situation profoundly touched the mind and heart of his hearers.

As a creative and imaginative storyteller, he used people's everyday experiences to open windows to the truth. His dialogic approach emphasized his accessibility to people. He expressed not only his willingness to be put on the spot but his confidence in letting them set the agenda for discussion. He continually extended to prostitutes and tax exploiters, some of the least desirable characters in his audience, an open invitation to learn from him. His actions revealed compassion for people in need. His miracles of healing and exorcism added to his credibility and dramatically showed that he cared. Jesus was the consummate teacher, effective in dialogue and sensitive to contextualize his message. He drew his analogies of spiritual reality from everyday life: a fisherman's net, a Samaritan well, current news reports, and the temple court. He disdained blind loyalty and shallow enthusiasm and worked to catalyze independent thought among his hearers.

But the nature and style of Jesus' teaching sharply contrasts with its radical message. Here is the paradox: everything we observe about the effectiveness and relevance of his message seems matched by its unyielding radical quality. Jesus refused to make truth easy. Consider the audacity of uttering such an inflammatory saying as "If anyone comes to me and does not hate his father and mother, his wife and children, his brother and sisters—yes, even his own life—he cannot be my disciple" (Luke 14:26–27). If a modern ethicist passionately insisted on nonretaliation, love of enemies, prayer instead of worry, and absolute marital fidelity, he or she would be judged hopelessly naïve and idealistic. Some Jewish scholars have argued that Jesus' ethical extremism frustrated his followers and resulted in the neglect of his teaching altogether.[3]

According to his critics, Jesus demanded more from his disciples than they could be reasonably expected to obey. Compared to rabbinic ethical teaching, Jesus neglected an individual's evil inclinations and overrated altruism. Besides that, they contend, Jesus confused a personal ethic with a social ethic. He seemed oblivious to the social ramifications of his personal ethical mandate. Consequently, Jesus' brand of revolutionary teaching threatened to rend the national moral fabric. Joseph Klausner, an influential Jewish scholar, is especially critical of Jesus' ethical radicalism. He writes,

> Jesus' moral teaching ceased to provide a firm basis for the life of human society. True Christianity, the Christianity of the Sermon on the Mount, cannot be practiced in an organized Society or State, where there must be law and justice, there must be family life, there must be security of life and property.[4]

In this regard the Jewish scholars are more faithful to the substance of Jesus' teaching than those Christians who equate the ethic of Jesus with cultural morality. The former at least recognize the absolute authority and radical challenge of Jesus' teaching. Jesus remains one of the most unlikely candidates for the moral majority we can imagine. He adamantly resisted pressure from the Pharisees, the masses, and even the disciples to domesticate his ethic. His teaching ran contrary to bad people as well as to good people who prided themselves on their enlightened ways and respectable behavior.

I doubt if Jesus would have been invited to speak at a presidential prayer breakfast. He was definitely not a "safe" speaker. Even with due consideration for the context, Jesus said many outlandish things. Consider his words to the rich young ruler: "Sell everything you have and give to the poor, and you will have treasure in heaven" (Luke 18:22); or his frequently repeated "all or nothing" challenge to his followers: "Any of you who does not give up everything he has cannot be my disciple" (14:33). When the scribes and Pharisees plotted Jesus' trial, they had plenty of his quotations to use against him, such as "I have come to bring fire on the earth, and how I wish it were already kindled!" (12:49). His extremism did not easily fit the conventions of hyperbole. "Anyone who says, 'You fool!' will be in danger of the fire of hell" (Matt. 5:22). Nor did his teaching seem very reasonable: "If your right eye causes you to sin, gouge it out and throw it away. It is better for you to lose one part of your body than for your whole body to be thrown into hell" (v. 29). Surely practical people judged his teaching to be naïve and idealistic. He taught them, for example, to "give to the one who asks you, and do not turn away from the one who wants to borrow from you" (v. 42). On occasion, he was completely incomprehensible to the majority of his audience, for example, when he said, "Whoever eats my flesh and drinks my blood has eternal life, and I will raise him up at the last day" (John 6:54).

Jesus' teaching was especially intriguing because he frequently chose the medium of parables. He drew his audience into his message by allowing them to recreate his word picture in their own imagination with themselves as the principle character or eyewitness. We sense an almost irresistible mental and emotional engagement in Jesus' teaching because we identify with the attitude of the prodigal son or the self-righteous ego of the elder brother. We feel like we are on the sidelines cheering for the good Samaritan or condemning the wicked tenants. Who would be so foolish as to build their house on the sand when they could build it on the rock? What would you do if you found a priceless treasure hidden in a field and all you had to do was buy an inexpensive field to claim it? If you were invited to a royal wedding banquet as an honored guest, would you go? By using parables, Jesus provoked thought and triggered an existential response. Through them he was able to pass judgment publicly on the scribes and Pharisees. Although his verdict may have been communicated indirectly, it was nevertheless unmistakably clear (Matt. 21:45).

As effective as the parables were, Jesus saw them paradoxically as a hidden means of communication. He demanded from his hearers a. deeper interpretation than that of simply a one-dimensional word picture. "He who has ears to hear let him hear" invited the hearer to enter into the spiritual reality of his teaching. He told his disciples,

> The secret of the kingdom of God has been given to you. But to those on the outside everything is said in parables so that they may be ever seeing but never understanding; otherwise they might turn and be forgiven! (Mark 4:11–12; cf. Isa. 6:9–10).

The medium Jesus chose was creative, effective, and provocative; everything was in favor of the listener. But the content of his teaching necessitated spiritual perception and life-transforming decisions. Jesus was under no illusion that his message would be easily understood and internalized. We will understand Jesus' teaching if we accept these three paradoxes: he was for the law completely but claimed to transcend the law; his concerns and passions were most compatible with those of the scribes and Pharisees, but he revealed his deepest antagonism especially against them; his open relationships, compassionate actions, and positive appeal to human understanding were as genuine as his absolute authority and radical commands.

BIBLICAL INTEGRITY

Jesus held the highest possible regard for the Old Testament. The authority of "the Law and the Prophets" was not an issue for Jesus—it was a conviction.[5] Did Jesus believe in the authority, historical reliability, and contemporary relevance of the Scriptures? Absolutely! But the evidence for this conclusion is found primarily in the way Jesus used Scripture rather than in propositional statements defending the text. As we have seen, Jesus used the Old Testament to shape and reflect his self-understanding and mission (Matt. 21:42; Luke 4:21; John 5:39). This fact alone is sufficient to demonstrate Jesus' high view of Scripture. But Jesus also used Scripture as the touchstone for his teaching. When he was questioned and challenged, he claimed the authority of Scripture for his words and actions. He expressed his submission to the authority of Scripture on several occasions by simply stating, "It is written." With this introductory formula, he called on the authority of Scripture to defend his righteousness against satanic opposition (Matt. 4:4, 7, 10), to reveal the fulfillment of prophecy (11:10; 26:24, 31), and to explain his moral outrage and action (21:13). Many of Jesus' explicit references to the Old Testament came in the heat of debate. When he was asked why he ate with tax exploiters and sinners, Jesus justified his behavior by quoting from Hosea 6: "It is not the healthy who need a doctor, but the sick. But go and learn what this means: 'I desire mercy, not sacrifice'" (Matt. 9:12–13).

On another occasion when he was challenged for permitting his disciples to do what the Pharisees judged unlawful on the Sabbath, he appealed to three separate biblical references. First, he told how David and his hungry companions "ate the consecrated bread—which was not lawful for them to do, but only for the priests" (Matt. 12:4; cf. 1 Sam. 21:1–6). Then he referred to the Pentateuch, asking, "Haven't you read in the Law that on the Sabbath the priests in the temple desecrate the day and yet are innocent?" (Matt. 12:5; cf. Num. 28:9–10). Finally, he quoted Hosea the prophet, "If you had known what these words mean, 'I desire mercy, not sacrifice,' you would not have condemned the innocent" (Matt. 12:7; cf. Hos. 6:6). Jesus fully intended to justify his actions on biblical grounds: what he permitted his disciples to do was consistent with David's historical precedent, faithful to the provision of the law, and obedient to the prophetic word. Far from proof-texting, Jesus used the Scripture incisively to make a twofold claim. Not only were his actions consistent with the true meaning of the Sabbath, but he clearly implied the fulfillment of the Sabbath through one greater than

David and the temple. By employing seemingly incidental citations he creatively summarized three streams of biblical tradition and alluded to his superior status as prophet, priest, and king.

Jesus' commitment to the Old Testament was evident in his discussion with the Pharisees over controversial ethical issues. In the divorce debate, Jesus upheld the teaching of both Genesis and Deuteronomy (Matt. 19:1–9).[6] He argued that God's will for the marriage relationship was from the beginning an exclusive and permanent relationship. Mosaic legislation in Deuteronomy did not change the will of God; it simply dealt with human sinfulness. Moses permitted the possibility of divorce with specific procedures and safeguards because of the Israelites' "hard hearts." The existence of divorce flowed from the reality of sin. Jesus interpreted divorce on the grounds of a biblical theology of marriage given in Genesis, together with the situationally sensitive and contextually relevant Deuteronomy passage. Jesus' judgments on divorce were both lighter (no capital punishment for adultery) and heavier (the sole basis being sexual sin) than those prescribed in Deuteronomy.[7] He did not repudiate the Mosaic ordinance. "What he objected to was the deductions people were drawing from the Bible to the effect that God approves divorce."[8] The guiding principle for Moses as well as for Jesus was God's abiding will for marriage. However, Jesus showed that he was not obligated to draw a one-to-one correspondence between Mosaic legislation and his own interpretation. He was free to go to the heart of the biblical theology of marriage. In his provision for divorce he recognized human sinfulness and its regrettable repercussions, yet he stressed absolute marital fidelity. His conclusions were based on the authority of God's Word.

Jesus did not play off one part of the law against another. He repeatedly stressed his commitment to the entire law. When Jesus denounced the scribes and Pharisees for neglecting "the more important matters of the law—justice, mercy and faithfulness," he used language reminiscent of Micah and seemed to prioritize the law's demands (Matt. 23:23; see Mic. 6:8).[9] But he did not relax the stipulation in the law regarding tithing. He claimed that the weightier matters of the law must be obeyed as a first priority, but less important commands could not be neglected (Matt. 23:23). The issue for him was a commitment to obey the entire law.

Jesus expressed the crux of his debate with the Pharisees by contending that the religious leaders violated the commands of God. He did not seek to change the law; he sought to obey it. So when the Pharisees and teachers of the law accused Jesus of permitting his disciples to break "the tradition of the elders," Jesus replied, "And why do you break the command of God for the sake of your tradition?" (Matt. 15:2–3). Instead of obeying the fifth commandment, to honor one's father and mother, the Pharisees as grown children shirked their responsibility by setting aside money for the temple treasury that would have gone to their parents.[10] "Thus you nullify the word of God for the sake of your tradition," condemned Jesus (Matt. 15:6). His passion for the integrity of God's Word became especially apparent in his debate with those who questioned his doctrine of Scripture. The most significant passage on Jesus' relationship to the law, Matthew 5:17–48, implies that Jesus' doctrine of Scripture was under fire from the experts in the law.

Among the biblicists of the day, Jesus' actions and teaching provoked a controversy about his faithfulness to the Scripture. He was challenged to defend his doctrine of Scripture before accusers who self-righteously believed they held a higher view of Scripture than he did, which is the most plausible explanation for his emphatic pronouncement,

> Do not think that I have come to abolish the Law or the Prophets; I have not come to abolish them but to fulfill them. I tell you the truth, until heaven and earth disappear, not the smallest letter, not the least stroke of a pen, will by any means disappear from the Law until everything is accomplished (Matt. 5:17–18).

Without reservation or qualification Jesus claimed absolute loyalty to the written Scriptures, but he did it in such an extremely unusual and provocative way that no Jew would have escaped the significance of his words. After Jesus spoke about the law, the issue shifted in the mind of his hearers from Jesus' attitude toward the law to the relationship of the law to Jesus.[11] This change helps to account for the growing opposition to Jesus. He pledged undivided loyalty to the law, but in doing so he made himself central to the law's relevance; thus giving to the law a radically new orientation. The law's significance was related to himself. The authoritative "I" became the focus of attention. He did not come to destroy the law but to fulfill it. "Jesus brings the Law and the Prophets to their intended meaning by providing the correct interpretation of the Law, i.e., by expounding the true meaning of the commandments and therefore the true measure of righteousness."[12]

Perhaps no single word is adequate to comprehend all the dimensions of Jesus' promised "fulfillment" of the law. He established the true ethical intent of the law, reaffirmed the law's continuing validity, and made genuine obedience a real possibility through his redemptive provision. It is misleading to argue that Jesus affirmed the moral commands of the law but neglected the ceremonial and cultic requirements. As the Matthaean passage shows, Jesus pledged loyalty to the full extent of the law, right down to its smallest letter and the least stroke of a pen. He did not distinguish between those elements of the law that were to be established and fulfilled and those that were obsolete. Nor did he diminish the significance of the law by implying that it was of little value. He emphatically claimed that the whole law must be fulfilled. Moreover, he taught that the whole law needed to be approached in a radically new way. According to Jesus, this new approach was implicit within the Old Testament itself. He placed the responsibility of spiritual perception squarely upon those who handled the law. "You are Israel's teacher . . . and do you not understand these things?" Jesus asked Nicodemus (John 3:10). This question is surprising, given the unusual subject matter.

How could Nicodemus be expected to understand Jesus' theology of the New Birth? Was Jesus expecting too much from this leading Pharisee? It is helpful to remember that Nicodemus was steeped in the Old Testament. He not only knew the tenets of the Levitical law and the commands of the Decalogue, but he prided himself on his thorough memorization of the Psalms and his intimate familiarity with the message of the Prophets. Why, then, was Nicodemus taken aback by Jesus' clear teaching that no one can enter the kingdom of God on one's own merit? Surely Nicodemus realized that knowing God was not an achievement of the flesh. Physical birth does not result in true spirituality, nor is righteousness derived from human systems. Jesus expected Nicodemus to know that compliance with laws does not make one holy. Was the language of spiritual rebirth so foreign to Nicodemus' concept of righteousness that his bafflement is excusable? Obviously, Jesus did not think so. He found it strange that Israel's teacher should be so slow to grasp spiritual truth.

Jesus linked his personal claim to authority with his commitment to the Old Testament. He believed that those who obeyed the law of Moses would accept his teaching. Rejecting him meant rejecting the testimony of Moses: "Your accuser is Moses, on whom your hopes are set. If you believed Moses, you would believe me, for he wrote about me. But since you do not believe what he wrote, how are you going to believe what I say?" (John 5:45–47; cf. v. 39; 7:16–19). In the parable of the rich man and Lazarus, Jesus stressed the sufficiency of Moses and the Prophets to lead people to the truth. The rich man asked Abraham to send Lazarus to warn his brothers of the torment they will experience if they follow in his example. Abraham replied, "They have Moses and the Prophets; let them listen to them." Knowing what little effect the Law and the Prophets had on his life, the rich man pleaded for a more convincing proof. "No, father Abraham . . . but if someone from the dead goes to them, they will repent." But Abraham replied, "If they do not listen to Moses and the Prophets, they will not be convinced even if someone rises from the dead" (Luke 16:19–31).

Jesus was not a negative biblical critic. From the evidence, we have no grounds for questioning his commitment to the integrity of God's Word. Far from setting it aside, he based his entire teaching, lifestyle, and self-understanding upon its authority, demonstrating his complete reliance upon the Scriptures on numerous occasions. He consciously integrated the Word of God with his life and actions, resulting in a faithful interpretation of the prophecies, promises, and commands of the Old Testament. He captured the essence of the law by dynamically drawing out its significance for the kingdom age. Instead of a static, casuistic interpretation, he read "the Law and the Prophets" in light of the new stage of salvation history which he himself inaugurated. Sadly, the Pharisees neither saw nor cared to see this new age.

HEART RIGHTEOUSNESS

We have become so accustomed to the antagonism between Jesus and the Pharisees that we often ignore their shared concerns and close affinity. Their continuous dialogue and debate evidences a presupposition with many of the same theological issues. On several occasions, Pharisees invited Jesus for dinner (Luke 7:36; 11:37). In spite of his close association with "undesirables" and his sometimes radical teaching, he was regarded with sufficient respect to be a recipient of hospitality. Obviously, his teaching was deemed worthy of serious consideration. In fact, much of what he said was echoed by the rabbis of his day. Perhaps the difficulty the Pharisees experienced in catching Jesus in some kind of heretical statement attests to the similarity in their biblical teaching.

When Jesus taught his disciples about forgiveness, he concluded by saying that the offended believer should treat the persistently unrepentant, sinning brother as if he were a pagan or a tax collector (Matt. 18:17; cf. 1 Cor. 5:1–5), which is something we might have expected a Pharisee to say. Jesus' hard line against sin and his sociological description of sin (pagans and tax collectors) were in keeping with the tradition of the Pharisees. However, they found it impossible to believe that they were indicted in Jesus' judgments along with common sinners (Luke 11:45). Jesus maintained respect for their office: "The teachers of the law and the Pharisees sit in Moses' seat. So you must obey them and do everything they tell you." But he qualified his respect for their authority by adding, "But do not do what they do, for they do not practice what they preach" (Matt. 23:2, 3).

Not all of the verbal exchanges between Jesus and the teachers of the law ended on a negative note. At least some of the Pharisees respected his teaching and admired his works of righteousness. When Jesus debated the Sadducees on the resurrection, his answer was received approvingly by at least one teacher of the law. After hearing it, this Pharisee sincerely sought to know which commandment Jesus believed to be the most important. When Jesus said to love God completely and our neighbor as ourselves (Deut. 6:6 and Lev. 19:18), the man replied enthusiastically, "Well said, teacher." Then he repeated the command, adding a significant line from the prophet Hosea that put the love of God and neighbor ahead of burnt offerings and sacrifices. From Mark's account, Jesus felt a kindred spirit with this teacher of the law: "When Jesus saw that he had answered wisely, he said to him, 'You are not far from the kingdom of God.'" (Mark 12:34).

Given the similarities between Jesus and the Pharisees, it is difficult to explain their deep, mutual antagonism, apart from discussing the unique and distinctive elements in Jesus' teaching. As we have seen, the most significant issue between them was Jesus' unparalleled claim to authority. By assuming the prerogatives of God, Jesus became an offense to most of the Pharisees. His commitment to the law and his zeal for righteousness were overshadowed by his radically new outlook toward the law. In addition, his growing popularity among the masses posed a practical problem to the chief priests and the Sadducees, who were concerned with the fragile balance of power. They knew all too well Rome's response to a perceived political threat. Jesus was a destabilizing influence. As his cultural penetration increased, so did their opposition. Even though there were sharp differences among the Pharisees, Sadducees, and chief priests, they joined in common cause against Jesus.

Nevertheless, the most significant contrast to Jesus' teaching was theological in nature rather than political and was articulated by the Pharisees. Their instruction on the kingdom was clearly different from Jesus' consciousness of the kingdom, and their approach to Scripture required a completely different hermeneutic from his. If Jesus had been a political revolutionary, opposition against him would not have arisen from the Pharisees and the teachers of the law. The fact that it did demonstrates that his revolution was theological and spiritual. I do not mean that a spiritual revolution implies political irrelevance and social conservatism. Just the opposite is true. The transformation proclaimed by Jesus was profoundly political as well as personal. Jesus held forth a new view of righteousness anticipated in the law and fulfilled in himself.

To anyone brought up in a culture that was enamored with the Pharisaic ideal, Jesus' standard of righteousness must have seemed excessive. How could those who had not committed themselves to a Pharisaic community which would obey the tithing laws scrupulously be expected to "surpass" the righteousness of the Pharisees? How could ordinary people go beyond the standard of their own respected religious leaders? Who, after all, was more committed to piety than the Pharisees? Jesus was not simply upgrading the requirements of righteousness. Instead, he authoritatively called for a whole new approach to righteousness. He did not suggest that there were weaknesses in the present order that needed alteration. He boldly and emphatically rejected the standard altogether: "I tell you that unless your righteousness surpasses that of the Pharisees and the teachers of the law, you will certainly not enter the kingdom of heaven" (Matt. 5:20).

The critical factor in Jesus' understanding of righteousness stemmed from his conviction that a decisive new stage in salvation history had begun. According to Jesus, "The Law and the Prophets were proclaimed until John. Since that time, the good news of the kingdom of God is being preached, and everyone is forcing his way into it" (Luke 16:16). There is considerable disagreement over the interpretation of the second half of this statement. Some scholars conclude that those who were forcing their way into the kingdom represent those who stood in evil opposition to the advancing kingdom, while others interpret the meaning of *force* positively, as an indication of whole-hearted support for the kingdom of God. In any case, the first half of the verse is clear; Jesus saw the history of salvation reaching a decisive turning point in and through his person and proclamation. The commencement of this new stage did not deny, discredit, or disqualify the law, but it brought God's revelation to its expected fulfillment (v. 17). Thus, the emergence of this new era reaffirmed the true nature of righteousness and dramatically showed up the mentality and practice of the Pharisees.

The Pharisees did not share Jesus' kingdom consciousness. Their fixation with the mechanics of the Scripture and the technicalities of the law revealed a shocking truth. They were more loyal to the minutiae of the law than they were to the fulfillment of God's promises (John 5:39–40). They made the "possession of the law" the essence of their religious experience. Legal compliance replaced heart righteousness (Mark 7:1–23). Rabbinic rules became more important than the reign of God. Consequently, the Pharisees were trapped in a piety which tended to degenerate into selfish pride and a performance designed to please others. (Luke 18:9–14). For all their sophisticated theologizing and zeal for the law, they missed the heart of righteousness.

Spiritual rigidity rather than maturity shaped their approach to God. They self-consciously sought to justify themselves (Luke 10:29). In contrast, Jesus declared, "Anyone who will not receive the kingdom of God like a little child will never enter it" (18:17). Jesus swept aside human effort and merit to make room for childlike faith and trust in a living God who forgives sin and fulfills his promises.

Unlike the Pharisees, Jesus interpreted the Word of God relationally and prophetically. Scripture was not perceived by him as an end in itself or as a text capable of fulfilling its purpose apart from drawing people to God. Jesus accepted Scripture as God's personal word to men and women. Therefore it was important to Jesus to read revelation according to its fulfillment trajectory. He brought the whole Word of God, including the experiences of Israel, the ethical commands, the ceremonial requirements, the messianic prophecies, and the kingdom hope, into the new era of salvation history. Just as we see the Word of God in light of Christ, he saw Scripture in the light of himself and the fulfillment of God's will.

Jesus initiated an extraordinary hermeneutic shift. In one sense he set Scripture in an entirely new theological context; in another sense he restored to biblical interpretation its original and intended purpose. He both established and transcended the meaning which had been lost by both the popular and the more rigorous biblical interpreters of his day. Jesus approached the text with a freedom foreign to rabbinic interpretation.

The Pharisees understood Old Testament law the way a lawyer views a legal contract. A precise and nuanced interpretation of the law took on crucial significance. By scrutinizing the wording of the text and carefully considering the history of interpretation, the Pharisees were prepared to define the requirements of the law in every conceivable situation. Scripture was the basis for a legal code, which required supplementing the biblical text with specific "bylaws" for conduct. It is not very difficult to see why attention shifted from the "weightier matters" of the law to the minutiae. A statutory and casuistic understanding of the law tended to reverse the priorities of the law by giving more attention to its finer points, such as Sabbath regulations, dietary laws, and tithing specification, than to the fundamental concerns of justice, mercy, and faithfulness. According to the Pharisees, right-eousness was clearly manifest in the detailed observance of the law. Obedience was measured against a check list of external indicators. Piety became calculable in an equation that quantified righteous perfection. Those who were especially serious about the law joined small communi-ties or associations of people with like-minded zeal for the finer points of the law and their tradition. By limiting their significant relationships to those who kept the law in the detailed, customary fashion of the Pharisees, they were able to preserve their ceremonial purity and fulfill their tithing obligations.

We can understand some of the dynamics involved in Pharisaic piety by its analogous relationship to contemporary denominationalism. We stand in the tradition of the Pharisees when sectarian pride and a false sense of importance is generated by complying with the measurable standards of *our* group. When we climb the ranks of denominational leadership and begin to glory in the attention and influence of our organization, we are guilty of the same charges Jesus leveled against the Pharisees. Although they were one of the most respectable groups in his day, Jesus condemned their negative traditionalism and their self-serving ethic. Righteousness had become a performance.

Both a symptom and a cause of this pathological spirituality was their approach to the Old Testament. Jesus never doubted their sincerity and loyalty to the text, but he strongly condemned their biblical hermeneutic and the distorted righteousness it produced. Ironically, Jesus' sharpest criticism was leveled against those who believed the Bible to be fully authoritative and inerrant. Yet these same interpreters twisted the Scripture by conforming it to their legal expectations. They defeated the purpose of the Sabbath by defining appropriate Sabbath observance apart from the humanitarian thrust of God's law.[13] Their casuistic system emphasized the technicalities of the law rather than the will of God. Through their severity and rigidity they missed the heart of the law, especially when it came to their Sabbath observance and association with sinners and others in need. But when it came to divorce, lust, anger, revenge, and lying, they carefully conditioned their interpretation of biblical requirements to traditional standards of practical conven-ience. Instead of the hard-line approach suitable to the law's ceremonial and ritual requirements, they softened their interpretation of the relational dimensions of righteousness. They compromised marriage fidelity by sanctioning divorce on inconsequential grounds. They limited the love command to Jews, and they defined lust and hate as outward acts and ignored the heart. People were held accountable for honest speech only if they had pronounced the right oaths. Thus, with all of their conservatism and fascination with the details of the law, they missed the meaning that God intended in the law. Instead, they sought to use the law to serve their own interests and convenience.

Jesus turned against this interpretative strategy with such effectiveness and passion that he exposed the emptiness of the Pharisees' formula for righteousness. He freely upheld the ethical challenge of the law in such a way as to encompass every dimension of the law. Jesus went to the heart of the commandments and revealed an approach to moral conduct alien to the Pharisees but consistent with the Law and the Prophets. He opened up a whole new way of obedience. He fulfilled what Jeremiah had prophesied, and through him God's new covenant was established (Jer. 31:31–34). Redemption and forgiveness paved the way for an in-depth internalization of God's ethic (Ezek. 36:25–27). Heart righteousness became a way of life that Jesus made possible.

THE NEW OBEDIENCE

Jesus' teaching sounds so radical and unyielding because it belongs to a new order of being. Jesus inaugurated a kingdom ethic, a new way of life consistent with the reign of God. Therefore anyone who seeks to follow Jesus faces the requirement of losing everything to gain Christ. A narrow view of religious life with is safe compartmentalizing of the sacred and the secular must go. Middle-class values and comfortable ideologies, of the left or right, need to be cast off.

The new wealth of the kingdom belongs to those who seek first God's kingdom and his righteousness, who know within themselves the transforming power of God's Spirit, who forgives, reconciles, purifies, and loves. If the teaching of Jesus appears hopelessly idealistic and frustratingly impractical, it is because we do not really believe Jesus is our Savior. We do not understand spiritually and practically what he has saved us from and what he has saved us for. Who would really love an enemy or lend to those in need without expecting repayment if they did not believe that there was more to life than worldly values? Who would have the power to forgive, if they have never sought or experienced forgiveness? Who would sacrifice economic security for spiritual reward if life consists primarily of material possessions? Who would love Christ more than family and friends who had not learned to love God wholeheartedly and their neighbor as themselves? Who would lay down their lives for others, apart from God's love shed abroad in their hearts? Genuine acts of love and sacrifice are obviously not confined to Christians, but ultimately all acts of human love belong to God. Just as all truth is God's truth, all acts of love issue from a human spirit made in God's image. God defines love the way an artist defines beauty. Divine love is expressed concretely in space and time as a historical reference point for the sake of human salvation. "This is love," wrote the apostle John, "not that we loved God, but that he loved us and sent his Son as an atoning sacrifice for our sins. Dear friends, since God so loved us, we also ought to love one another" (1 John 4:10–11).

The Christian ethic is exclusively dependent upon Christian redemption. The command to become like Jesus is always "deeper than the external duplication of the words and deeds of Jesus." We respond to Jesus' ethic out of gratitude and thanksgiving. Jesus is much more than an example to us. We do not only read, "Love because you have seen me love," but, "Love . . . as I have loved you" (John 15:12). Not only does the Bible encourage believers to forgive as Christ forgave his enemies; it also says, "Forgive as the Lord forgave you" (Col. 3:13). Nor do we read "lay down your life because you have seen me lay down my life" without the reminder that "Jesus Christ laid down his life for us" (1 John 3:16).[14] We would be caught in a tragic dilemma if Jesus described for us a new lifestyle but failed to make a new life possible. "He not only embodies the truth but he also grants the condition to receive the truth. We are saved not by a teaching that is universally accessible to the mind of man but by a teacher who converts the will of man."[15]

We are born into Christian ethics, a family ethic nurtured among those who are at home in the household of faith. As Jesus said, "If you love me, you will obey what I command" (John 14:15, 23). If we reject the way of salvation provided through Jesus, we end up rejecting his ethic. And if we reject the ethics of Jesus, we confirm that we never knew his salvation (1 John 3:16–24; Matt. 7:21–23). In the final analysis the Pharisees who rejected Jesus turned away from both his ethics and his redemption. They rejected him and his message of the reign of God.[16] They spurned his consciousness of the kingdom. Unwilling to see Jesus as the fulfillment of messianic prophecies, they could not grasp the profound insight and joy of Jesus' kingdom ethic.

A passion for Christ engages the believer in a dynamic openness to the biblical text. Eternal verities were meant to intersect our contemporary situation, bringing to bear the wisdom and power of God's revelation in daily life. Jesus' teaching had exactly that effect, and so should ours. If we read the Bible the way Jesus did, we will become like Jesus both in the content as well as the style of our communication. There will be a freshness and vitality in our exposition of the truth which will expose the redundancy of worn-out liberal and reactionary theologies.

The teaching of Jesus was provocative rather than predictable, honest instead of manipulative, always relevant, never boring. His popularity waned, but the cutting edge of his teaching never became dull. He fused love and truth in a passionate proclamation of good news. Through the gift of the Spirit, Jesus made provision for the on-going interpretation and proclamation of God's Word. He anticipated new situations by assuring his followers that the Spirit of truth would guide them in all truth (John 16:13). He prepared his disciples for the privilege and the responsibility of interpreting the gospel for various new circumstances facing Christians.[17] "Every teacher of the law who has been instructed about the kingdom of heaven is like the owner of a house who brings out of his storeroom new treasures as well as old" (Matt. 13:52).

The apostles followed in Jesus' tradition, not as understudies copying an actor's performance, but as sons internalizing the wise counsel of their father. We do not hear parables in the Book of Acts, but we hear the passion and wisdom of Jesus in the apostolic proclamation of the gospel. The disciples there were gripped by the life and message of Jesus, which is seen in everything from their interpretation of the Old Testament to their ethical counsel. The apostles were convinced of the wisdom and power of the gospel to bring about new life in Christ. It is not surprising, therefore, that those who heard the apostles noticed that they had been with Jesus (Acts 4:13). This observation should be true today for all those who seek to follow Jesus. People will take note that we have been with Jesus when we share in his faithfulness to God's Word, discern his will through the power of God's Spirit, enter into his kingdom consciousness, communicate with his integrity, and commit ourselves to his passion for the truth. Then we will know what it is to become like our Teacher.

11

the crucified messiah

Devotion to Christ ultimately rests on a biblical theology of the Cross worked out in daily experience. The more we become like Jesus, the more central the Cross becomes in our lives. Every aspect of Jesus' life—his spirituality, self-understanding, and kingdom ethic—points to a path of obedience marked by the Cross. As we walk that path we share his passion.

The Cross has profound theological meaning.[1] Apart from this theological and historical significance, we are left with a minimal Jesus who bravely took his cause to its bitter end. But this end holds no future for us. Minus its biblical meaning, the Cross is a tragedy without peace and hope and without explanation.

Even though Jesus' violent death looked imminent, the disciples were horrified at the extravagant waste when Mary poured out expensive perfume on Jesus' feet and wiped his feet with her hair. But Jesus recognized her costly gift as an act of worship. Mary had faith to see in his life and death a meaning which transcended heroism and martyrdom. Unlike the disciples, who resisted the inevitable climax of Jesus' earthly ministry, she shared Jesus' expectation of death. She laid aside nationalistic expectations of a triumphant Messiah who would lead a righteous uprising against Rome. She went beyond her sentimental attachment to a great teacher and sensitive friend and accepted the harsh reality that the one who had the power to raise people from the dead was destined for the cross.

Jesus interpreted her actions as an act of spiritual solidarity. Mary entered into the experience of his cross. She faced the reality of the Cross, and so must we. As long as the death of Jesus remains a religious abstraction or a mere symbol of innocent suffering, we are no better than the disciples who condemned Mary (John 12:4–5). Jesus repeatedly warned the disciples of his suffering and death, but they chose to ignore him. Hoping for a fortuitous turn of events, they suppressed the truth. The Cross was not on their agenda. But before we condemn them for their inability to hear and respond to Jesus' predictions about the Cross, perhaps we should question the place of the Cross in our own lives. We may find that the Cross is not on our agenda either.

It can be argued convincingly that much of contemporary Christianity holds no theology of the Cross. Even though we may have a doctrine of the Crucifixion, celebrate the Lord's Supper, and wear a gold cross around our neck or on our suit lapel, it does not mean we have a theology of the Cross. We may enjoy Christianity because it solves some nagging questions about life after death and self-acceptance. It gives us hope that, if there is a God, he will accept us because Jesus died for our sins. But the practical reality of being crucified with Christ escapes us. Like the disciples, we hear about the Cross, but we choose to ignore it or suppress it. We may even assimilate the jargon of the Cross into a theology of success. But only by avoiding the meaning of the Cross could anyone say that "the cross is the down payment for my prosperity" or that "Jesus suffered so I can prosper."[2] Clearly, the gospel according to success is not the gospel according to Jesus.

Perhaps we dwell on the *religious* significance of the Cross, feeling a strong emotional attachment to it, but deny its ethical impact in our lives. Then someone confronts us like Mary, a woman who perceived, deeply and passionately, that the death of Jesus was at the very center of *her* existence. We almost instinctively want to ridicule her. It only makes it worse that her devotion to Jesus is completely humble and self-effacing. Because human nature is the way it is, we would be delighted to find some mixed motives in her passion in order to write her off as an impractical idealist.

The cross of Jesus was never intended to give the Christian a martyr's complex, but neither was its significance meant to be lost in rhetoric and ritual. Jesus infused the cross with profound theological meaning. God's eternal plan of salvation was at stake when Jesus went to the cross. Centuries of blood sacrifices and altars of repentance foreshadowed the cross. And now we remember his shed blood and broken body as God's gracious provision for a New Covenant. But the story of the Cross does not end there. We do not diminish the meaning of the Cross in salvation history nor compromise the uniqueness of

Jesus' passion when we realize that the Cross is not only in the past but in the present. The many-sided dimensions of the Atonement are matched by the full significance of taking up our cross daily and following Jesus. The spiritual proof of redemption and regeneration, justification and reconciliation, is evident in the Christian's self-denial, death to sin, obedient submission to the will of God, and intimate devotion to the living Lord Jesus.

Jesus' cross is planted squarely at the center of the believer's existence, providing both the means of salvation and the challenge of a new lifestyle. The meaning Christ gives to the Cross is betrayed when we refuse to become like Jesus. We may have all the right words and be an expert on the doctrine of the Atonement, but if we do not share in his sufferings, "becoming like him in his death" (Phil. 3:10), we reject the Cross. Rejection, of course, can take the form of doctrinaire hypocrisy, self-inflicted pain administered to reproduce a literal imitation of the pain of Jesus, or mental fascination with Jesus' agony on the cross. Obviously, the Cross can be made to represent the wrong thing. Its significance can become distorted and twisted as it is wrenched from its biblical meaning and reshaped by popular sentiment or political ideologies.

Probably no other symbol in Latin America has been more important than the crucifix. For many it is a religious ethic which stirs the emotions as it superstitiously advances their prayers for safety and success. In popular Latin American art there is a fascination with the death of Jesus. Statues, carvings, and paintings depict the agony of Jesus on the cross. I remember seeing some years ago a slide presentation by a Peruvian missionary depicting the crucifixion. The viewer was mentally transported back to the cross to behold in vivid detail the horror and pain of Jesus' death. The art was repulsive not because Jesus' death was any less gruesome than portrayed but because his death had been misunderstood. Bowing before gory replicas of a dying Jesus, sincere people testified to their continued anguish and spiritual turmoil. Filling their mind with the hideous vision of cruel torture, they reduced the meaning of the Cross to the idolatry of their own imagination. Religious aspirations, severed from the Scripture principle, pervert the meaning of the Cross and turn it into a religious relic. In effect the Cross becomes a pagan symbol for people who have yet to hear the good news of Christ crucified (1 Cor. 1:23–24).

CONTEMPORARY VIEWS

When the meaning of the Cross becomes subject to the modernity principle, theological truth is invariably sacrificed for political relevance or existential impact. If superstition and magic reduce the Cross to a religious relic, secularism shapes the contemporary view of Jesus' death according to values that are compatible with the spirit of the age. According to such theologians, Christianity requires updating. What Christians have believed for centuries needs to be exchanged for a new view of the Cross without a lot of worn-out theological baggage. Thus, those who view the death of Jesus as an atoning sacrifice offered to God to avert his wrath are not so much wrong as out of date. It follows, then, that concepts such as expiation and propitiation, which may have been popular in the Middle Ages, are directly misleading today.[3]

Hans Küng, the popular Roman Catholic theologian, advises that the term *sacrifice* be avoided "as much as possible in modern proclamation." He argues that the concept of sacrifice must be understood in the Old Testament sense, with its emphasis on sin and the cultic practice of animal sacrifices. The temptation is too great, he contends, to link the Jewish sacrificial system with pagan sacrifice. He asks, "Is God so cruel, even sadistic, that his anger can be appeased by the blood of his Son? Does an innocent person have to serve as scapegoat, whipping boy and substitute for the real sinners?" Averting the wrath of a holy God may have been a viable interpretative scheme for the early Jewish Christians, argues Küng, but it holds no relevance for modern people. It is better to see the death of Jesus not as a sacrifice for sin but as an act of personal self-surrender and self-giving. Jesus reveals once and for all that God can be encountered, "not only in light and joy, but also in darkness, sorrow, pain and melancholy." According to Küng, this insight is the hidden meaning of Jesus' suffering and death. Beyond the fact that God can be encountered in the midst of pain, Jesus' cross offers no explanation. At least for Küng, the doctrine of the penal substitutionary atonement offers no appeal to modern men and women.[4]

Historically the meaning of the Atonement has been sought in the rich complexity of biblical revelation. No one theme or emphasis has adequately encompassed Christ's accomplishment on the cross. Through his death and resurrection, Christ triumphed over the cosmic powers of evil (Heb. 2:14; 1 John 3:8). He suffered the punishment we deserved (Isa. 53:5, 10–12; Rom. 3:23–25; 1 John 2:2; 4:10). He took upon himself our sin and through his perfect sacrifice satisfied the just requirement of God's holiness. He died not only on our behalf but in our place (Gal. 3:13; Mark 10:45). He identified with us in our pain and suffering by becoming a victim of injustice and oppression. His voluntary death remains for us the ultimate challenge to genuine discipleship. His death, however, was not only exemplary but also propitiatory. He provided for our liberation from the bondage of sin and death and for our reconciliation with God (2 Cor. 5:18–19; Col. 1:13–14, 20). The different "theories" of the Atonement should not be compartmentalized into neat, conceptual categories. The meaning of the Cross should be explored comprehensively, giving due recognition to the triumphal, identificational, and substitutionary significance of Christ's death.

The traditional doctrines of the Atonement are frequently dismissed sarcastically by many modern theologians. "Better Skid Row than the endless round of empty speculations that run from the implausible to the irreligious," writes Michael Goulder, who labels the traditional theories of the Atonement as "rubbish." He places Jesus alongside Gandhi and Martin Luther King as preeminent examples of love.

> Had Jesus merely lived and taught agape and died for it, it is difficult to think that his community would have lasted a fortnight. But by the completeness of his faithfulness unto death Jesus achieved unwittingly the destiny which he had followed all his ministry. . . . For there are locked within the human psyche strong forces which an event of this quality can set in motion.[5]

Goulder finds the modernity principle more intelligible than the Scripture principle and the history of Christian conviction and simply views Jesus' love as having set in motion a powerful chain reaction of human conversion. The world is different because of Jesus the way the world is different because of Gandhi and King. Goulder has brought Jesus down to a scale of human experience he hopes people today can still appreciate.

Another British theologian, John Robinson, agrees with Goulder that understanding Jesus' death in the customary language of the Atonement must change.

> Most people would genuinely *like* to believe the Christmas story, but wonder whether it *can* be true with the world as it is after nearly two thousand years. But in the case of the Atonement they ask with some impatience how anything done two thousand years ago on the Cross *could* "affect me now." As a description of some metaphysical *opus operatum* the "full, perfect and sufficient sacrifice, oblation, and satisfaction for the sins of the whole world" supposed to have been "made" on Calvary requires, I believe, for most men today more demythologizing even than the Resurrection.

His conclusion is blunt: "At no point does the supranaturalist scheme appear less compelling."[6]

How does Robinson propose to reinterpret the Cross for modern men and women? Drawing on the writings of Paul Tillich, Robinson finds two important dimensions of the Cross which can be freed from any religious or supernatural connotation. The Cross vividly expresses humanity's feelings of estrangement—all of its despair, pain, loneliness, and meaninglessness. The death of Jesus symbolizes the agony of human existence. But it also symbolizes life and hope. For at the moment of our deepest despair, we can experience acceptance with the "Ground of our being." Suddenly, the darkness is penetrated by a wave of light. Robinson describes the experience using Tillich's words:

> It is as though a voice were saying: "You are accepted. *You are accepted,* accepted by that which is greater than you, and the name of which you do not know. Do not ask for the name now; perhaps you will find it later. . . . *Simply accept the fact that you are accepted!*"

> If that happens to us, we experience grace. After such an experience we may not be better than before, and we may not believe more than before, . . . And nothing is demanded of this experience, no religious or moral or intellectual presupposition, nothing but *acceptance.*[7]

Robinson's reinterpretation of the Cross frees people from the supposed "burden" of having to believe anything about Jesus. The Cross is for him a profound existential experience without biblical content or theological meaning.

Liberation Theology generally presents another model of the Cross. It endeavors to take seriously the historical path of Jesus which led to his violent political death. According to Jesuit priest Jon Sobrino, the history of the interpretation of the Cross has been marred by the persistent effort to "mollify" Jesus' death and to "soften the edges of this scandalous happening." Sobrino is certain that the death of Jesus has nothing to do with "a more or less magical conception of redemption." Nor should the Cross be understood as providing salvation through "some mysterious supra-historical reality (akin to what has traditionally been called the 'supernatural')."[8] Sobrino endeavors to strip the Cross of its "alienating mystifications" by exposing the various ways the scandal of the Cross has been misinterpreted.[9] He begins with the New Testament, citing the difficulty encountered by the first Christians in preserving the scandal of the Cross. According to Sobrino, the impact of Jesus' suffering is lessened when his death is described "majestically" in the Gospel of John and when Luke replaces the "scandalous phrase" "My God, my God, why have you forsaken me?" (Mark 15:34) with the "triumphant strains," "Father, into your hands I commit my spirit" (Luke 23:46). Sobrino contends that the cutting edge of Jesus' death is lost in the honorific titles used by the New Testament writers to express Jesus' personal dignity and to describe the nature of his mission in positive terms. The Cross becomes little more than "a preliminary and provisional stage leading up to the resurrection."[10]

The note of scandal disappears for Sobrino as the New Testament focuses on the "why" and "wherefore" of the Cross. The early Christians elaborated the meaning of salvation in terms of God's eternal design, inappropriately implying, contends Sobrino, that the Cross could be explained in terms of a supernatural redemption. Sobrino is not opposed to the New Testament theme of sacrifice and expiation as long as we understand that it is simply a mythical thought form used by early Christians to communicate the absolute importance of Jesus' death. Consequently, biblical teaching on expiation does not *explain* the Cross or infuse the suffering of Jesus with theological *meaning*.

Sobrino articulates a theology of the Cross which he believes preserves its true scandal. Jesus' historical path to the cross reveals a questioning search for God in the midst of pain and injustice. But Jesus preserves the mystery of God by accepting the Cross, even when there are no answers for human suffering. For Sobrino, the Cross produces a crisis for all human knowledge of God and exposes the selfish interest and manipulative intent of all our efforts to explain God in a world of misery. Jesus dies in total "theological abandonment."

We do not understand the Cross, argues Sobrino, by believing in the Bible's teaching on redemption. In a world of suffering and pain, the Cross shows us that the only way to know God is through those whose very humanity is questioned and denied. To understand the Cross we must take seriously the "death of the other human being." God does not approach the problem of suffering from outside history. On the contrary, God becomes immersed in human suffering. Thus the Cross is not a fixed historical moment, necessary in God's design to assure redemption. Sobrino writes, "God himself must go by way of the cross in the midst of countless historical crosses."[11] The uniqueness of Jesus' cross thus does not lie in the fact that God, at a particular point in space and time, experienced the suffering intrinsic to the sinfulness of humanity in order to provide a way of redemption.

Sobrino denies that Jesus made a vicarious offering on behalf of men and women deserving of God's wrath. "The cross is not an altar, and there is no sacrificial lamb on it."[12] Jesus' death remains unique, according to Sobrino, because Jesus historicizes in exemplary fashion the suffering experienced by God in all the crosses of the oppressed. Through his historical path of suffering and death, we are brought to the liberating conviction that God does not remain outside of history indifferent to the present course of evil events. God reveals himself through the authentic medium of the poor and oppressed. If we want to know God, Sobrino challenges us to experience the God-forsakenness that Jesus felt on the cross. We can take this position today by sharing in the political struggle of the oppressed poor.

These contemporary views of Jesus' death share a common rejection of a supernaturalistic world view. The many dimensions of the Atonement which have occupied Christian theologians through the centuries are summarily dismissed as archaic thinking. It is argued that each generation must reinterpret the absolute significance of Jesus' death in the myths and relationships which best express God's relevance to the human situation. The modernity principle overrides a biblical theology of the Cross to interpret the content of Jesus' death in intellectual categories acceptable to the spirit of this age. The soteriological significance of Christ's vicarious sacrifice to reconcile us to a holy and righteous God is consequently replaced with a relational emphasis. The meaning of the Cross is found in identification with those who suffer and in solidarity with the poor. It is expressed in the hope of encountering God in the midst of despair.

While these themes are important, they do not capture the full significance of the Cross. Unquestionably, sacrificial identification with those who suffer is a biblical imperative that has sadly been rejected by many conservative, orthodox Christians. This fact does not justify, however, using Jesus' solidarity with the poor to obscure the full meaning of the Cross intended by Jesus and the apostles. The problem with many of the contemporary views of the Cross is that its real scandal is ignored.

THE SCANDAL OF THE CROSS

Death by crucifixion is offensive by anyone's standards. It was a state punishment reserved for rebellious slaves, political traitors, violent offenders, and dangerous criminals. Rated as the severest Roman penalty, followed by burning and decapitation, "It symbolized extreme humiliation, shame and torture." The repugnancy of "this cruelest of all penalties" can be attested by the paucity of references to crucifixion in Hellenistic and Roman literature and led to its early elimination as a form of capital punishment.[13] Not until the fourth century, when Constantine abolished crucifixion as a death sentence, did the cross begin to appear as a public symbol for Christianity.

Our mental imagination of the cross is colored by a majesty and dignity completely foreign to the fear and dread associated with crucifixion in the first century. It was designed to maximize the public disgrace and physical torture of the sufferer. Usually death came excruciatingly slow, with the naked victim finally succumbing to exposure, disease, hunger, shock, and exhaustion.[14] The cross bore a social stigma comparable to the ignominy of the guillotine or the electric chair. It was the most unlikely symbol imaginable to become meaningful for God-fearing men and women.

The real offense of Jesus' cross, however, was not the form of execution but the person who died. It would have been hard enough to convince the world that a crucified man was noble and decent, but to proclaim that this man was God incarnate violated every sensibility of people in the first century. Therefore if the biblical meaning of the Incarnation is eliminated or in any way compromised to become more appealing to the modern mind, the significance of Jesus' death is bound to be reduced and the scandal of the Cross obscured. The early Christians faced scorn and mocking from both Jews and Greeks every time they proclaimed "Christ crucified" (1 Cor. 1:23). "Madness" was the verdict of the ancient world, according to Justin, who described the offense of the crucified Son of God: "They say that our *madness* consists in the fact that we put a crucified man in second place after the unchangeable and eternal God, the Creator of the world."[15]

Those who wish to make the cross of Jesus less offensive to modern men and women by eliminating the alleged "superstition" and "magic" of redemption ought to consider how offensive the death of God incarnate was to the first-century world view. Given the moral and intellectual climate, it was not surprising for Suetonius to describe the Christian message as "new and pernicious superstition."[16] After all, if Christians had the audacity to commend a "crucified criminal" as the Savior of the world, they deserved ridicule. An example of such derision is illustrated by a painting from the Palatinate of a crucified figure with an ass's head. The head of the ass represented Christianity's roots in Judaism. Apparently, a longstanding joke against Jews was that they worshiped an ass in the temple.[17] The Cross only added to the scorn pagans felt toward this offensive "Jewish cult."

The real scandal before the world was not that the founder of Christianity was martyred but that Christians claimed that the Lord of the Universe was crucified. In one of the earliest Christian sermons extant, Melito of Sardis captured the awesome paradox of the cross:

Listen and see, all families of the nations! An unprecedented murder has come to pass in the midst of Jerusalem, in the city of the Law, in the Hebrew city, in the prophet's city, in the city adjudged righteous. And who has been killed? . . . It is a heavy thing to say, and a most fearful thing to refrain from saying. But listen, as you tremble in the face of him on whose account the earth trembled. He who hung the earth in place is hanged. He who fixed the heavens in place is fixed in place. He who made all things fast is made fast on the tree. The Master is insulted. God is murdered.[18]

We look in vain for the meaning of the Cross in the mass of human suffering. As bare historical fact, Jesus' suffering and death does not give to the Cross the profound significance that it has always possessed for Christians. We are dependent upon the apostolic witness for a two-pronged theology of the Cross. Docetically inclined Christians have traditionally considered the primary meaning of the Cross by extracting it from its historical reality. Reinstating the full meaning of the Cross does not happen by denying what the history of the church has always affirmed and the Bible reveals. But neither can we understand the Cross apart from the political realities of Jesus' situation. It is misleading to jump from the birth of Jesus to his death without considering the impact of his kingdom ethic. His actions and teaching placed him on a collision course with the political and religious authorities. We need to ask if Jesus' political impact is not scandalous to conservative Christians who neglect Jesus' passion for justice. Jon Sobrino correctly observes, "The cross is the outcome of Jesus' historical path"; and if we are going to follow the path of Jesus, "we must take a stand vis-à-vis the sinfulness that gives configuration to a given situation."[19] In other words, the Cross has ethical impact.

Those who seek to live first for the kingdom of Christ will suffer various forms of persecution. They will *not* be ostracized simply because they are committed to what the world considers to be an offensive idea. They will be resisted for taking seriously Jesus' path of obedience. Just as we cannot legitimately reduce the Cross to the relational themes of identification and solidarity with the poor, neither can we turn the Cross into a religious abstraction. If the cross remains an external transaction between the Father and Son without affecting our daily lives, we are as guilty of heresy as one who denies the doctrine of the Atonement. Nor should we reduce the Cross to an emotional phenomenon. Although the Cross may move us deeply, if it ends up leaving our worldly values and business ethics intact, the death of Jesus has had little real impact in our lives. A biblical theology of the Cross unites its soteriological and ethical dimensions. Jesus is fully God and fully man. He provides the means of salvation and authenticates genuine ethical action. Followers of Christ cannot look to the Cross for redemption without becoming subject to the way of the Cross ethically.

A consideration of Jesus' historical path to the cross leads to several important observations. It is scandalous that one who healed the sick, loved the outcast, and transformed the sinner should die a hideously cruel death by Roman crucifixion. What kind of world do we live in that sentences holy and compassionate men and women to die? Jesus exposes the fact that the political and religious authorities are not always on the side of righteousness. Greed, pride, and hate often control the power brokers of society. Jesus became a victim for the sake of righteousness. It was impossible for anyone living in the first century to gloss over the practical social consequences of following Jesus. The Cross made sure of that. Early Christians knew that their lives were marked by the Cross, but many contemporary, conservative Christians give the impression that a decision for Jesus simply involves submitting mentally to the idea that Jesus died for their sins.

On the other hand, those who wish to emphasize the political side of Jesus' death tend to ignore the circumstantial evidence of the Gospels. Jesus' message clearly had political impact, yet he was completely different from the Zealots and decidedly less dangerous. He resisted violence (Luke 9:54–55; John 18:10–11), rejected popular support (2:24; 6:15), and flatly denied that his kingdom was of the world (18:36). He neither defended the status quo nor encouraged revolution. He refused to be tricked into nationalism. He insisted on God's authority over all of life, without making a secular-spiritual dichotomy (Mark 12:17; John 19:11). He narrowed his loyal supporters down to a small band of men and women but remained accessible to the public through his daily teaching right up to the end (Mark 14:48–49). The meaning of his life simply cannot be exhausted politically. Although his death has tremendous political significance, he lived and died for something more significant than a political cause. This truth is part of the confusion and tragedy of the Cross. From a political point of view Jesus did not have to die. It is true that the Jewish Sanhedrin feared for their social privilege and political influence, but this fear alone was not sufficient to account for his death (John 11:48).

To contend that Jesus' strategy of nonviolence and his condemnation of those who wielded the sword resulted in the death penalty goes beyond the evidence. It is difficult to support the conclusion that Jesus was a greater political threat than Barabbas. John Yoder's observation seems exaggerated: "His alternative was so relevant, so much a threat, that Pilate could afford to free, in exchange for Jesus, the ordinary Guevara type insurrectionist Barabbas."[20]

The Gospels do not develop the political impact of Jesus sufficiently to lead logically and inevitably to the Cross. Jon Sobrino admits as much when he suggests that, if the early Christians had a clearer understanding of the "over-all nature of Jesus' mission," the Gospels would have treated Jesus' relationship to the political realm more explicitly.[21] This inability to explain Jesus' death simply in political terms is part of the frustration and despair of the Cross. Pilate did not have to kill Jesus. Nowhere is it suggested that he considered Jesus a greater threat to Roman rule than Barabbas. If anything, he probably released Barabbas and sentenced Jesus only to pacify the Jews. His judgment was not decided because he feared the political impact of Jesus' civil disobedience. In all likelihood, much of what Jesus said and did escaped Pilate's notice. The death of Jesus was a relatively small matter for Pilate. Politically speaking, Jesus may just as likely have walked away a free man as been nailed to the cross.

Part of the scandal of the Cross is that God's purposes are accomplished and his Word is fulfilled in the midst of political ambiguity and seemingly accidental circumstances. I remember being troubled as a young boy by the death of Dr. Paul Carlson, a medical missionary in the Belgium Congo when fighting broke out in 1960 between the colonial government and independence factions. He was caught in the cross fire between the rebels and Belgian troops. Seconds before he was able to scale a wall to safety he was killed—a bullet through his brain. His body was graphically shown through the world on the glossy pages of *Life* magazine. At the time he seemed more a victim of tragic circumstances than an ambassador for Christ who gave his life for the gospel. Since then, I have come to see that the Christian's cross, like Jesus' cross, must be interpreted on two levels. On one level, confusion and ambiguity appear to be the order of the day. From this perspective, Dr. Carlson's death was nothing more than meaningless circumstances leading up to a tragedy that might easily have been averted.

The same could be said about Hernando Hernandez, who was one of Latin America's promising Christian leaders. He was killed in Ecuador when his car swerved to avoid a bus on a narrow road along a mountain range and then plummeted down the cliff. Hernando impressed me as a courageous Christian who would have affirmed his allegiance to Jesus Christ no matter how dire the consequences. But instead of dying in direct confrontation with those who oppose Jesus

Christ, he was the victim of unsafe roads and the reckless driving of a bus driver. His death seemed so accidental and unnecessary. Nevertheless, he died for Christ. His death must be interpreted beyond the circumstances and infused with the meaning of his life in Christ and of his obedience to God's will. Jesus' situation guides our thinking. There is nothing heroic about the Cross.

On the one hand, Jesus appears as the victim of circumstances—a friend betrays him, popular sentiment turns against him, a ruler concerned only with political expediency hears his case, and his disciples abandon him. On the other hand, Jesus dies (in accord with Old Testament prophecy) as the lamb who was slain from the foundation of the world (Luke 24:25–27; 1 Peter 1:20; Rev. 13:8). There is an inevitability about his death that lies outside historical circumstances and human arrangements. It is impossible to adequately understand the suffering and death of Jesus apart from God's interpretation of this event. God infuses the Cross with meaning from three primary sources: the history of God's revelation to Israel, Jesus' self-disclosure, and the apostolic witness. There is a tremendous redemptive purpose arising out of the muddle of historical circumstances. This glorious purpose is not the product of human imagination and wishful thinking. It is the fulfillment of God's eternal plan of redemption. The real scandal of the Cross lies in the fact that God in Christ, the Savior of the world, was crucified.

GOD'S LOVE

Are we to understand God's love in terms of modern self-understanding or in terms of God's revelation in Scripture?[22] Modern men and women have scaled down their expectation of salvation. Today's definition of happiness includes a positive self-image, relationship fulfillment, career satisfaction, economic well-being, and physical health. Sin is thought to be an old-fashioned concept. Eternity no longer matters. God, if considered at all, is a remote deity who is ultimately responsible for the way things are but irrelevant to daily life. Because of these cultural trends and intellectual patterns, the biblical meaning of the Cross sounds strange to modern ears. The loss of the sacred order is evident in numerous ways, but it becomes especially obvious when Christians try to explain why Jesus died. How could the death of a man who lived two thousand years ago change my life? History is filled with heroic martyrs. Great men and women have lived exemplary lives, suffered unjustly, and died for their convictions. Why should Jesus' death mean anything more?

For most people today the answer to that question lies in a whole new and secular interpretation of reality. But common modern assumptions about the meaning of life and the nature of human destiny need to be questioned. The god of popular imagination and cultural convention requires a reality test! Perhaps notions of sin and morality have never been subject to careful scrutiny. Now may be the time for such a test. Many have accepted a "one-dimensional" universe that practically denies the supernatural order. In the so-called scientific age the pressure has been great to confine truth questioning to empirical issues that can be tested in a laboratory. What exists outside of this realm has been quietly dismissed. Consequently, ultimate issues of life and death have been pushed aside. Knowing God in a personal, life-transforming way may have never entered many people's mind as a real possibility.

Our society is vexed with a host of very real problems: loneliness, family breakdown, addictions, racism, terrorism, poverty, the threat of nuclear destruction, sexism, abortion, and pornography. But we tend to wrestle with these besetting evils superficially because we do not deal with the root cause of evil. The power of positive emotions and massive funding from federal budgets will not remove these plagues from society. Like secondary cancer cells, these sins point to a primary tumor. In the human heart there is a willful rejection of God and his will (Jer. 17:9; Isa. 64:6). Regardless of how much we may deny it, we are spiritual beings *created* in God's image. Our indignation over pain and suffering and the inhumanity of individuals to each other is in itself a witness to our spiritual being. But we realize that the problem of evil does not lie outside of us. As Aleksandr Solzhenitsyn puts it, "the line separating good and evil passes right through every human heart."

It is a strange paradox that, in an age of growing scientific, technological, military, political, and commercial complexity, modern men and women should be so satisfied with simplistic answers to our moral and spiritual crisis. Is it not becoming evident that salvation is not to be found in education, economic success, sexual freedom, or self-actualization? Even political peace, technological breakthroughs, and positive support groups do not resolve the human predicament. Christians believe that, apart from God's love personally applied in the life of the individual, salvation in this world and the next is impossible. Human fulfillment is ultimately understood in spiritual terms, revealed in God's Word and accomplished in concrete history through the death and resurrection of Jesus. Reconciliation with God through Jesus' substitutionary death on the cross paves the way for a reordering of life. God in Christ recreates us to fulfill our true humanity.

Is this truth too much for modern men and women to accept? Ironically, the ancients also found it difficult to understand. Imagine yourself sitting in the Jewish synagogue in Capernaum. You have followed Jesus' public career with keen interest. For a while now you have been impressed with his teaching and marveled at his miracles of healing. You respected his integrity and felt inspired by his compassion. From the beginning you witnessed his solidarity with the poor and outcasts and agreed inwardly with his critique of religious hypocrisy. You were not ashamed to be identified with Jesus—at least not until now. But this afternoon Jesus went too far. He crossed the line of rational thought and claimed explicitly that he was "the bread of life." He said outlandish things such as, "I am the living bread that came down from heaven. If anyone eats of this bread, he will live forever. This bread is my flesh, which I will give for the life of the world" (John 6:51). He went beyond his usual provocative teaching and made the unmistakable claim that our future destiny was dependent upon our mystical union with himself. He promised eternal life to those who were willing to enter into a relationship with himself. He described this union in what seems to be the most repugnant and graphic terms possible: he said we must eat his flesh and drink his blood.

> I tell you the truth, unless you eat the flesh of the Son of Man and drink his blood, you have no life in you . . . whoever eats my flesh and drinks my blood remains in me, and I in him. Just as the living Father sent me and I live because of the Father, so the one who feeds on me will live because of me (vv. 53, 56–57).

No one has ever found Jesus' theology of the Cross easy. It is a profound mystery from within a Christian world-and-life view and an object of ridicule from without. As the apostle Paul said: "For the message of the cross is foolishness to those who are perishing, but to us who are being saved, it is the power of God" (1 Cor. 1:18). There is no reasonable cause for the Cross to continue as an object of scorn to the modern man or woman, but there is every reason for the Cross to remain a mystery to the Christian. Christians are convinced that the mystery of "Christ crucified" coheres with the nature of reality. We are confronted by the primary mystery of the living God who discloses himself in Scripture and creation. The God of all creation makes his presence known to us in wise and powerful ways. God is personal, loving, holy, and just. His law is written in our conscience. His image is stamped on our character. Whether or not we acknowledge God, our personal uniqueness, together with our capacities for love, worship, thinking, and communication, are derived from God. God is simultaneously knowable and incomprehensible. We cannot fathom "the depth of the riches of the wisdom and knowledge of God!" Therefore Christians share Paul's doxology:

> How unsearchable his judgments, and his paths beyond tracing out! Who has known the mind of the Lord? Or who has been his counselor? Who has ever given to God, that God should repay him? For from him and through him and to him are all things. To him be the glory forever! Amen. (Rom. 11:33–36).

Such praise flows from knowing God. Letting God be God involves a twofold challenge: First, submitting to God's self-disclosure and the central authority of his revealed Word; second, rejecting a narrow caricature of God's truth in neat conceptual categories. God's truth is comprehensible and reasonable. It appeals to our head and heart. It convinces our mind even as it stirs our emotions. It leads us in the way everlasting. But at every point God's truth defies a rationalistic reduction. James Packer warns against a defensive rationalistic methodology that ends up polarizing genuinely biblical dimensions of the doctrine of the Cross.

> The passion to pack God into a conceptual box of our own making is always strong, but must be resisted. If we bear in mind that all the knowledge we can have of the atonement is of a mystery about which we can only think and speak by means of models, and which remain a mystery when all is said and done, it will keep us from rationalistic pitfalls and thus help our progress considerably.[23]

The consequence of refusing to heed this wise advice is spiritual arrogance and an "abstract Christ." Our conservative theologies may construct the meaning of the Cross to a safe list of propositional statements about Jesus' death without any practical impact or mystical power, thus making one's approach to the Cross cold and doctrinaire. Like Job's orthodox friends who failed to enter into the passion of his suffering, we may lose our sensitivity toward God's truth and use it against those who really bear the cross of Jesus. Possessing the doctrine of the Cross is a far cry from experiencing the power of the Cross.

The mystery of the Cross also coheres with the mystery of the Incarnation. The same rationale behind God sending his Son is at work in the meaning of the Cross. If God is remote and distant, incapable of penetrating space and time, then a biblical theology of the Cross is just as impossible as the birth narratives. On the contrary, Christians believe that in both contexts God showed his love among us. "He sent his one and only Son into the world that we might live through him. This is love: not that we loved God, but that he loved us and sent his Son as an atoning sacrifice for our sins" (1 John 4:9–10). If we hold to the ontological reality of the Incarnation by faith, the meaning and the mystery of Jesus' death must be understood in the most profound terms. What does it mean for God to go to the cross? Can we ever exhaust this mystery? In the words of Charles Wesley:

> Tis mystery all! Th' Immortal dies!
> Who can explore His strange design?
> In vain the first-born seraph tries
> To sound the depths of love divine!

We explore this mystery by taking our lead from Jesus. Becoming like him involves believing what he believed about the Cross and sharing his conviction about the meaning of his death. His thoughts about the Cross become our theology of the Cross. The apostles took a certain position, and so should we. Jesus saw his death as "a necessity beyond human comprehension grounded in the will of God."[24] "The Son of Man," declared Jesus, "did not come to be served, but to serve, and to give his life as a ransom for many" (Mark 10:45). The centrality of the Cross in Jesus' self-consciousness ought to be interpreted according to the theological meaning he gave to his death. He conveyed this meaning in several significant ways: by speaking of his death as a "ransom," by believing in the divine necessity of the Cross, by his explicit interpretation of the Last Supper, and by his cry of God-forsakenness from the cross. Jesus explained the life-giving significance of his own death according to the redemptive analogies of the Old Testament. He saw himself as the Passover Lamb, destined to take away the sin of the world, whose blood established the New Covenant. Furthermore, his promises of rest (Matt. 11:28), peace (John 14:27), and abundant and eternal life (10:10; 3:16) were consciously tied to the concrete action of the Cross.

The apostles did not invent a meaning of the Cross alien to Jesus' interpretation of his death. They inherited the meaning of the Cross primarily through Jesus and subsequently through Old Testament revelation and the wisdom of the Holy Spirit. Thus the centrality of the Cross in Jesus' life parallels the significance of the Cross in apostolic proclamation and lifestyle. Following the Resurrection, the apostles developed the significance of the Cross in doctrine and in praxis under the guidance of the Holy Spirit. They proclaimed the meaning of the Cross passionately. Far from speculating about theories of the Atonement, they reflected deeply on the mystery of God's love so that others might know "this love that surpasses knowledge" (Eph. 3:19).

The Cross confronts us with the love of God in ways we would never have imagined. Perhaps for the first time we begin to grasp God's passionate hatred for sin. The love of God is holy and just. He strikes no compromise with evil. Ultimately the cosmic problem of pain and evil must be resolved. Characteristic human attitudes toward sin, ranging from indifference, denial, expediency, and suppression to indulgence, fascination, and glorification, are not found in our Creator. For this reason the mystery of the Cross cannot be understood from the human attitude toward sin. On the cross God's verdict against sin is handed down. The holy and just God took upon himself the judgment we deserve. He vicariously assumed our role as sinner in order to turn away his just wrath. He who knew no sin was made sin for us (2 Cor. 5:21). Since all have sinned and fallen short of the glory of God (Rom. 3:23), God's wrath needed to be averted. If we were ever to experience God's forgiveness and fellowship, his wrath required propitiation. While the logic of the Cross may escape the modern mind, it is consistent with moral necessity which takes seriously human opposition to God's will. In ourselves we have no power to bring about moral satisfaction. We cannot right the wrongs intrinsic to our sinful nature. As the apostle Paul wrote, "When we were still powerless, Christ died for the ungodly. . . . God demonstrates his own love for us in this: While we were still sinners, Christ died for us" (Rom. 5:6, 8).

God incarnate suffered the consequences of divine wrath against human sin, the full implications of which we cannot fathom. How can God be against God? Yet we know that, for our sakes, God-in-the-flesh experienced the pain and spiritual agony of separation from God the Father. This fact explains his dread in the Garden of Gethsemane. The Cross reveals not only the love of God but the pain of God as well. Just as the fullness of God cannot be "telescoped into the figure of Jesus,"[25] the Father cannot be removed from the pain of the Son. Donald Bloesch writes, "God himself takes upon himself in the person of his Son our sin and guilt so that his justice might be executed and our sins might be forgiven. God is moved toward this self-sacrifice by his infinite compassion."[26] Thus, the mutual motivation of the Father and Son leading up to the Cross corresponds to their shared experience of broken fellowship. The chasm between God's holiness and humanity's sin needs to be measured by God's ultimate sacrifice. Coming from the Incarnate One, the cry of dereliction, "My God, my God, why have you forsaken me?" reminds us that God's abandonment of Jesus was the necessary means of bridging the distance between God and ourselves. "The Atonement cannot be understood merely as the genesis of societal reform," writes David Wells. "It must be seen centrally and primarily, as God's provision for averting his own anger."[27]

By taking the penalty we deserved upon himself, Jesus Christ, who was "moved by a love that was determined to do everything necessary to save us, endured and exhausted the destructive divine judgment for which we were otherwise inescapably destined, and so won us forgiveness, adoption and glory."[28] God's redemptive strategy expresses the wisdom and power of God. In a single act climaxing a life of complete righteousness, Jesus accomplished a perfect sacrifice. Through his humanity he satisfied the requirements of divine law for us, and through his deity he applied this perfect sacrifice on our behalf (Gal. 3:13; Heb. 10:14; 1 Peter 3:18).

In his manhood Christ redeemed every aspect of our human existence. In his deity he triumphed over Satan and all other demonic personalities (Heb. 2:14; 1 John 3:8; Matt. 16:18). The power of the Cross lies in both its personal as well as its universal dimensions. Every application of God's redemptive love is personal and specific. Paul could say, "I live by faith in the Son of God, who loved me and gave himself for me" (Gal. 2:20). God in Christ deals with every individual on a personal basis. God not only does for us what we cannot do for ourselves, but he creates the power within us to respond to his love (John 6:65).

God's love, demonstrated on the cross, has universal scope as well. In Hebrews we are told that, by the grace of God, Jesus tasted death for everyone (Heb. 2:9). God's gracious provision of salvation excludes no one—"God so loved the world that he gave his one and only Son"— which does not mean that all are saved. For we are also told that "whoever believes in him shall not perish" (John 3:16). But God does not want "anyone to perish, but everyone to come to repentance" (2 Peter 3:9). Jesus' invitation, "Come to me, all you who are weary and burdened" (Matt. 11:28), is extended to all. And the promise is true that "everyone who calls on the name of the Lord will be saved" (Rom. 10:13). What Jesus accomplished on the cross is the ground for God's new society and the consummation of the kingdom. The victory over sin and evil has already been assured. One day everything will be reconciled to God. "For God was pleased to have all his fullness dwell in him, and through him to reconcile to himself all things, whether things on earth or things in heaven, by making peace through his blood, shed on the cross" (Col. 1:19–20; see also Rom. 8:22).

Jesus' death cannot be understood in terms of powerlessness and suffering alone. The love displayed on the cross is not only sacrificial but victorious. And "His victory is the basis of every man's reconciliation."[29] The God of all creation, with its order, beauty, and majesty, is also the

God of the cross, with all its physical suffering and spiritual despair. Otherwise, the powerlessness Jesus experienced on the cross would not have been powerful to redeem. Christians believe that the power of the crucified Messiah has effectively liberated, justified, and redeemed those who turn to Christ in faith and that it has conquered the powers of darkness.

God's love is an objective reality. Christ's victory over sin and death is an accomplished fact. No one has an excuse for remaining in bondage to sin and death. He "has destroyed death and has brought life and immortality to light through the gospel" (2 Tim. 1:10). The work of the Cross is a finished work. Christ sacrificed for sins "once for all when he offered himself" (Heb. 7:27; cf. 1 Peter 3:18). Through this single historical act he "obtained eternal redemption" (Heb. 9:12). Now we wait for the final consummation of Christ's achievement, but we know he has already "disarmed the powers and authorities" and "made a public spectacle of them, triumphing over them by the cross" (Col. 2:15).

The objective basis of salvation calls for a personal response from us. God's love is not abstract and impersonal but has a subjective dimension. The work of the Cross needs to be appropriated and applied in the life of each and every believer. God's passion for us, accomplished once and for all at the cross and confirmed daily by his Spirit, stirs within us a passion for God. "Christ suffered and atoned for all vicariously," an objective fact, "but man remains bound to the powers of sin and corruption until he is brought by the Spirit into personal contact with the saving work of Christ." Being reborn by the Spirit needs to be our subjective experience. "Christ on the cross" and "Christ in our hearts" are equally important.[30] Jesus emphasized the mystical dimension of the Atonement when he spoke of us "eating his flesh and drinking his blood." Jesus' theology of the Cross needs to be applied to our lives emotionally as well as cognitively. It must be felt in our heart, observed in our lives, and publically confessed.

The believer's sense of self-worth and personal fulfillment needs to be consciously bound to the victory of the Cross. When Jesus hung on the cross the power of the plague of sin was broken. He nailed to the cross our sinful nature, our dread of loneliness, our false ambitions—even our fear of God-forsakenness. We have explored the life of Jesus as a model for our lives. The importance of our christological study has been to take more seriously the historical life of Jesus so that we become like Jesus in our spirituality, self-awareness, and kingdom righteousness. This approach is based on the conviction that Jesus' life before the Cross and leading up to the Cross is what we should be like after the Cross. His substitutionary sacrifice for us makes becoming like him possible through the indwelling Spirit of Christ.

Apart from the objective accomplishment of the Atonement and the subjective experience of Christ's victory, the imitation of Christ is a religious fantasy sure to frustrate and destined to fail. Even though the hard facts of our existence may be oppressive, there is one objective fact which grounds our subjective experience in hope. No stranger to emotional anguish and physical persecution, the apostle Paul could write, "But thanks be to God, who always leads us in triumphal procession in Christ and through us spreads everywhere the fragrance of the knowledge of him (2 Cor. 2:14). Perhaps Paul's outlook on life is best expressed by two rhetorical questions which reveal the reason for his confidence: "If God is for us, who can be against us? He who did not spare his own Son, but gave him up for us all—how will he not also, along with him, graciously give us all things?" (Rom. 8:31–32). The apostle John shared this confidence. He wrote, "For everyone born of God overcomes the world. This is the victory that has overcome the world, even our faith. Who is it that overcomes the world? Only he who believes that Jesus is the Son of God" (1 John 5:4–5).

Through the centuries Christians have evidenced in their daily existence the personal conviction that "The one who is in you is greater than the one who is in the world" (1 John 4:4). They have demonstrated this passion for Christ in their pursuit of justice, in their worship, in their family life, and in their use of material goods. They have borne their cross in joy and confidence. However, when they have failed to live in Christ, as so often has been the case for confessing Christians, they have witnessed against Christ and brought his cross into disrepute.

CROSS-BEARING

Becoming like Jesus means sharing his conviction about the unique meaning of the Cross. It also means following his *path* to the Cross. All that we have to say about cross-bearing is by way of response to what God in Christ has done for us. The death we die in him is not of the same order as the death he died for us.[31] Only Christ can atone for our sins. But what Christ does for us radically changes our approach to life.

We therefore affirm with the apostles a two-pronged theology of the Cross. First, Christ's penal substitutionary death saves us from God's judgment of sin and the experience of God-forsakenness. Second, Christ calls us to take up our cross and follow him. The words of Jesus are final; discipleship follows salvation absolutely. "If anyone would come after me, he must deny himself and take up his cross daily and follow me" (Luke 9:23). Bonhoeffer warned against turning the costly grace of Christ's cross into the cheap grace of religious abstractions and empty piety. He wrote, "Cheap grace is grace without discipleship, grace without the cross, grace without Jesus Christ, living and incarnate."[32]

The apostles were not only convinced of the doctrine of the Crucifixion: they were committed to the way of the Cross. They were more concerned to work out the reality of the Cross practically than they were to repeat a theological formula. When Paul wrote to the Corinthians, saying, "I resolved to know nothing while I was with you except Jesus Christ and him crucified" (1 Cor. 2:2), he had no intention of reducing the gospel to an abbreviated form of the "plan of salvation." On the contrary, Paul saw the relevance of the Cross in every conceivable sphere of the Christian's life. He saw the Cross of Jesus as the basis for Christian unity (1:13) and the rationale for church discipline (5:7), and he even advised refraining from eating meat on the basis of the Cross. Since eating meat which had first been offered to idols was an offense to some of the Christians in Corinth, Paul warned believers not to continue this practice because it might confuse and destroy their weaker brothers and sisters "for whom Christ died" (8:11). Paul was prepared to go meatless for the sake of the Cross. Knowing nothing except Jesus Christ and him crucified meant that every challenge and every problem was seen in terms of the Cross of Jesus. Paul bore it into every life situation, from lawsuits and singleness to the exercise of gifts and the practice of the Lord's Supper.

Instead of circumscribing the relevance and power of the Cross, the apostles were concerned to live up to its full implications. They took the example of Jesus seriously. Through the power of the Spirit of God, they committed themselves to his path of self-denial, suffering, and obedience. In view of the criminal and political significance of the cross in the first century, the initially strange and unthinkable command to take up a cross and follow Jesus took on practical meaning. Believers were called to suffer for the sake of the gospel. Apostolic conviction followed Jesus' promise, "Blessed are you when people insult you, persecute you and falsely say all kinds of evil against you *because of me*" (Matt. 5:11; italics added). In fact, behind the Beatitudes in Matthew's Sermon on the Mount is an applied theology of the Cross. Herein lies a concise summary of the way of the Cross, including repentance, humility, peacemaking, and persecution for the sake of righteousness.

The apostles were under no illusion that living and proclaiming the gospel would meet with social acceptance. But neither did they cultivate a martyr's complex. Cultural respectability was not one of their expectations. But they were able to anticipate hard times without the usual neurosis and prejudice associated with persecuted minorities. Believers who follow their example see suffering as the Christian's privilege and responsibility. "For it has been granted to you on behalf of Christ not only to believe on him, but also to suffer for him" (Phil. 1:29). Christians should therefore have the same attitude as Christ Jesus, who "humbled himself and became obedient to death—even death on a cross!" (2:5, 8). The apostle Peter reminded believers that suffering for the sake of righteousness, not unrighteousness, was commended by Christ. The death of Jesus was the ultimate example: "To this you were called, because Christ suffered for you, leaving you an example, that you should follow in his steps" (1 Peter 2:21). Suffering confirms the believer's partnership with Jesus Christ and demonstrates visibly that the principle of the Cross is actually applied in one's life. Yet, according to Paul, the suffering is "not worth comparing with the glory that will be revealed in us" (Rom. 8:17–18).

The apostles did not lose sight of the dignity and hope in "bearing the disgrace he bore" (Heb. 13:13). Cross-bearing puts an end to triumphalism, with its shallow appraisal of sin and its cheap grace (Gal. 6:14). The old self with it sinful nature has been crucified with Christ so that the bondage of sin may be broken (Rom. 6:6; Gal. 5:24). But the new self shares in Christ's ministry of reconciliation and rejoices in the opportunity of sharing in Christ's suffering on behalf of the body of Christ, the church (2 Cor. 5:17–19; Col. 1:24). The best definition for love refers specifically to the body-life implications of cross-bearing. "This is how we know what love is: Jesus Christ laid down his life for us. And we ought to lay down our lives for our brothers" (1 John 3:16).

Accepting the Cross of Jesus Christ is not a passive act. It is a personal, passionate public commitment to become like Jesus. Jesus issued the command to take up the Cross publicly (Mark 8:34). He made his point in the midst of the crowd and did not simply whisper the command in secret or hint at it in the privacy of the Upper Room. He chose to let everyone know what it meant to follow him. Even the world can detect a disciple on the basis of the Cross.

Cross-bearing means obedience to everything that Jesus and the gospel of the kingdom stands for. Self-denial means following a course of action determined by the gospel. Jesus' life and message become the ground for our actions. Death to self assumes a specifically Christ-centered focus. The Cross is not simply an illness or an accident or a difficult family situation. It is not the hectic pace one may be expected to keep at work or a frustration of personal ambition. It is not increased mortgage rates. Nor is the Cross some inward psychological feeling of empathy with Jesus' suffering. We trivialize the Cross if we define it according to the array of everyday calamities that come upon us, irrespective of our commitment to Christ and his kingdom. The Cross has a more definite, specifically Christian meaning, which rules out any superficial equating of negative circumstances with the practical reality of taking up our cross and following Jesus.

Taking up our cross in this culture may specifically mean for us rejection by other believers because we have seemingly taken Jesus and his teaching too seriously and passionately. It may result in scorn and ridicule from those who deny God's clear principles regarding sexuality and the maintenance of physical and psychological health. Taking up our cross may result in a job demotion because we are not willing to sacrifice our life and family for the sake of the company. It may result in dismissal because we will not permit a specific injustice to go unnoticed.

Undoubtedly, it will mean the real sacrifice of our material possessions for the sake of the body of Christ. Taking up our cross may mean the costly inconvenience of practicing law in the inner city or medicine in Zaire for the sake of the gospel. For many of our missionaries and third-world Christian brothers and sisters, taking up Jesus' cross may lead to being falsely accused regarding political motives because of their opposition to social and political injustices. Taking up our cross may mean courageously facing the reality of a mentally disabled son or daughter in the spirit of love and confidence that Jesus both wills and provides.

The Lausanne Covenant rightly states, "A church which preaches the Cross must itself be marked by the Cross."[33] Jesus' cross provides not only the message of salvation but the message of judgment against every form of alienation, exploitation, and oppression. Whether believers act today against injustice is determined not by expediency or convenience but by whether they really believe that at the cross of Jesus the world has been radically changed. The unfolding of the new world is not here yet, but it is at the right hand of the Father and is in the Word of Jesus.[34]

12

---

the Risen Lord

The crucified Messiah *is* the risen Lord. To divorce Jesus from the biblical testimony of the Resurrection effectively annuls Christian faith and practice. At no other point is the continuity between the historical Jesus and the Christ of faith more crucial. If the bodily resurrection of Jesus did not take place, then all that has been said about the *fact* and *meaning* of the Incarnation, kingdom ethic, and Atonement would have to be discounted. The Resurrection is the major premise of the early Christian faith.[1] If the bones of Jesus disintegrated in a Palestinian tomb, then becoming like Jesus is a sad delusion. If the Resurrection is reduced from historical fact to myth and metaphor, then the biblical meaning and the supernatural character of the imitation of Christ is canceled.

The centrality of the Resurrection is evident in the mind of Jesus and in the theology of the apostles. It is impossible to interpret Jesus' death according to the biblical accounts without the foundational conviction that Jesus did in fact fulfill his predictions that he would rise from the dead. All four Gospels clearly teach that the goal of Jesus' mission was death *and* resurrection. Jesus declared to his disciples not only the inevitability of his death but the reality of his resurrection (Mark 9:31; 10:33–34; 14:27–28; John 10:11, 18). He attempted to prepare his disciples for both eventualities. He did not consider the one without the other, because he considered the Resurrection as "the essential completion of his death."[2]

Apostolic preaching emphasized the resurrection of Jesus as the justifying and the motivational ground for the gospel. Since Jesus was "not abandoned to the grave, nor did his body see decay," the apostle

Peter boldly affirmed, "God has made this Jesus, whom you crucified, both Lord and Christ" (Acts 2:31, 36). The character of the early Christian community, reflected in its unity, worship, and economic sharing, was shaped by the apostles, who continued to testify "with great power . . . to the resurrection of the Lord Jesus" (4:33). It was inconceivable to the apostles to explain away or deemphasize the bodily resurrection, even though it provoked hostility from the Jews and mockery from the Greek intelligentsia (v. 2; 17:32). Like Jesus, the apostles saw death and resurrection in factual as well as theological continuity. When they spoke of Jesus' death, they declared his resurrection (Rom. 4:25; 8:34). The historicity of the Resurrection was considered in the same terms as the historicity of the Cross, without bifurcating reality into fact and symbol or reality and poetry. The apostles had no intention of "spiritualizing" the historicity of the Resurrection, even though mythologizing it would have spared them considerable disrespect in the religious and intellectual communities.

They also linked Jesus' death and resurrection theologically. The Resurrection infused the Cross with salvific meaning (Rom. 6:5–10; 1 Pet. 3:18, 21). Without the reality of the Resurrection, the apostle Paul admitted that Christian preaching was useless, their faith was futile, and their lives were still steeped in sin. As far as he was concerned, Christianity without the Resurrection had no credibility. If God did not raise Jesus from the dead, believers were false witnesses of God, without hope, who ought to be "pitied more than all men" (1 Cor. 15:14–19). "But Christ has indeed been raised from the dead," argued Paul. His resurrection had tremendous theological meaning and anthropological significance. "For since death came through a man, the resurrection of the dead comes also through a man. For as in Adam all die, so in Christ all will be made alive" (vv. 20–22).

The Resurrection does not reverse the meaning of the Cross. It confirms the real scandal of Jesus' death. The one who died on the cross was none other than the Anointed One of God. The nameless Suffering Servant was the firstborn of all creation (Col. 1:15). The same one who was nailed to a cross by the hands of godless men has now been exalted to the right hand of God (Acts 2:23, 33). The victim of the cross conquered death, once and for all, and now brings new life to those who confess "Jesus is Lord" and believe in their heart "that God raised him from the dead" (Rom. 10:9). The early Christian community was confident that the humiliated Jesus of Nazareth was the same as the risen Lord.[3]

The Resurrection not only established the meaning of the Atonement; it provided the rationale for Christian cross-bearing Shallow Christians who use the victory of the empty tomb to justify a life of worldly happiness and success have failed to grasp the meaning of the Resurrection. They want the glory of the Resurrection without the fellowship of Christ's suffering. They have little intention of walking the same path Jesus did. They want a heavenly crown without an earthly cross. The Resurrection of Jesus does not cancel out the Cross. Jesus died for our sins and experienced God-forsakenness on our behalf, which does not mean that believers are released from the responsibility of cross-bearing and can live carefree and self-directed lives. Perhaps our observance of Easter contributes to the misconception that the Cross is to be relegated to a mental idea rather than a personal experience. We may move from the grief of Good Friday to the exuberance of Easter too quickly and superficially, with the result that we fail to appreciate that believers' genuine experience of resurrection hope takes place as they take up their cross daily to follow Jesus. Human nature would like nothing better than to "get over the Cross" in three days and get into new clothes and a new mood on Easter Sunday. But this reduces the Cross and the Resurrection to a caricature in the popular imagination of religious tradition.

Following the Resurrection, Jesus took the initiative to meet with Peter (John 21:15–23). He sought to restore their relationship, which had been disrupted by Peter's denials and Jesus' death. Three times he asked this feisty, outspoken Galilean fisherman, "Do you love me?" and three times Peter responded, "You know that I love you." Standing before the risen Lord, Peter felt the pain of repentance. He was hurt by Jesus' repeated question, "Do you love me?" But his remorse was necessary if his self-doubt and guilt were to be removed from his deepest thoughts and feelings. Jesus proved to Peter that Peter's love was worth restoring and renewing. The Lord of Glory considered Peter's love significant.

First, Jesus defined this love in terms of humble, sacrificial service: "Feed my sheep." To love Jesus was to serve his followers. Then he applied the practical consequences of this love to Peter's life. Jesus gave a sobering scenario to Peter's future ministry: "I tell you the truth, when you were younger you dressed yourself and went where you wanted; but when you are old you will stretch out your hands, and someone else will dress you and lead you where you do not want to go. . . . Follow me!" (John 21:18–19). From first to last, the call of discipleship is the same: "Follow me!" But now the sacrificial impact of the command is obvious, much more so than when Andrew first introduced Peter to

Jesus. Contrary to a spirit of triumphalism or a popular messianic crusade, Peter heard the "facts of life" for a follower of Jesus. The Resurrection did not remove the Cross from discipleship, but it gave meaning to cross-bearing. Therefore it made sense for Jesus to speak about "the kind of death by which Peter would glorify God" (v. 19), precisely because of the Resurrection. Peter was to become like his Lord, "who for the joy set before him endured the cross" (Heb. 12:2).

Resurrection joy and cross-bearing belong together in the believer's life. Peter emphasized this theme in his epistle when he praised God for the "new birth into a living hope through the resurrection of Jesus Christ from the dead," adding, "In this you greatly rejoice, though now for a little while you may have had to suffer grief in all kinds of trials" (1 Pet. 1:3, 6). For Paul, knowing Christ involved experiencing the "power of his resurrection and the fellowship of sharing in his sufferings" (Phil. 3:10). In his understanding of the Christian life, the two dimensions were inseparable. The apostles were convinced that, on this side of eternity, Jesus promised a cross. They believed what Christians today should affirm, namely, that the risen Lord will not permit his followers to forget the definite and practical path of discipleship. Jesus is alive. He is present in the fullness of his Spirit, and he is powerful at the right hand of the Father, challenging men and women to take up the cross and invest their lives in the kingdom of God.

RESURRECTION REALITY

Christians believe that the best explanation for a small band of disciples turning the world upside down is the bodily resurrection of Jesus. This account sounds implausible to those who limit history to events with natural causes and rule out a priori the possibility of God's direct intervention. If we confine our thinking to our ordinary experience or to the limits of modern scientific knowledge, it will always be easier to believe that the disciples lied or were tricked than to believe that the biblical record is true. The Bible admits that "there can be no purely historical explanation for the rise of the resurrection faith. It is due to an act of God which happened in history but did not happen in terms of historical causality."[4] Hence the explanation for the reality of the Resurrection must be found in God and believed by faith. But the Bible also admits that resurrection faith is reasonable. The Resurrection is a supernatural act without historical causality; nevertheless, it is a historical reality which helps explain the convictions and actions of the early Christians.

Apart from the history of the Resurrection, significant questions remain. How do we explain the empty tomb, knowing that the authorities would have made every attempt possible to produce the body of Jesus in order to discredit the preaching of Jesus' resurrection? Is there an explanation for the radical change in the discouraged and bewildered disciples? Would these same men, who failed so miserably to stand with Jesus during his trial, face persecution and death for the sake of a lie? Why do the biblical accounts of the Resurrection draw significantly on the witness of women, when, "according to Jewish principles of evidence, women were notoriously invalid witnesses"?[5] If the disciples were concerned only with a "symbolic" resurrection, why did they go out of their way to claim the historicity of Jesus' resurrection? Why would they have documented his appearances and described their disbelief, if they wanted to say only that the spirit of Jesus' life survived his death and lived on in the proclamation of the gospel?

Christians have argued that the most reasonable answer to these questions is the reality of the bodily resurrection of Jesus. But it has never been easy to believe in the Resurrection. The disciples had great difficulty coming to terms with the Resurrection. It was easier for them to believe that the body of Jesus had been stolen than to believe that Jesus had risen from the dead.

We cannot blame Thomas for his skepticism. As far as he was concerned, his experience with Jesus was a closed book. Just as the two disciples did on the road to Emmaus, he thought and spoke of Jesus in the past tense. The "Jesus phase" of his life was over. Understandably, Thomas resisted the pressure to conform to the enthusiasm of the disciples. He discounted what seemed to him to be strange and unfounded reports of Jesus' appearance first to women and then to the disciples behind locked doors (John 20). Thomas would have nothing to do with their wishful thinking. Against their appeal he issued a challenge: "Unless I see the nail marks in his hands and put my finger where the nails were, and put my hand into his side, I will not believe it" (v. 25). If he is going to believe in the Resurrection, it must be a *real* resurrection. He gave his ultimatum. If Jesus did not personally confront him with an actual body, he would reject any notion of resurrection. It is either a bodily resurrection or nothing at all. A modern writer expresses Thomas's feelings: "Let us not mock God with metaphor, analogy, sidestepping, transcendence; making of the event a parable, a sign painted in the faded credulity of earlier ages."[6]

The factuality of the Resurrection mattered a great deal to Thomas, as it did to all the apostles. Nothing is said in the biblical accounts to imply otherwise. Nor is there any hint that the disciples were either intellectually or theologically prepared to believe in the Resurrection. It took them all by surprise. "It is naive," writes Colin Brown, "for modern man to think that miracles were somehow much easier to accept in the ancient world than they are today. . . . The miraculous was still miraculous for ancient man."[7] The skepticism of Thomas was as characteristic of his age as our own, with the possible exception that he was more open to further evidence. But it is doubtful whether he expected anything to come of his challenge. After all, dead people do not come back to life.

Theologically, the disciples were ill prepared for the resurrection of Jesus (Luke 24:37; John 20:19). Perhaps if they had been exposed to explicit prophecies on the resurrection of the Messiah they might have anticipated Jesus' resurrection. But they were not, and Jesus' repeated reference to his own death and resurrection did not penetrate their preconceived notion of a victorious Messiah. The disciples were not adequately conditioned by Jesus' predictions to expect his bodily resurrection. The Jews, with the notable exception of the Sadducees, believed in a general eschatological resurrection of the righteous and unrighteous at the end of history (Dan. 12:2). The Old Testament provided glimpses of a future life in the presence of God, but the biblical emphasis was placed on the enduring faithfulness of God rather than human immortality (Ps. 16:9–11; 49:15; 73:24; Hos. 6:1–2; Ezek. 37:11–13).[8]

Given the lack of Old Testament references to the Resurrection, what was the apostle Paul's thinking when he wrote, "that he was buried, that he was raised on the third day *according to the Scriptures*" (1 Cor. 15:4; italics added)? Or what biblical passages did John refer to when he explained the disciples' confusion of Easter morning with a parenthetical comment, "They still did not understand from Scripture that Jesus had to rise from the dead" (John 20:9; cf. Luke 24:25–27)? The answer to these questions lies in the fact that, until the resurrection of Jesus had actually taken place, the disciples were unable to apply passages of Scripture such as Hosea 6:2; 13:14; Psalms 16 and 110; and Job 19:25–27 to the Messiah. They simply did not understand the application of these texts to Jesus. The death and resurrection of Jesus resulted in a Spirit-inspired reinterpretation of Scripture. For the first time they saw the messianic meaning of many texts. The resurrection of Christ was a new revelatory event which infused the text with a deeper meaning. It motivated the disciples to interpret the Scripture the way Jesus did in the light of himself.

Precisely because the disciples were not preconditioned to expect the Messiah's death and resurrection, their testimony was enhanced. Contrary to their personal trauma, biblical interpretation, and intellectual outlook, they came to believe in the reality of the Resurrection. Something had to *happen* to make the *risen* Lord Jesus central to their powerful preaching. Christians have believed that, in light of the whole history of Jesus, the most reasonable explanation of the empty tomb, the disciples' courage, and the biblical description of his appearances was in fact the resurrection of Jesus. Faith did not create the Resurrection; the Resurrection created faith.

Jesus was under no obligation to prove himself to Thomas, but he did. For the sake of Thomas and for future believers, Jesus accepted the challenge of doubt and confronted Thomas. "Put your finger here," he ordered. "See my hands. Reach out your hand and put it into my side. Stop doubting and believe" (John 20:27). Whether Thomas actually felt his side and held his hand we do not know, but Thomas immediately went far beyond a grudging acknowledgment of the Resurrection by exclaiming, "My Lord and my God!" (v. 28). Doubt resolved, Thomas freely worshiped. Jesus humbly met the terms of credibility set by Thomas. He proved the historical reality of his resurrection, but more than that, he affirmed that the faith of Thomas mattered a great deal to him. One of the salient points emphasized in the conclusion of the Gospel of John, both with Peter and Thomas, is that their love and faith are of enduring significance to the risen Lord. They do not believe in an abstract concept of theology. They entrust themselves to a risen Lord who from the beginning has given himself completely to them.

Resurrection faith does not call for a sacrifice of the believer's intellect. Neither can it be adequately explained in terms of the believer's intellectual satisfaction about the Resurrection. Unless there is a personal encounter with the risen Lord, eliciting the exclamation of worship, "My Lord and my God," the evidence ultimately matters little. Unquestionably Thomas' situation was unique. He actually saw the body of Jesus. Consequently the requirement of faith becomes greater for those who follow Thomas. As Jesus said, "Blessed are those who have not seen and yet have believed" (John 20:29). But belief in the historical reality of the Resurrection remains unchanged and central to the gospel, regardless of the intellectual climate. Thomas experienced the concrete appearance of Jesus for his sake as well as ours, that we might "believe that Jesus is the Christ, the Son of God, and that by believing [we might] have life in his name" (v. 31).

MODERN INGENUITY

What if the body of Jesus were discovered in an ancient tomb? How would the church react? Would it mark the end of the Christian faith? Canadian author Charles Templeton develops this scenario in a novel entitled *Acts of God.* He imagines the intrigue and conspiracy of church leaders who cover up the discovery of Jesus' bones for fear that, if the truth were known, Christianity would be destroyed.

Templeton's plot depends on the central hypothesis that positive evidence against the physical resurrection of Jesus would do irreparable damage to the Christian faith. Surprisingly, however, many theologians and church leaders do not share Templeton's assumption. They argue that the discovery of Jesus' bones would have no effect whatever on their belief in the Resurrection.[9] Ernest Howse, a well-known United Church pastor in Toronto, feels that people threatened by such an eventuality have confused poetry with fact. The meaning of the Resurrection, he argues, should not be taken in a literal, physical sense. For Howse, the spirit of Jesus lives on in spite of his death. The "empty tomb" and "appearances" are symbols of his powerful sustaining influence and were never intended to be interpreted as facts.

The dilemma facing many contemporary theologians is how to remain faithful to modern notions of historicity and at the same time maintain the historicity of the Resurrection. Since a literal, physical resurrection is impossible, how can it be reinterpreted to make sense to the modern reader? Many agree with Rudolf Bultmann's judgment: "An historical fact which involves a resurrection from the dead is utterly inconceivable!" The empty tomb and the appearances "are most certainly embellishments of the primitive tradition."[10] For those unacquainted with theological doublethink and the customary use of one set of words with two sets of meanings, Bultmann's conclusion is confusing. He denies the resurrection of Jesus insofar as it means the return of a dead human being to life, but he affirms Jesus' resurrection as an existential experience of freedom and self-understanding in response to the proclamation of the gospel.

Along a similar line, Jon Sobrino, a proponent of Liberation Theology, argues that the key to understanding the Resurrection is what took place not "in" history but "for" history. He attempts to define a "historical" dimension that is beyond the realm of fact. What is important, he argues, is not the evidence of an empty tomb or the postresurrection appearances, but the presence of hope in the current sociopolitical situation. We cannot say what *resurrection* meant in Jesus' history because it escapes all historical verification, remaining as yet unknown and hidden in obscurity. It is beyond the bounds of historical judgment to lay hold of the resurrection as such. The historical aspect of Jesus' resurrection is to be grasped insofar as we see it in terms of promise that opens up a future.[11]

We sense an embarrassment among many contemporary theologians over the historicity of Jesus' bodily resurrection. Their discomfort with New Testament teaching triggers ingenious evasionary tactics designed to soften the scandal of the Resurrection. The modernity principle takes precedence over the creative development of sophisticated "mythical" versions which retreat from the historical uniqueness and physical concreteness of Jesus' resurrection.

Harvard theologian Gordon Kaufmann insists that the Resurrection has nothing to do with Jesus' body. Suffering from hallucinating visions of the risen Christ, the disciples were mistaken in their initial interpretation. When all the confusion and misconceptions are cleared away, argues Kaufmann, the Resurrection really means that God's action never ceases. God's presence in Jesus' ministry continues to work in the believing community.[12]

The interpretative strategy in vogue today strives to *dematerialize* resurrection faith, without eliminating its centrality in Christian theology. Hans Küng has many important things to say about the meaning of the Resurrection for Christians. But he denies that the power and mission of the Resurrection is linked with God's supernatural intervention to cause the bodily resurrection of Jesus.

> We tried to understand the numerous miracle stories of the New Testament without assuming a "supernatural" intervention—which cannot be proved—in the laws of nature. It would therefore seem like a dubious retrogression to discredited ideas if we were now suddenly to postulate such a supernatural "intervention" for the miracle of the resurrection: this would contradict all scientific thinking as well as all ordinary convictions and experiences. Understood in this way, the resurrection seems to modern man to be an encumbrance to faith, akin to the virgin birth, the descent into hell or the ascension.

"Faith in the risen Christ . . . is independent of the empty tomb," Küng continues, for

> historical criticism has made the empty tomb a dubious factor and the conclusions of natural science have rendered it suspect. To maintain the identity God does not need the relics of Jesus' earthly existence. We are not tied to physiological ideas of the resurrection. . . . The

corporality of the resurrection does not require the tomb to be empty.
God raises the person in a new, different, unimaginable "spiritual
corporality."[13]

Christians can hold to the witness of the apostles and agree with
Küng that the resurrection of Jesus was not the resuscitation of a corpse.
His resurrection was not a restoration to a normal state of life, for Jesus
received a new, glorified body. Christians can also agree with Küng that
there is no verification in the sense prescribed by the modern historical
method. But Christians through the centuries have not been willing to
sever resurrection faith from historical evidence. We agree with George
Ladd that "there can be no purely historical explanation for the rise of
the resurrection"—Not because the Resurrection did not take place in
history but because it was an act of God "which happened in history but
did not happen in terms of historical causality."[14] Faith in the risen
Lord is a response to what was actually accomplished in history. Belief
does not result from empirical proof, but it is a response to the historical
evidence. Hence we are unwilling to say with Küng that "the historicity
of the empty tomb and the Easter experience cease to count beside the
question of the significance of the resurrection message."[15] This
mentality betrays the testimony of the apostles and confuses the
contemporary seeker. It depreciates what God has done in history for
the sake of making God more appealing.

Is the Resurrection more believable when it is desupernaturalized,
dematerialized, and reduced to a symbol for hope? Do we commend the
truth of God when we disown the scandal of the Resurrection for fear
that the world will sneer (Acts 17:32)? It is either an act of God in
history, without historical casuality and scientific explanation, or a
colossal deception. We are unwilling to reinterpret the empty tomb and
postresurrection appearances as fictional embellishments creatively
imagined to illustrate the subjective experiences of the disciples. The
historian looks in vain for a sequence of events which will explain the
Resurrection. But he does not look in vain for events which testify to it.
Historians will be unable to find the historical cause for the Resurrection, but they are challenged to judge its subsequent historical impact.

I am convinced that the historical facts available to us in the biblical
narratives lead us to the faith conclusion "that the only rational
explanation for these historical facts is that God raised Jesus in bodily
form from the realm of mortality into the world of God."[16] These facts
include the remarkable reversal in the disciples' outlook, their sacrificial
commitment to the gospel mission, the authenticity of the biblical

narratives (i.e., the testimony of women), the undisturbed grave clothes, Jesus' appearances to the disciples, and the conversion testimony of the apostle Paul. Combined, these facts lead to the faith conviction that the crucified Jesus is indeed the risen Lord. The continuity between the historical Jesus and the Christ of faith is established by God in history and for history. We are left with only two alternatives. The Resurrection is either superstitious folly or a mandate for faith.[17]

RESURRECTION POWER

A passion for Christ must be energized by the power of the risen Christ. Resurrection power is the only reason we can participate in the spirituality of Jesus, pray in his name, obey his teaching, claim his victory over sin and death, seek his kingdom, and anticipate his coming. The faith and mission of the body of Christ is defined by the suffering love of the crucified Messiah *and* the sovereign power of the risen Lord.

The powerlessness of God on the cross must be understood in light of the power of God to raise Jesus from the dead. If death is the last word, then love has not triumphed. Love, to be victorious, "requires power stronger than death, man's last enemy."[18] Two facts must be kept in mind. First, the love of God demonstrated through solidarity with the needy is powerful and effective. Second, nothing God does can be divorced from his holy love. Whenever God acts he does so in love. But an additional truth needs to be asserted. When we speak of God raising Jesus from the dead, we cannot substitute *love* for *power*. Christ's victory over death is not fully explained by love, even the outpouring of God's love for us on the cross. The Resurrection reminds us that God is all-powerful and sovereign over creation. He is the Lord of the Universe. He has the power to vindicate the suffering of the Son and make him the Lord of Glory.

Some will depreciate this truth by stressing that the "power" of God resides exclusively in weakness, humility, suffering, and power-lessness. It is claimed that God's love is comprehended totally by sacrificial identification with the oppressed and the incarnational lifestyle. But such a claim represents only one side of the picture. The resurrection of Christ challenges us to acknowledge historically and personally the victory of the Cross. Russell Aldwinckle correctly affirms, "No Christology which uses the concept of love to destroy the power of God as Creator and Sustainer of the world can be satisfactory." He continues,

Not only does such a procedure call into question the eternal reality of this love itself. It ignores undoubted elements in the New Testament witness and leaves the believer with a basic uncertainty about the triumph of the very Lord who has brought him the message of God's love and secured his reconciliation.[19]

The resurrection of Jesus made the message of the Cross the power of God unto salvation (Rom. 1:16; 1 Cor. 1:18).

Before the apostle Paul was encountered by the risen Lord on the road to Damascus, he did not know the meaning of God's power. Until then he gloried in the worldly power of self-achievement and self-righteousness. He relied on the power of family pride and cultural privilege. He wielded the power of violence by persecuting the followers of Jesus. Then suddenly he was struck down by a blinding flash of light. In a moment he went from power to powerlessness. Encountered by Jesus, he yielded to the greater power of the risen Lord.

People who are spiritually perceptive enough to know that demons and supernatural forces are real look for a demonstration of power when the gospel of Jesus Christ is proclaimed. The most convincing testimony to native peoples in Canada is the overcoming power of Jesus to destroy the domination of evil. They need no one to tell them that human life struggles "against the powers of this dark world and against the spiritual forces of evil in the heavenly realms" (Eph. 6:12). If Jesus is unable to help them triumph over the powers and principalities of the world, then they have no interest in the gospel. Their real-world experience cannot afford an abstract Christ. They need to know that the kingdom of God proclaimed in the gospel of Jesus "is not a matter of talk but of power" (1 Cor. 4:20).

Secular versions of power predominate in Western culture. By repressing the truth of spiritual existence, the West seeks to "humanize" existence, reducing problems to environmental causes, sociological upheavals, and psychological disorders. Secular humanism mythologizes the world by making human beings the locus of authority. We are intrigued by power. Sales promoters describe the "power lunch," executives are advised to project a "power image," and hockey players go for the "power play." But on a deeper level the West has begun to realize that the problems confronting us are no longer on a human scale. This conclusion has always been the case, but the truth is only now beginning to emerge. Human beings left to their own ends work out the power of the demonic in new ways. The tragic impression communicated by many Christians is that all the power belongs to the world. They are like the disciples who unknowingly encounter Jesus on the road to Emmaus.

Their life perspective is shaped by the disillusionment of the world. They are unaware that their victory has already been assured in Christ. Their experience of power is in the past. Jesus is only a memory. As far as they are concerned, Jesus *was* "a prophet, powerful in word and deed" (Luke 24:19). The two disciples going to Emmaus did not recognize the risen Lord. But today's believer cannot share their excuse. We cannot sit idly by, the guardians of the untapped power of Christianity, when our world, racked by evil powers and satanic forces, desperately needs resurrection power.

What is the meaning of resurrection power, and what significance should it have in the believer's life? Is it definable in practical terms and applicable to daily life? The answer lies in the Christian's personal appropriation of all that the resurrection of Jesus accomplished and all that it anticipates. Becoming like Jesus follows the lead of the apostles, who consciously applied the meaning of Jesus' resurrection to the life of the believer. They were convinced that what had transpired in Jesus' life was meant for them as well. Through the Spirit of God they shared his resurrection experience. They did not confuse or compromise the uniqueness of Jesus' resurrection as the risen Lord. His resurrection meant the declaration of his lordship (Rom. 1:4), the commencement of his exaltation, his ascension into glory, his enthronement "at the right hand of the throne of the Majesty in heaven" (Heb. 8:1), and the sending of the Holy Spirit. All the benefits of the Father's ultimate vindication of the Son are laid out by the apostles in direct relationship to the believer's life in Christ. The risen Lord empowers prayer, secures salvation (7:25; 1 Pet. 3:18), commissions gospel ministry (Matt. 28:18–20), and conquers the powers and authorities (Col. 2:15).

Resurrection power is both a present and future reality. The apostles maintained a dialectic between the personal experience of resurrection power in the present and the resurrection of a new and glorified body at the end of the age when Christ returns. Paul strongly opposed efforts to dematerialize the Resurrection. He condemned Hymenaeus and Philetus for teaching that the resurrection had already taken place (2 Tim. 2:17–18). With the Corinthians, he worked through the meaning of the transformed, glorified body (1 Cor. 15:35–57). He told them he longed to be "clothed" with his "heavenly dwelling, because when we are clothed, we will not be found naked" (2 Cor. 5:2–3). The expectation of the resurrection at the end of the age did not relegate resurrection power to the future. It was meant to be the believer's immediate spiritual experience. "If we have been united with him like this in his death, we will certainly also be united with him in his resurrection" (Rom. 6:5). Since we have died to sin and been buried with him through baptism, we are able to live a new life because Christ was raised from the dead (v. 4). Paul's desire "to know Christ and the power of his resurrection" was a daily spiritual experience, one he found compatible with "the fellowship of sharing in his sufferings" (Phil. 3:10). For Paul, resurrection power did not remove the rationale for cross-bearing but instead accentuated it.

Resurrection power, experienced by believers as a living hope, sustains Christian obedience and perseverance. Christ has taken away the sting of death and has broken the power of sin (1 Cor. 15:54–55). Naïve optimism and triumphalism have no place in the Christian life; the hope that nothing shall separate us from the love of Christ does. The spiritual struggle cannot be slighted nor the personal sacrifice minimized, but in the end victory is assured. We "groan inwardly as we wait eagerly for our adoption as sons, the redemption of our bodies. For in this hope we were saved" (Rom. 8:23–24). The ethical implications of this resurrection hope are essential for any believer who seeks to obey the teachings of Jesus. Obedience takes place in a definite historical situation, not because Christ's lordship is a theoretical premise, but because it is a fact, "established in history by his resurrection."[20] Praxis begins with the enduring fact of Jesus' eternal lordship over the principalities, powers, and rulers of darkness. What more can motivate the Christian to live in this world as Jesus did than faith's conviction that, in Jesus' bodily resurrection, the tyranny of evil, injustice, and death has been overcome? We work and pray for the coming of God's kingdom with the assurance that Christ will be there at the end of history. For this reason we can heed the challenge to stand firm, fully committed to the work of the Lord, knowing that our labor in the Lord is not in vain (1 Cor. 15:58).

The pastoral dimension of resurrection hope is also significant. Christians ought to face death differently from those who believe physical death ends all. We sorrow not as those without hope. The test of resurrection faith comes when we face death squarely and renew our conviction that God does not abandon those to the grave who place their trust in him but raises them to eternal life. The Incarnate One has destroyed "him who holds the power of death—that is, the devil" and has freed those "who all their lives were held in slavery by their fear of death" (Heb. 2:14–15). Yet many of us need a deeper grasp of resurrection hope in order to liberate us from the anxiety of sickness and death. Martin Luther wrote:

He who fears death or is unwilling to die is not a Christian to a sufficient degree; for those who fear death still lack faith in the resurrection, since they love this life more than they love the life to come. . . . He who does not die willingly should not be called a Christian.[21]

Luther was not advocating here a casual view of death. He did not trivialize the "valley of the shadow of death," but he was convinced that the rays of resurrection hope should shine through the darkest despair. Death is the believer's passage to glory. Facing death in Christ is an act of obedience that allows us to share with Jesus the hope he experienced prior to death.

Father, the time has come. Glorify your Son, that your Son may glorify you. . . . I have brought you glory on earth by completing the work you gave me to do. And now, Father, glorify me in your presence with the glory I had with you before the world began (John 17:1–5).

These words belong uniquely to the preexistent Lord, but they also apply to believers who face death like their Lord. Even in death believers become like Jesus. They share his expectation of glory as an act of faith—a demonstration of resurrection power.

Resurrection hope is best expressed in the promise of Christ's second coming. "When he appears," wrote the apostle John, "we shall be like him, for we shall see him as he is. Everyone who has this hope in him purifies himself, just as he is pure" (1 John 3:2–3). Until Christ comes again we accept the challenge of making our life passion to become like Jesus. Precisely because the joy is set before us and we are empowered by the Holy Spirit, we are convinced that the example of Jesus is the practical pattern for the Christian life. The aim of this study has been to "fix our eyes on Jesus, the author and perfecter of our faith" (Heb. 12:2). We have explored the meaning and impact of Jesus' life on our own lives for the purpose of deepening and authenticating our Christian commitment.

We look forward to that day when we shall see him "face to face" and experience the unimaginable glory of his presence; when our faith will be turned to sight and we will know fully, even as we are fully known (1 Cor. 13:12). But until that day we strive to be like Jesus *now*. The apostle John left no room for doubt that this goal should be primary for each and every believer: "Love is made complete among us so that we will have confidence on the day of judgment, because in this world we are like him" (1 John 4:17). The way to know Christ and to continue his ministry in the latter part of the twentieth century is to become like Jesus through the power of his Spirit. For this reason, "Within the limits of our prayers and with no messianic pretensions," we will follow his pattern of self-awareness, spirituality, and biblical interpretation.[22] We will commit ourselves to his ministry of kingdom righteousness that was manifest in his teaching, healing, and cross-bearing.

> Jesus, Name above all names,
> Beautiful Savior, Glorious Lord.
> Emmanuel, God is with us,
> Blessed Redeemer, Living Word.[23]

summary

The major themes of this book have been used not only to inform but to challenge. I have endeavored to interpret the Bible faithfully and relevantly in the formulation of a doctrine of Christ that serves as a catalyst for cultivating a passion for Christ. The following brief summary of these themes may aid the reader in tracing the flow of thought and the path of responsibility facing the follower of Jesus Christ.

1. North American Christianity faces a crisis of meaning and relevance. Social pressures, religious habits, and intellectual trends have compromised an authentic knowledge of Christ. The passions of this age are trivializing Jesus and crippling the spirit and the practice of contemporary Christians. To know Christ is to discern and defeat everything that comes between us and a personal, passionate relationship to Jesus Christ.
2. Submitting to Christ as he is revealed in Scripture by the power of the Holy Spirit is the hallmark of classical Christianity. Subjecting Jesus to the creative imagination of contemporary theorists conforms Christ to the spirit of the age. The modernity principle arbitrarily dictates what is authentic or unauthentic about the historical Jesus as he is presented by the apostolic witness. A passion for Christ depends upon a Spirit-inspired life response to the Scripture principle.
3. Reinterpreting the meaning of Jesus' identity exclusively according to the functional and relational categories acceptable to the modern world view betrays an antisupernatural bias. We must be willing to let the history of Jesus and the testimony of the apostolic witness determine our understanding of his substantive self. Neither dead orthodoxy nor the modern outlook does justice to the conservative and contemporary poles of authentic christology.

4. Becoming like Christ is the key to understanding both the person of Christ and the path of discipleship. The high christology of the Epistles is closely linked with the portraits of Jesus Christ in the Gospels. The absolute uniqueness of the person of Christ must be affirmed together with the absolute relevance of his example for our lives. Models of imitation may abound, but the true essence of Christlikeness is found in the full biblical pattern laid down by the apostles.

5. The name of Jesus was consciously linked by the apostles with all the authority, power, and wisdom represented by the name of God in the Old Testament. To define a christology authentically we must include the Old Testament understanding of the reality of God. True confession involves knowing the name of Jesus in the fullness disclosed by God through the life and teaching of Jesus as well as through Spirit-inspired prophecy and salvation history.

6. Jesus was genuinely dependent upon the Father for power and wisdom. He experienced human ignorance and spiritual growth, suffered temptation, learned obedience, and was required to exercise faith in God. Theological perspectives that defend the deity of Christ at the expense of his genuine humanity dehumanize the Incarnation and distort the Christian life. Jesus identified with us in the full range of human experiences, including suffering, temptation, and death. In him the full human significance of spirituality becomes evident, as he shows us what life is like when lived in complete dependence upon God.

7. Jesus' spirituality shows us the true nature of God-centeredness. He exemplifies the fear of God in his profound understanding of God's holiness, in his prayer life, and in his submission to the authority of God's Word. Sharing in the example of Jesus' spirituality leads us into an emotional oneness with him. We identify with his anger against sin, love for the lost, and compassion for the downtrodden. We experience his determination to obey the Father's will.

8. The meaning of the Christ-event cannot be separated from Jesus' personal disclosure of his self-identity. Apart from the meaning of his person, it is difficult to understand the history of Jesus or explain his significance. An analysis of the life of Jesus that dismisses his self-understanding as a fabrication of the early church has difficulty explaining his impact. Critical presuppositions have influenced scholars to deny or discount Jesus' messianic self-consciousness.

9. The contrast made between John the Baptist and Jesus proves that the early church knew the difference between a great prophet and the Incarnate One. Jesus accepted John's testimony but was reluctant to claim the messiahship explicitly until after his passion and resurrection. Through his teaching, kingdom-consciousness, and miracles, Jesus clearly presents himself as absolutely decisive for humanity's eternal destiny. Accepting Jesus' revelation about himself is central to accepting his revelation about anything. If he is not who he claimed to be, then his teaching and actions lose their integrity, his death is stripped of theological significance, and his resurrection is mythological.

10. Through his powerful and provocative teaching, Jesus inaugurated a kingdom ethic. Jesus went to the heart of the commandments and revealed a heart of righteousness alien to the Pharisee but faithful to God's Word. The content of his teaching necessitated a new obedience, made possible through the power of God's Spirit, as well as a new commitment to his passion for the truth.

11. Jesus infused the cross with profound theological meaning. God's eternal plan of salvation was at stake when Jesus went to the cross. Nothing can diminish the uniqueness of Jesus' passion or the scandal of his death. His cross is planted squarely at the center of the believer's existence, providing both the means of salvation and the challenge of radical discipleship. Many contemporary views of Jesus' death dismiss the biblical meaning of the Atonement and reduce its significance to the relational and ethical categories compatible with modernity. The apostles affirmed a two-pronged theology of the Cross. First, Christ's penal substitutionary death saves us from God's judgment of sin and the experience of God-forsakenness. Second, Christ calls us to take up our cross and follow him. Becoming like Jesus means sharing his conviction about the unique meaning of the Cross. It also means following his path to the Cross.

12. The Resurrection not only established the meaning of the Atonement but provided the rationale for becoming like Jesus. Christians have believed that, in the light of the whole history of Jesus, the most reasonable explanation of the empty tomb, the disciples' courage, and the biblical description of his appearances is in fact the resurrection of Jesus. The modern mentality betrays the testimony of the apostles and confuses the contemporary seeker by reinterpreting the Resurrection as a desupernaturalized, dematerialized symbol of hope. On the contrary, the apostles were convinced of

the historical uniqueness and physical concreteness of Jesus' resurrection. Resurrection power, experienced by believers as a living hope, sustains Christian obedience and perseverance. Resurrection faith enables them to face death squarely and to renew their conviction that God does not abandon them to the grave but raises them to eternal life.

notes

Chapter 1: To Know Christ

[1] See Daniel Yankelovich, *New Rules: Searching for Self-Fulfillment in a World Turned Upside Down* (New York: Bantam, 1981).

[2] Albert C. Outler, "Loss of the Sacred," *Christianity Today*, January 2, 1981, 17.

[3] Ibid., 16.

[4] Yankelovich, *New Rules*, 5-6.

[5] R. E. O. White, "Salvation," in *Evangelical Dictionary of Theology*, ed. Walter A. Elwell (Grand Rapids: Baker, 1984), 968.

[6] Alvin Toffler, *The Third Wave* (New York: Morrow, 1980), 407, 382, 383, 26.

[7] Ibid., 395.

[8] Christopher Lasch, *The Minimal Self: Psychic Survival in Troubled Times* (New York: Norton, 1984), 15.

[9] Ibid., 16.

[10] C. S. Lewis, *Surprised by Joy* (London: Fontana, 1959), 176-77.

[11] Jon Sobrino, *Christology at the Crossroads: A Latin American Approach* (Maryknoll, N.Y.: Orbis, 1978), xv.

[12] *Christianity Today*, December 11, 1981.

[13] Saúl Trinidad and Juan Stam, "Christ in Latin American Preaching," in *Faces of Jesus: Latin American Christologies*, ed. José Miguez-Bonino (Maryknoll, N.Y.: Orbis, 1984), 40-41.

[14] Joseph Weizenbaum, quoted in *Time*, January 3, 1983, 16.

[15] James Orr, *Christian View of God and the World* (Grand Rapids: Eerdmans, 1954), 4.

[16] E. D. Schmitz, "Knowledge," in *The New International Dictionary of New Testament Theology*, ed. Colin Brown, 3 vols. (Grand Rapids: Zondervan, 1976), 2:393.

[17] Gerald Hawthorne, *Philippians*, vol. 43 of *Word Biblical Commentary* (Waco: Word, 1983), 143-44.

Chapter 2: The Scripture Principle

[1]Ernest Renan, *The Life of Jesus* (New York: Modern Library, 1927), 285–94; quoted in *Jesus,* ed. Hugh Anderson (Englewood Cliffs, N.J.: Prentice-Hall, 1967), 100–101.

[2]Quoted in Anderson, *Jesus,* 88, 106.

[3]Harold O. J. Brown, *Heresies: The Image of Christ in the Mirror of Heresy and Orthodoxy, from the Apostles to the Present* (Garden City, N.Y.: Doubleday, 1984), 8.

[4]John Hick, ed., *The Myth of God Incarnate* (London: SCM, 1977), x.

[5]Adolf Harnack, *What Is Christianity?* (1901; reprint, New York: Harper and Row, 1957), 12–13.

[6]Ibid., 14, 29.

[7]Rudolf Bultmann, "New Testament and Mythology," in *Kerygma and Myth,* ed. Hans Werner Bartsch (New York: Harper and Row, 1961), 2–3.

[8]Rudolf Bultmann, *Jesus Christ and Mythology* (New York: Scribner, 1958), 17.

[9]Rudolf Bultmann, *Jesus and the Word* (1934; reprint, New York: Scribner, 1958), 8.

[10]Norman Perrin, *Rediscovering the Teaching of Jesus* (London: SCM, 1967), 222.

[11]John A. T. Robinson, *Honest to God* (London: SCM, 1963), 8, 78.

[12]Ibid., 124.

[13]John A. T. Robinson, "Our Image of Christ Must Change," *Christian Century,* March 21, 1973, 339.

[14]Ibid., 342.

[15]James Packer, "Reconstituting Authority," *Crux* 18:4 (1982): 8.

Chapter 3: Truth and Relevance

[1]Don Posterski, "Making Jesus News Again," *Faith Alive,* November 1982, 54.

[2]Langdon Gilkey, *Naming the Whirlwind: The Renewal of God-Language* (Indianapolis: Bobbs-Merrill, 1969), 51.

[3]Morton T. Kelsey, "Is the World View of Jesus Outmoded?" *Christian Century,* January 22, 1969, 112–15.

[4]George Orwell, *Nineteen Eighty-Four* (1949; reprint, New York: Penguin, 1983), 39, 35.

[5]John A. T. Robinson, *The Human Face of God* (London: SCM, 1973), 117.

[6]Frances Young, "A Cloud of Witnesses," *The Myth of God Incarnate,* ed. John Hick (London: SCM, 1977), 34.

[7]Ibid., 37.

[8]Jon Sobrino, *Christology at the Crossroads: A Latin American Approach* (Maryknoll, N.Y.: Orbis, 1978), 334, 385, 387.

[9] Rudolf Bultmann, *History of the Synoptic Tradition* (Oxford: Blackwell, 1972), 205.

[10] Rudolf Bultmann, *Jesus and the Word* (1934; reprint, New York: Scribner, 1958), 13.

[11] Reginald Fuller, "The Criterion of Dissimilarity: The Wrong Tool?" in *Christological Perspectives*, ed. Robert F. Berkley and Sarah A. Edwards (New York: Pilgrim, 1982), 48.

[12] Edward Schillebeeckx, *Jesus: An Experiment in Christology* (New York: Seabury, 1979), 94.

[13] Ibid., 96.

[14] Norman Anderson, *The Mystery of the Incarnation* (Downers Grove: InterVarsity, 1978), 30.

[15] Norman Pittenger, *Christology Reconsidered* (London: SCM, 1970), 87.

[16] Juan Segundo, *The Liberation of Theology* (Maryknoll, N.Y.: Orbis, 1976), 120, 87.

[17] Sobrino, *Christology at the Crossroads*, 351, xviii.

[18] Cf. Donald M. Baillie, *God Was in Christ* (New York: Scribner, 1948), 11, 20.

[19] On this point, see Donald G. Bloesch, *Essentials of Evangelical Theology*, 2 vols. (New York: Harper and Row, 1978), 1:135.

[20] Aloys Grillmeier, *Christ in Christian Tradition: From the Apostolic Age to Chalcedon*, 2d ed. (Atlanta: Knox, 1975), 1:77.

[21] Robert E. Webber, *Common Roots: A Call to Evangelical Maturity* (Grand Rapids: Zondervan, 1978), 16–17.

[22] Clark H. Pinnock, "An Evangelical Theology: Conservative and Contemporary," *Christianity Today*, January 5, 1979, 23.

[23] Donald G. Bloesch, *The Evangelical Renaissance* (Grand Rapids: Eerdmans, 1973), 46.

[24] Charles H. Kraft, *Christianity in Culture: A Study in Dynamic Biblical Theologizing in Cross Cultural Perspective* (Maryknoll, N.Y.: Orbis, 1979), 38–39.

[25] Samuel Escobar, "The Social Responsibility of the Church in Latin America," *Evangelical Missions Quarterly* 6 (Spring 1970): 145.

[26] J. Andrew Kirk, "The Use of the Bible in Interpreting Salvation Today: An Evangelical Perspective," *Evangelical Review of Theology*, October 1977, 2.

[27] Cf. Geoffrey W. Bromily, "The Limits of Theological Relativism," *Christianity Today*, May 24, 1968, 6–7.

[28] John R. W. Stott, *Christian Mission in the Modern World* (Downers Grove: InterVarsity, 1975), 59, 43.

[29] Webber, *Common Roots*, 147.

Chapter 4: The Imitation of Christ

[1] Cf. Russell F. Aldwinckle, *More Than Man: A Study in Christology* (Grand Rapids: Eerdmans, 1976), 13.

[2] William Wrede, *Paul* (London: Green, 1907), 151.

[3] F. F. Bruce, *Paul and Jesus* (Grand Rapids: Baker, 1974), 20–21.

[4] I. Howard Marshall, *Luke: Historian and Theologian* (Grand Rapids: Zondervan, 1971), 48.

[5] Bruce, *Paul and Jesus,* 20.

[6] Rudolf Bultmann, *Faith and Understanding* (London: SCM, 1969), 241.

[7] Gerald F. Hawthorne, *Word Biblical Commentary: Philippians,* vol. 43 (Waco: Word, 1983), 78–79.

[8] Ibid., 79. Hawthorne writes, "Hence although this hymn is unquestionably a christological gem unparalleled in the New Testament, although it may be considered soteriological in character, and although it may have been originally composed for christological or soteriological reasons, Paul's motive in using it here is not theological but ethical. His object is not to give instructions in doctrine, but to reinforce instruction in christian living. And he does this by appealing to the conduct of Christ. The hymn, therefore, presents Christ as the ultimate model for moral action."

[9] I. Howard Marshall, *I Believe in the Historical Jesus* (Grand Rapids: Eerdmans, 1977), 75.

[10] Richard F. Lovelace, *Dynamics of Spiritual Life: An Evangelical Theology of Renewal* (Downers Grove: InterVarsity, 1979).

[11] Thomas à Kempis, *The Imitation of Christ,* trans. C. Bigg (London: Methuen, 1898), bk. 1, ch. 1, 45.

[12] Francois Vandenbroucke, Louis Bouyer, and Jean Leclercq, *The Spirituality of the Middle Ages,* vol. 2 of *A History of Christian Spirituality* (New York: Seabury, 1982), 439.

[13] Ibid., 438.

[14] R. E. O. White, *Christian Ethics* (Atlanta: Knox, 1981), 166.

[15] Ibid., 168.

[16] Ibid., 269.

[17] Myron Rush, *Management: A Biblical Approach* (Wheaton: Scripture Press, 1983), 38.

[18] Robert Schuller, *Self-Esteem: The New Reformation* (Waco: Word, 1982), 20, 44.

[19] Ibid., 39.

[20] Ibid., 155, 156 (quoted).

[21] John Alexander, "True Confessions," *Other Side,* July 1983, 9.

[22] Dallas Willard, "Discipleship: For Super-Christians Only?" *Christianity Today,* October 10, 1980, 25.

Chapter 5: The Name of Jesus

[1] Copyright © 1970 by William J. Gaither. Reprinted by permission of William J. Gaither.

[2] Albert Schweitzer, *The Quest of the Historical Jesus,* trans. W. Montgomery (London: A. and C. Black, 1910), 310–11.

[3] Peter O'Brien, *Colossians and Philemon*, vol. 44 of *Word Bible Commentary* (Waco: Word, 1982), 211.

[4] H. Bietenhard, "Name," in *The New International Dictionary of New Testament Theology*, 3 vols. ed. Colin Brown (Grand Rapids: Zondervan, 1976), 2:654.

[5] Ibid.

[6] Ibid., 649; cf. also T. E. McComiskey, "Names of God," in *Evangelical Dictionary of Theology*, ed. Walter A. Elwell (Grand Rapids: Baker, 1984), 464–65.

[7] Cf. McComiskey, "Names of God," 464.

[8] Ray S. Anderson, *Historical Transcendence and the Reality of God: A Christological Critique* (Grand Rapids: Eerdmans, 1975), 131.

Chapter 6: The Human Spirituality of Jesus

[1] James Houston, "Spirituality," in *Evangelical Dictionary of Theology*, ed. Walter A. Elwell (Grand Rapids: Baker, 1984), 1046.

[2] Wayne Dyer, *Your Erroneous Zones* (New York: Avon, 1976), 68.

[3] Theodore Roszak, "The Crisis of Culture," *Toronto Star*, October 19, 1980.

[4] Aloys Grillmeier, *Christ in Christian Tradition*, 2d ed. (Atlanta: Knox, 1975), 1:332.

[5] Norman Anderson, *The Mystery of the Incarnation* (Downers Grove: InterVarsity, 1978), 48.

[6] Richard A. Norris, ed., *The Christological Controversy* (Philadelphia: Fortress, 1980), 23.

[7] Cf. Robert H. Stein, "A Limit on Jesus' Omniscience?" *Standard* [Baptist General Conference], December 1981, 35.

[8] Philip E. Hughes, *A Commentary on the Epistle to the Hebrews* (Grand Rapids: Eerdmans, 1977), 53.

[9] C. F. D. Moule, *The Cambridge Greek Testament Commentary: The Epistles to the Colossians and to Philemon* (Cambridge: Cambridge University Press, 1957), 65.

[10] Hughes, *Commentary on Hebrews* 50.

[11] V. L. Walter, "Arianism," in *Evangelical Dictionary of Theology*, ed. Elwell, 74.

[12] Donald M. Baillie, *God Was in Christ* (New York: Scribner, 1948), 70.

[13] J. N. D. Kelly, *Early Christian Doctrines* (London: A. and C. Black, 1958), 229; (the quotation is from Athanasius's "Contra Arianos," 1. 6.

[14] Anthony A. Hoekema, *The Four Major Cults* (Grand Rapids: Eerdmans, 1963), 327–30.

[15] Walter, "Arianism," 75.

[16] Kelly, *Early Christian Doctrines*, 232.

[17] Dyer, *Your Erroneous Zones*, 68.

[18] Jon Sobrino, *Christianity at the Crossroads: A Latin American Approach* (Maryknoll, N.Y.: Orbis, 1978), 161, 92, 94, 71.
[19] Thomas F. Torrence, *God and Rationality* (London: Oxford University Press, 1971), 157.

Chapter 7: God-Centeredness

[1] Robert Roberts, "The Strengths of a Christian," *Reformed Journal* 34:8 (August 1984): 14.
[2] Origen, *The Classics of Western Spirituality* (New York: Paulist, 1979), 112–13.
[3] Ray S. Anderson, *Historical Transcendence and the Reality of God: A Christological Critique* (Grand Rapids: Eerdmans, 1975), 178.
[4] Ibid., 179.
[5] R. T. France, *Jesus and the Old Testament* (Downers Grove: InterVarsity, 1971), 223.
[6] Dietrich Bonhoeffer, *The Cost of Discipleship* (New York: Macmillan, 1963), 41.
[7] Ray Anderson, "Burnout as a Symptom of Theological Anemia," *Theology, News and Notes,* March 1984, 13.

Chapter 8: Jesus' Self-Understanding

[1] Russell F. Aldwinckle, *More Than Man: A Study in Christology* (Grand Rapids: Eerdmans, 1976), 193.
[2] Ibid., 16.
[3] Royce Gruenler, *New Approaches to Jesus and the Gospels: A Phenomenological and Exegetical Study of the Synoptic Christology* (Grand Rapids: Baker, 1982), 71.
[4] R. H. Fuller, *The Foundations of New Testament Christology* (London: Collins, 1965), 18.
[5] John Knox, *The Death of Christ* (London: Collins, 1959), 58.
[6] Jon Sobrino, *Christology at the Crossroads: A Latin American Approach* (Maryknoll, N.Y.: Orbis, 1976), 73–74.
[7] Ibid., 366, 50, 69.
[8] Leonardo Boff, *Jesus Christ Liberator: A Critical Christology for Our Time* (Maryknoll, N.Y.: Orbis, 1978), 196–97.
[9] James Dunn, "In Defense of a Methodology," *Expository Times* 96 (July 1984): 296.
[10] James Dunn, *Christology in the Making: A New Testament Inquiry into the Origins of the Doctrine of the Incarnation* (Philadelphia: Westminster, 1980), 32.
[11] According to Dunn (239–47), John 1:1–18 is the only explicit statement of the Incarnation in the Bible. Dunn argues that, outside of the prologue of the fourth Gospel, including passages such as Phil. 2:6–11; Col. 1:15–20; Heb. 1:1–3, the concept of the Incarnation is not to be found.

12 I. Howard Marshall, "Book Reviews," *Trinity Journal* 2 (Fall 1981): 244. See Leon Morris, "The Emergence of the Doctrine of the Incarnation," *Themelios* 7 (September 1982): 15–19; Donald Hagner, "Christ Before Christmas," *Reformed Journal* 32 (December 1982): 19–20; Bruce Demarest, "Book Review," *Journal of the Evangelical Theological Society* 25 (1982): 107–8.

Chapter 9: God Incarnate

1 William Wrede, *The Messianic Secret,* trans. J. C. Greig (1901; reprint, London: James Clarke, 1972).

2 Helmut Thielicke, *The Evangelical Faith,* 3 vols. (Grand Rapids: Eerdmans, 1977), 2:352.

3 Richard N. Longenecker, *The Christology of Early Jewish Christianity* (London: SCM, 1970), 74.

4 See R. T. France, *Jesus and the Old Testament* (Downers Grove: InterVarsity, 1971), 134.

5 Immanuel Kant, *Philosophical Correspondence, 1759–99,* ed. and trans. Arnulf Zweig (Chicago: University of Chicago Press, 1967), 80.

6 I. Howard Marshall, *The Origins of New Testament Christology* (Downers Grove: InterVarsity, 1976), 45.

7 See Thielicke, *Evangelical Faith,* 2:361; and France, *Jesus and the Old Testament,* 223.

8 Philip B. Payne, "Jesus' Implicit Claim to Deity in His Parables," *Trinity Journal* 2 (Spring 1981): 3, 9.

9 Ibid., 18, 20.

10 See Walter Kasper, *Jesus the Christ* (New York: Paulist, 1977), 96.

11 James Dunn, *Christology in the Making* (Philadelphia: Westminster, 1980), 27.

12 Marshall, *Origins of New Testament Christology,* 45.

13 Aloys Grillmeier, *Christ in Christian Tradition: From the Apostolic Age to Chalcedon,* 2d ed. (Atlanta: Knox, 1975), 1:11.

14 F. F. Bruce, "The Background to the Son of Man Sayings," in *Christ the Lord,* ed. Harold H. Rowdon (Downers Grove: InterVarsity, 1982), 70.

15 Longenecker, *Christology of Early Jewish Christianity,* 89.

16 France, *Jesus and the Old Testament,* 223, 148.

17 Marshall, *Origins of New Testament Christology,* 76.

18 France, *Jesus and the Old Testament,* 121.

Chapter 10: Kingdom Righteousness

1 R. E. O. White, *Biblical Ethics* (Atlanta: Knox, 1979), 65.

2 Ibid.

3 Donald Hagner, *The Jewish Reclamation of Jesus* (Grand Rapids: Zondervan, 1984), 161.

4 Joseph Klausner, "Christian and Jewish Ethics," *Judaism* 2 (1953): 23.

[5]Cf. John Wenham, *Christ and the Bible* (Downers Grove: InterVarsity, 1972); Clark Pinnock, "The Inspiration of Scripture and the Authority of Jesus Christ," in *God's Inerrant Word*, ed. John W. Montgomery (Minneapolis: Bethany Fellowship, 1974).

[6]Douglas J. Moo, "Jesus and the Authority of the Mosaic Law," *Journal for the Study of the New Testament* (Sheffield, England) 20 (1984): 12.

[7]Donald A. Carson, "Matthew," in *The Expositor's Bible Commentary*, ed. Frank E. Gaebelein, 12 vols. (Grand Rapids: Zondervan, 1984), 8:417.

[8]Pinnock, "Inspiration of Scripture," 210.

[9]Moo, "Jesus and Authority," 11.

[10]Carson, "Matthew," 349.

[11]Cf. Robert Banks, "Matthew's Understanding of the Law: Authenticity and Interpretation in Matthew 5:17–20," *Journal of Biblical Literature* 93 (1974): 226–42.

[12]Hagner, *Jewish Reclamation of Jesus*, 123.

[13]Cf. Moo, "Jesus and Authority," 9; Stephen Westerholm, *Jesus and Scribal Authority*, Coniectanea Biblica, New Testament Series, no. 10 (Lund, 1978), 102–3.

[14]White, *Biblical Ethics*, 376 (quoted), 112–13.

[15]Donald G. Bloesch, *Essentials of Evangelical Theology*, 2 vols. (New York: Harper and Row, 1978), 1:122.

[16]Westerholm, *Jesus and Scribal Authority*, 131–32.

[17]Richard N. Longenecker, *New Testament Social Ethics for Today* (Grand Rapids: Eerdmans, 1984), 18.

Chapter 11: The Crucified Messiah

[1]P. T. Forsyth writes, "The only Cross you can preach to the whole world is a theological one. It is not the fact of the Cross, it is the interpretation of the Cross, the prime theology of the Cross, what God meant by the Cross, that is everything. That is what the New Testament came to give. That is the only kind of Cross that can make or keep a Church" (*Work of Christ* [Toronto: Westminster, 1909], 48).

[2]Cynthia Schaible, "The Gospel According to Success," *Christian Reader* 19:4 (1981): 35–41.

[3]Hans Küng, *On Being a Christian* (Great Britain: Collins, 1974; Fount Paperback, 1978), 420–21.

[4]Ibid., 424–26, 434.

[5]Michael Goulder, "Jesus, the Man of Universal Destiny," in *The Myth of God Incarnate*, ed. John Hick (London: SCM, 1977), 58–59.

[6]John A. T. Robinson, *Honest to God* (London: SCM, 1963), 78–79.

[7]Ibid., 81, quoting Tillich, *The Shaking of the Foundations*.

[8]Jon Sobrino, *Christology at the Crossroads: A Latin American Approach* (Maryknoll, N.Y.: Orbis, 1979), 184–85, 179, 227.

[9] Hugo Assmann, *Practical Theology of Liberation* (London: Search, 1975), 86.

[10] Sobrino, *Christology at the Crossroads*, 185–86.

[11] Ibid., 196, 190.

[12] Ibid., 304.

[13] Martin Hengel, *Crucifixion* (London: SCM, 1977), 33, 62, 14.

[14] Julius Scott, "Cross," in *Evangelical Dictionary of Theology*, ed. Walter A. Elwell (Grand Rapids: Baker, 1984), 287.

[15] Hengel, *Crucifixion*, 1; the quotation is from Justin's Apology 1. 13. 4.

[16] Hengel, *Crucifixion*, 5; the quotation is from Nero 16. 3.

[17] Hengel, *Crucifixion*, 19.

[18] Melito of Sardis, "A Homily on the Passover," in *The Christological Controversy*, ed. Richard A. Norris (Philadelphia: Fortress, 1980), 46–47.

[19] Sobrino, *Christology at the Crossroads*, 215.

[20] John H. Yoder, *The Politics of Jesus* (Grand Rapids: Eerdmans, 1972), 112.

[21] Sobrino, *Christology at the Crossroads*, 211.

[22] David Wells, *The Search for Salvation* (Downers Grove: InterVarsity, 1978), 166.

[23] James Packer, *What Did the Cross Achieve? The logic of Penal Substitution*, reprinted from Tyndale Bulletin no. 25 (London: Billing and Sons, 1974), 12–13.

[24] C. E. B. Cranfield, *The Cambridge Greek Testament Commentary: The Gospel According to St. Mark*, ed. C. F. D. Moule (Cambridge: Cambridge University Press, 1963), 272.

[25] Russell F. Aldwinckle, *More Than Man: A Study in Christology* (Grand Rapids: Eerdmans, 1976), 88.

[26] Donald G. Bloesch, *Essentials of Evangelical Theology*, 2 vols. (New York: Harper and Row, 1978), 1:150.

[27] Wells, *Search for Salvation*, 12.

[28] Packer, *What Did the Cross Achieve?* 25.

[29] Bloesch, *Essentials of Evangelical Theology*, 1:162.

[30] Ibid., 163–64.

[31] Packer, *What Did the Cross Achieve?* 34.

[32] Dietrich Bonhoeffer, *The Cost of Discipleship* (New York: Macmillan, 1963), 47.

[33] J. D. Douglas, ed., *Let the Earth Hear His Voice: International Congress on World Evangelization, Lausanne, Switzerland* (Minneapolis: World Wide Publications, 1975), 5.

[34] John H. Yoder, "The God of the Poor," (Address given at Fuller Theological Seminary, Pasadena, Calif., January 13, 1978).

Chapter 12: The Risen Lord

[1] George Eldon Ladd, *I Believe in the Resurrection of Jesus* (London: Hodder and Stoughton, 1979), 42.

[2] Ibid., 34.

[3] Russell F. Aldwinckle, *More Than Man: A Study in Christology* (Grand Rapids: Eerdmans, 1976), 76.

[4] Ladd, *I Believe in the Resurrection*, 25.

[5] Ronald J. Sider, "Jesus' Resurrection and the Search for Peace and Justice," *Christian Century*, November 3, 1982, 1105.

[6] Richard Lischer, " 'Resurrexit': Something to Preach," *Christian Century*, April 2, 1980, 372, quoting John Updike, *Telephone Poles and Other Poems* (New York: Knopf, 1963).

[7] Colin Brown, *Miracles and the Critical Mind* (Grand Rapids: Eerdmans, 1984), 281.

[8] Ladd, *I Believe in the Resurrection*, 46–48.

[9] Cf. Clark H. Pinnock, "The Incredible Resurrection: A Mandate for Faith," *Christianity Today*, April 6, 1979, 12–17.

[10] Rudolf Bultmann, *Kerygma and Myth*, ed. Hans Werner Bartsch (New York: Harper and Row, 1961), 39.

[11] Jon Sobrino, *Christology at the Crossroads: A Latin American Approach* (Maryknoll, N.Y.: Orbis, 1978), 252–53.

[12] Gordon Kaufmann, *Systematic Theology: A Historicist Perspective* (New York: Scribner's, 1968).

[13] Hans Küng, *On Being a Christian* (Great Britain: Collins, 1974; Fount Paperback, 1978), 346, 366.

[14] Ladd, *I Believe in the Resurrection*, 25.

[15] Küng, *On Being a Christian*, 379.

[16] Ladd, *I Believe in the Resurrection*, 141.

[17] Cf. Pinnock, "Incredible Resurrection," 13.

[18] Aldwinckle, *More Than Man*, 100.

[19] Ibid., 101.

[20] Samuel Escobar, *Christian Mission and Social Justice* (Kitchener, Ontario: Herald, 1978), 54.

[21] Quoted in Raymond Brown, *The Message of Hebrews* (Downers Grove: InterVarsity, 1982), 71.

[22] Vernon Grounds, "Goodness: Reflections on the Incarnation," *Christianity Today*, June 26, 1981, 29.

[23] Naida Hearn, "Jesus, Name Above All Names," in *Scripture in Song*, vol. 2 (New Zealand: Scripture in Song, 1978; dist. Benson Co., Nashville), 21. Reprinted by permission of Scripture in Song.

subject index

scripture index

SCRIPTURE INDEX   217